Managing Children in Disasters

Planning for Their Unique Needs

Managing Children in Disasters

Planning for Their Unique Needs

Jane A. Bullock
George D. Haddow
Damon P. Coppola

CRC Press
Taylor & Francis Group
Boca Raton London New York

CRC Press is an imprint of the
Taylor & Francis Group, an **informa** business

CRC Press
Taylor & Francis Group
6000 Broken Sound Parkway NW, Suite 300
Boca Raton, FL 33487-2742

Printed in the United States of America on acid-free paper
10 9 8 7 6 5 4 3 2 1

International Standard Book Number: 978-1-4398-3766-5 (Hardback)

Library of Congress Cataloging-in-Publication Data

Bullock, Jane A.
Managing children in disasters : planning for their unique needs / Jane A. Bullock, George Haddow, Damon P. Coppola.
p. cm.
Includes bibliographical references and index.
ISBN 978-1-4398-3766-5
1. Child disaster victims--United States. 2. Child disaster victims--Services for--United States. 3. Disaster relief--United States. I. Haddow, George D. II. Coppola, Damon P. III. Title.

HV555.U6B85 2011
363.34'80830973--dc22 2010027399

Visit the Taylor & Francis Web site at
http://www.taylorandfrancis.com

and the CRC Press Web site at
http://www.crcpress.com

Contents

CHAPTER 5 — Response 161

CHAPTER 6 — Recovery 197

Introduction

According to the U.S. Census Bureau, children ranging in age from 0 to 18 years constitute nearly one-quarter of the U.S. population (U.S. Census Bureau, n.d.). These 74 million infants, toddlers, adolescents, and teenagers together comprise one of the most vulnerable population groups not only in normal conditions, but also (and especially) in times of disaster.

On a day-to-day basis, there exist organizations and agencies in the governmental, private, and nonprofit communities that together form a complex structure of networks on which children depend for their mental, physical, and psychological development, health, and safety. These children also depend heavily on the parents, guardians, or primary caregivers who provide them with the safe, structured, and supervised environment they depend on virtually twenty-four hours a day.

Once a disaster occurs, however, many, if not all, of these foundations can suddenly collapse. Their child care centers and schools may be damaged, destroyed, or converted into emergency shelters. If their parents or guardians are not directly injured or killed, they may be so overwhelmed by their own and their family's response and recovery needs to adequately address the special day-to-day needs children have.

The child victims, who are generally incapable of managing their own needs, can suffer disproportionately and may fall behind their peers in development and education. Additionally, the physical and psychological damage sustained by children can far outweigh the same effects inflicted on fully grown members of society, often requiring years of physical, psychological, and other therapy to address.

With proper planning and guidance, emergency management agencies can minimize the risk faced by the community's children. Children, families, and those tasked with the care of children (teachers, day care centers, etc.) can all take action before disasters occur to prepare for and mitigate their effects. Response and child stewardship organizations that are most likely to assume the protective role of children in the immediate aftermath of a disastrous event can be equipped for and provided with proper training to manage the specific needs of this special population. And finally, the community can plan for the specific needs that children will face in the longer-term recovery phase when these vulnerable lives are gradually brought back to normalcy.

For every aspect of emergency management, without exception, and inclusive of planning and preparedness, mitigation, response, and recovery, there are special considerations unique to the needs of children that are not adequately addressed in standard industry practice. Failing to become cognizant of and likewise plan for these special considerations only ensures shortfalls in care, inadequate levels of preparedness and protection, and the risk of failing the community's children in their time of greatest need.

The purpose of this book is to provide guidance for emergency managers and others involved with working with children before, during, and after a disaster on how best to address the unique needs of children in disasters. This book provides detailed information concerning the unique needs of children in disasters, the family, community, and educational infrastructure that support children in their everyday lives, and the types of efforts that can be undertaken in all phases of emergency management.

Chapter 1 identifies the unique needs of children in disasters. These needs include physical security, emotional stability, family unity, and ongoing education. Information taken from a variety of sources makes clear that children are not just small adults, and that their needs in disasters vary greatly from the adult population and must be both acknowledged and planned for accordingly.

Chapter 2 details the infrastructure that supports the everyday existence of children growing up in a safe and secure community. A child depends greatly on parents, grandparents, siblings, and friends for physical security and emotional stability. Child care centers and the school system play significantly roles in the growth and development of every child, as do the medical professionals and facilities that ensure their good health.

Chapter 3 examines how hazard mitigation actions can reduce the impacts of future disasters on the everyday lives of children and the infrastructure that supports them. Based on an understanding of the unique needs of children in disaster and the infrastructure that supports children, emergency managers and community leaders are better able to identify how community hazards can impact their children, how to best mitigate these community hazards, and how to reprioritize mitigation actions in light of this knowledge.

Chapter 4 outlines the many steps that can be taken by parents, emergency managers, school officials, child care providers, and others involved in children's lives to prepare for the next disaster. Examples are provided of existing programs and guides that help children to understand how disaster can impact their lives and what they can do with their families to prepare for the next disaster.

Chapter 5 reviews those actions that should be taken by agencies and organizations involved in responding to a disaster to ensure that children are protected and families remain intact during a disaster. This chapter examines evacuation plans and processes, how children and families are best served in emergency shelters, and what is required to meet the physical, medical, and psychological needs of children during a disaster.

Chapter 6 details what has to be done in the recovery phase of a disaster to rebuild children's lives. This includes reuniting families that have been separated, rebuilding schools and child care centers so that children have a safe and secure place to learn and grow, allowing parents to return to work, and helping children to cope with the psychological impacts of a disaster.

Chapter 7 provides a listing of the full spectrum of resources available to emergency managers and others concerning children in disasters. Resources are listed in the following areas: emergency planning, sample plans, psychosocial recovery, training and education courses and materials, technical assistance, reports, and organizations.

Each year, hundreds of thousands of children are impacted by disasters spanning a spectrum from house fire or automobile accident to the levels of devastation witnessed in the 2004 Boxing Day Tsunami and Hurricane Katrina. Emergency planners have to date largely failed to adequately recognize and accommodate the unique needs that children have in times of disaster. Thankfully, this is changing not only in the United States but also elsewhere around the world.

It is our intention that this book serve as a valuable and comprehensive addition to the growing list of materials available to parents, emergency managers, community leaders, school administrators, child care providers, and the many other individuals and organizations that care for and about the disaster needs of children. Our goal is thus to provide each of these groups with the knowledge and context necessary to build better, stronger, and more effective emergency plans and operations. In the words of the seventeenth-century novelist Miguel de Cervantes Saavedra, “Forewarned, forearmed; to be prepared is half the victory.”

About the Authors

Jane A. Bullock is a partner in Bullock & Haddow, LLC, disaster management consulting firm. Ms. Bullock has over twenty-five years of private and public sector experience culminating in responsibility, as chief of staff, for the daily management and operations of the Federal Emergency Management Agency (FEMA), the federal agency responsible for disaster prevention, response, and recovery. In the course of her career at FEMA, she directed the restructuring and streamlining of the agency, set policy and programmatic direction for the nation's emergency management systems, served as the agency's spokesperson, and worked with the U.S. Congress and the nation's governors to enhance disaster management throughout the United States. She was chief architect of Project Impact: Building Disaster Resistant Communities, a nationwide, grassroots effort by communities and businesses to implement prevention and risk reduction programs. Since leaving FEMA, Ms. Bullock has worked with a variety of organizations to design and implement disaster management and homeland security programs, including the Corporation for National and Community Service, the Annie E. Casey Foundation, DRII International, and county and municipal governments throughout the United States. Ms. Bullock served on the Obama Homeland Security/FEMA transition team.

George D. Haddow is a principal in the Washington, D.C.-based disaster management consulting firm of Bullock & Haddow, LLC. He has worked on disaster management projects with Good Harbor Consulting, Save the Children, the World Bank, the Global Partnership for Preparedness, FEMA, the Corporation for National and Community Service, the U.S. Chamber of Commerce Business Civic Leadership Center, the Annie E. Casey Foundation, and the Humane Society of the United States. Mr. Haddow serves as an adjunct professor at the Institute for Crisis, Disaster and Risk Management at George Washington University in Washington, D.C., and the Baton Rouge (LA) Community College. He is the coauthor of three university-level textbooks concerning emergency management, homeland security, and disaster communications. Mr. Haddow is the former deputy chief of staff to James Lee Witt during his tenure as FEMA director, responsible for policy formulation in the areas of disaster response and recovery, public–private partnerships, public information, environmental protection, and disaster mitigation. Mr. Haddow was one of the principal architects of FEMA's national disaster mitigation initiative entitled Project Impact: Building Disaster Resistant Communities.

Damon P. Coppola is an emergency management analyst with more than ten years practical experience serving clients in the international, governmental, nongovernmental, and private sectors. Mr. Coppola has authored several leading emergency management academic and professional texts, most recently *Communicating Emergency Management: Strategies for Creating a Disaster Resilient Public* (CRC Press, Boca Raton, FL). Mr. Coppola developed national-level guidance for communities interested in including the unique needs of children in their municipal, county, and parish emergency operations plans, and has helped to lead a number of programs focused on limiting disaster vulnerability in the United States and around the world, including the National Catastrophic Disaster Planning Program, the FEMA Gap Analysis Program, and the International Recovery Platform. Mr. Coppola holds a master's degree in engineering management in crisis, disaster, and risk management from The George Washington University.

Chapter 1
Unique Needs of Children in Disasters

Introduction

Children suffer disproportionately from the impacts of emergencies and major disasters.

This simple fact is well understood by the many nongovernmental, nonprofit, and faith-based response and recovery organizations that have traditionally focused their efforts on children. However, the greater emergency response community has largely overlooked the plight of children in emergencies for decades, primarily out of a poor understanding of the topic and an almost absolute lack of institutional guidance regarding comprehensive emergency management. In 1997, a study conducted by the Federal Emergency Management Agency (FEMA) concluded that not one state's disaster plan included pediatric-specific considerations (Mailman School of Public Health, 2003).

In 2001, following the September 11 terrorist attacks, several organizations (including the American Academy of Pediatrics) initiated studies regarding the ways in which the needs of children might be incorporated into the emergency planning process. Their efforts focused primarily on the terrorism hazard, reflecting the perception of risk at the time, and little action was taken at the local, state, or even national levels (see Sidebar 1.1). In August 2005, however, the unique vulnerabilities of children could no longer be denied or disregarded. Hurricane Katrina, with brutal force, displaced an estimated three hundred thousand children from New Orleans and the Gulf Coast. The disaster event exposed the problems of a strained emergency management system that is fundamentally incapable of addressing disaster-affected children.

SIDEBAR 1.1 PEDIATRIC PREPAREDNESS

Dr. Steven Krug, in a July 26, 2006, testimony on pediatric preparedness to a congressional committee, stated, "As long ago as 1997, the Federal Emergency Management Agency raised the concern that *none* [speaker's emphasis] of the states it had surveyed had pediatric components in their disaster plans. That same year, the American Academy of Pediatrics issued its first policy statement, entitled "The Pediatrician's Role in Disaster Preparedness," with recommendations for pediatricians and communities. In 2001, the American Academy of Pediatrics formed its Task Force on Terrorism and issued a series of detailed recommendations on various aspects of chemical, biological, radiological, and blast terrorism. In 2002, Congress created the National Advisory Committee on Children and Terrorism to prepare a comprehensive public health strategy related to children and terrorism. In 2003, the federal government sponsored a National Consensus Conference on Pediatric Preparedness for Disasters and Terrorism that, again, issued a laundry list of dozens of specific recommendations. Just last month, the IOM issued its report on the pediatric aspects of the emergency care system. Despite all of this, progress in pediatric preparedness has been slow, fragmented, disorganized, and largely unmeasured and unaccountable" (Krug, 2006).

Ultimately, many of the needs of these Katrina-affected children were addressed by the community-based nongovernmental and faith-based organizations that responded in the storm's aftermath. However, most community leaders understand, and many grapple with the reality, that it is the local government that is responsible for this function. In fact, local governments are tasked

FIGURE 1.1 **Marianna, Florida, May 12, 2009. FEMA Voluntary Agency Group (VOLAG) Supervisor Jerry Harfoot presents information about FEMA services to the Jackson County School Board as FEMA Community Relations (CR) Specialist Maribel Rovira listens. This FEMA outreach effort is to get information to families through schoolchildren about services available for those affected by a recent storm or flood. (George Armstrong/FEMA)**

by their constituents to perform or coordinate *all duties* associated with the mitigation, preparedness, response, and recovery of disasters, as they pertain not only to the population as a whole, but to the special needs of the community's children (Figure 1.1).

Like any vulnerable population, children have special, particular needs both prior to and following the occurrence of a disaster. These needs are generally not adequately addressed in the community's base emergency operations plan (EOP) (Save the Children, 2005a). Children, because of their age, cognitive abilities, and dependence upon parents and other adult caretakers, require a distinctive set of procedures and protections that the general population might otherwise disregard. Children have unique needs that cannot be discounted simply because a disaster has occurred.

According to the American Academy of Pediatrics (AAP), "Children have unique needs (physical, physiological, developmental and mental) that place them at increased risk when emergencies or disasters occur" (American Academy of Pediatrics, 2002). Disasters can upset the everyday routine that children rely on and can both put a child at physical risk and frighten him or her. This chapter will discuss the unique needs of children in disasters as they relate to physical security, emotional stability, and family unity (see Sidebar 1.2).

SIDEBAR 1.2

Save the Children has identified seven critical types of protection that children require in disaster areas and war zones:

- Protection from physical harm
- Protection from exploitation and gender-based violence
- Protection from psychosocial distress
- Protection from recruitment into armed groups
- Protection from family separation
- Protection from abuses related to forced displacement
- Protection from denial of children's access to quality education

Source: Save the Children. 2005b. *Policy brief—Protecting children in emergencies*. http://www.savethechildren.org/publications/policy-briefs/policy_brief_final_1.pdf.

The AAP discovered after Katrina that "two major deficiencies have been identified that are of special concern to pediatricians: (1) the inadequacy of existing planning in addressing the unique needs of children, and (2) the need for individual physicians to develop or revise their own disaster plans" (Needle, no date).

The purpose of this chapter is to identify and define the unique needs of children in disasters. This chapter will focus primarily on three basic areas: physical security, emotional stability, and family unity.

Children as a Special Population

It is often said that children are not small adults. This statement certainly holds true when it comes to emergency planning. The differences between children and adults are both diverse and pervasive, falling into physical, psychological, social, cognitive, physiological, and other areas. Every part of a child's life differs from that of adults—his or her routines, diets, sleep patterns, wants, and fears. What is most important to consider is that all of these characteristics combined result in a level of vulnerability that is greatly magnified (see Sidebar 1.3 and Figure 1.2).

SIDEBAR 1.3 CHILDREN IN DISASTERS

Losing your home is a horrible thing. No matter how meager your home, no matter how few possessions, losing it all of a sudden is an emotional shock. Home is where we can be ourselves, in all our quirky individuality. You can open the refrigerator and get a drink, turn the lights on or off, sift through the photographs and mementos that chronicle your past. You can be silly or noisy or crabby. Home is where you have family, pets, plants, closets, toys, and your own blanket and bed.

When children lose their homes in a disaster or personal catastrophe, they may also lose pets and cherished possessions (their collections, trophies, gifts from special people). They might also lose friends, routines, rituals, and even their school. The whole architecture of their lives has collapsed. Children's lives usually have a parent, but a parent in distress, who may be tired from heroic efforts to just make it through the day, or who may be sad or depressed. And when they find shelter, they usually have lost even more: the ability to sleep easily, to keep clean, to get a snack or pocket money, and to move around freely without the constant presence of an adult.

What have children usually found? Crowded conditions, uncertainty and fear, no place to play or do homework, no private space to pause and be off the beaten path. It's hard to keep clean and look good. And older children may have found a social stigma leading to a sense of embarrassment, shame, or anger.

Source: Greenman, J. 2005. What happened to my world? Helping children cope with natural disaster catastrophe. Watertown, MA: Comfort for Kids. http://www.mercycorps.org/sites/default/files/file1134070665.pdf.

In order to fully address the needs of a special population, it is important to first have a good understanding of the demographics of that group as a whole. While there are some characteristics that translate across the entire nation regardless of location, each community will have a unique situation with regards to their children's socioeconomic and other conditions—information that is maintained by various town or city offices (including the office of vital records, department of education, social services, etc.).

FIGURE 1.2 **Even something as basic as a nap or sleep schedule, in the midst of a disaster, can disrupt a child's routine and sense of well-being.**

As a national group, recent census data indicate that there are approximately 74 million children aged 0–17 living throughout the United States. This group is almost equally divided among those who are aged 0–5, 6–11, and 12–17 (approximately 24.5 million in each)—three subgroups each of which has its own special set of needs, vulnerabilities, and preparedness requirements. Together, this special population makes up approximately 25% of the total population of the country—almost double that of senior citizens (13%), a special population that has traditionally received much more consideration by emergency management efforts in the past.

Other important statistics that help to paint a picture of this group and its individuals include:

Children 0–6 in nonparental child care	60.8% (2005)
Children who live with only one or no parents	33% (2005)
Children who speak another language at home	18.9% (2004)
Children with less than good health	18% (2004)
Children living in poverty	17% (2004)

Children suffering from asthma	13% (2005)
Children taking regular prescription medicine	13% (2005)
Children with limitation of activity caused by chronic condition	7% (2006)
Children with a learning disability	7% (2005)
Children who receive special education or early intervention services	5.6% (2005)
Children who have difficulty speaking English	5.2% (2004)

Source: ChildStats.Gov, CDC.Gov.

One of the most important defining characteristics of children is their location dependence, specifically as it relates to schools and day care facilities. The vast majority of children spend up to 80% of their waking hours in school or out-of-home care. Other locations where children congregate include sports facilities, camps, and entertainment venues (movie theaters, arcades, playgrounds). While in-school hours help to reduce the vulnerability of children (in that they are together and accounted for), many children in families with working parents remain alone or unsupervised between the hours when the school day ends and parents return home. During summer months, when school is not in session, this period may persist throughout the entire workweek.

The massive evacuation surrounding Hurricanes Katrina and Rita in 2005 showed that planners need to look beyond the population of children within their own communities when preparing for disasters. Influxes of as many as three hundred thousand evacuees (as was the case in Houston, Texas) quickly resulted in disaster responses in those other locations that were otherwise unaffected by the initiating hazard. In these situations, many of the same response mechanisms are initiated (shelter, emergency nutrition, reunification, first aid, and medical care), and these processes can quickly overwhelm existing normal capacities. Therefore, planners must look most closely at the population of children within their jurisdiction, but also understand that there may be children and families from outside areas who arrive looking for assistance.

Additionally, many systems of classification, including that utilized by the child-focused international organization UNICEF, include pregnant women in the special population category of

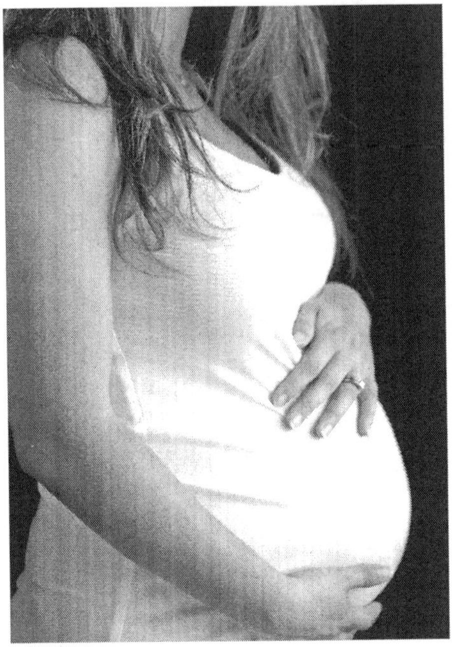

FIGURE 1.3 **In disaster scenarios, planners should consider the vulnerabilities and needs of pregnant women in much the same way as they would a child.**

children. Because an unborn child is dependent upon its mother's ability to maintain proper health and nutrition, and to stay safe and healthy, pregnant mothers have many needs similar to those of children. Planners should consider the vulnerabilities and needs of pregnant women when developing disaster response plans and the functional annex as described in this guide (Figure 1.3).

Physical and Physiological Vulnerabilities

One of the most imporant physical characteristics contributing to the vulnerability of children is their smaller size. For biological and chemical hazards, for instance, their small size results in greater absorbtion of toxic agents, as a result of their thinner skin, greater skin surface-to-mass ratios, faster breathing rates, and other factors. Their smaller total body mass can also result in greater force applied per unit of body area inflicted by flying objects, falls, and blunt or blast trauma (proven to result in a higher frequency of injury to multiple organs than adults).

Children's bodies contain lower absolute volumes of blood than adults and, likewise, a smaller reserve of fluids. Injuries resulting in blood loss become critical much sooner in children, and dehydration from diarrheal illnesses or a lack of rehydration lead to shock and death much faster as well. And because children's bones are smaller, more pliable, and not yet fully formed, they are more likely to fracture. Children are more likely to sustain spinal and cranial injuries in events that would not normally cause a severe injury to an adult. Brain injuries in a developing child can result not only in immediate effects, but have long-lasting implications on the future development of the child. Because children's rib cages are much thinner and more fragile, injuries to the liver, spleen, and lungs are more likely from blunt force trauma (see Sidebar 1.4).

SIDEBAR 1.4 PHYSICAL HARM

There are many ways that children can be physically harmed in a disaster:

- Injury from building collapse
- Injury motor vehicle crashes
- Injury from debris
- Infection from spilled chemicals or pollutants in standing water
- Ingesting spoiled food or polluted water
- Injured in transit during an evacuation
- Injured or assaulted in an evacuation shelter
- Extended periods without proper nutrition or water
- Exposure to inclement weather (hot or cold)
- Attack by feral animals
- Existing or chronic illness aggravated by disaster disruption in medical attention
- Lack of access to appropriate health care professionals, medicine, and equipment

The physiological reaction of children differs significantly from that of adults, which can result in misdiagnosis or incorrect treatment by untrained emergency technicians. For instance, children's bodies are able to compensate for and maintain a relatively steady heart rate even while suffering from shock. Other vital signs, including temperature, respiratory rates, and blood pressure, can differ significantly from adults' in the same emergency situations, and vary by age group as well.

Children, especially small babies, do not yet have fully formed immune systems. Because of this, they are much more susceptible to infection, whether from a biological agent or from the decreased health conditions present in the aftermath of a major disaster. Children are much more likely to contract food- and water-borne illnesses during the response and recovery of a disaster, and those who do fall ill tend to have much more pronounced reactions to these pathogens (Figure 1.4).

Children are different from adults in the type of health care they require in a disaster. The AAP notes, "Children require appropriate pediatric care, and disaster planning must be customized to meet children's needs. Awareness of pediatric guidelines, and training related to these guidelines, are both key. When children are critically ill or injured, their bodies will respond differently than adults in similar medical crises. Children need different doses of medicine, customized equipment, and special considerations during decontamination efforts" (American Academy of Pediatrics, 2002).

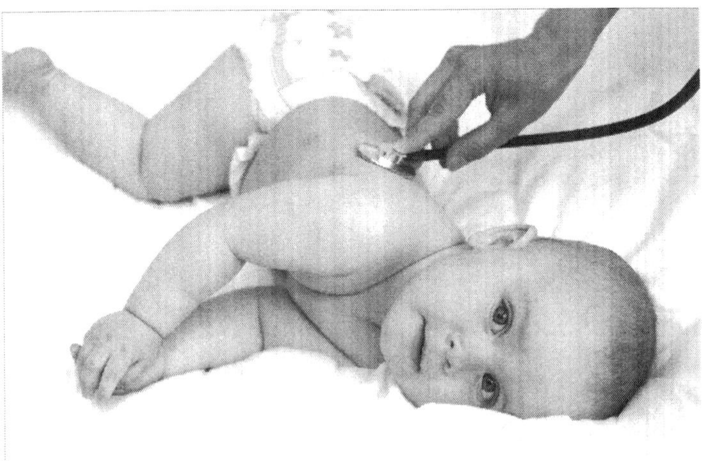

FIGURE 1.4 Children, especially small babies, are far more susceptible to contract illnesses or infection than adults.

Developmental and Social Vulnerabilities

Because of their immature state of development, children are often unable to describe, or even comprehend, their physical and emotional health conditions and needs. This is especially true of children who are very young, including newborns and toddlers. Children may not recognize injury or illness, and likewise may not be able to tell responders, caregivers, or physicians about their pain or other symptoms. Children may even struggle against or otherwise resist the efforts of responders out of a lack of understanding or fear of what is going on (see Sidebar 1.5).

SIDEBAR 1.5 CHILDREN'S VULNERABILITY TO DISASTERS

Physically, how children are more vulnerable in a disaster:

Children have less fluid reserves and, thus, are more susceptible to dehydration if vomiting occurs due to illness or from exposure to toxins.

Young children, babies, and toddlers largely cannot flee danger as quickly as adults, or flee at all, due to (a) their stature and motor skills, (b) their inability to understand commands, and (c) their lack of cognitive awareness to escape imminent danger.

In a biological or chemical scenario, since children breathe more times per minute than adults, they will be exposed to higher doses of toxins over same time period.

Some toxic agents are heavier and will lie more directly in the path of children.

Children's thinner skin may result in higher absorption in addition to the higher surface-to-mass ratio, as compared to adults.

Psychologically, how children are more vulnerable in a disaster:

The level of physical and cognitive development and experience plays an important role in how children at any age will react to a disaster.

The psychological well-being of their parents and/or caregivers can significantly impact the psychological well-being of an individual child.

Source: Based on information available from the American Academy of Pediatrics.

Because of their rapid development, children have very different and constantly changing dietary, sleep, recreation, and medical regemens that must be tracked and addressed regularly. During times of disaster, especially in situations where primary caregivers are injured or unable to reach their children, these routines can become disrupted and result in physical and stress-related reactions in children in a very short period of time. Children with special dietary needs or with allergies may not fully understand these needs and may not be able to communicate them to alternate or emergency caregivers (such as in shelters) (see Sidebar 1.6 and Figure 1.5).

SIDEBAR 1.6 PROTECTING KIDS: SAFE SPACES

Safe Spaces is one of Save the Children's "signature programs" in U.S. emergencies and around the world. Under the supervision of caring adults, **Safe Spaces** provides children with a special area where they can play, socialize, express themselves and begin to recover through a variety of games and activities. In the U.S., Save the Children distributes kits with materials to help set up **Safe Spaces** in evacuation shelters and other locations. The kits can be used by staff and volunteers to set up structured activities for children, or in shorter-term scenarios, to provide ways for families and children to play together. The kits contain materials to mark off a special area for children; activity supplies such as art materials, books, blocks, scarves and balls; and materials to help schedule activities, check children in and out, and sanitize toys.

Source: Save the Children. Safe Spaces—A signature program. http://www.savethechildren.org/programs/us-programs/safe-spaces-us.html.

A child who has lost or become separated from a primary caregiver, or whose caregiver is incapable of providing adequate care, will face immediate life safety-critical vulnerabilities. Most children are completely incapable of addressing their own basic needs, be they for shelter, food, water, clothing, medication, pyschological comfort, or other. They also may be unable to remove themselves from dangerous pre- or postdisaster situations. Infants and toddlers who have lost caregivers, and who have not been located by responders or other caregivers, are most at risk, and likely to suffer severe injury or death within days or hours (depending upon climatic and other

FIGURE 1.5 **Houston, Texas, September 12, 2005. The George R. Brown Convention Center has several areas with extensive play facilities for the children of evacuees. Hundreds of displaced New Orleaneans are being housed here. (Ed Edahl/FEMA)**

conditions at the time of the disaster event). Finally, their lower cognitive abilities can hinder their capacity to comprehend and follow warnings and directions, or to recognize and distance themselves from dangerous situations (see Sidebar 1.7).

SIDEBAR 1.7 AMERICAN RED CROSS—CHILDREN

Disasters may strike quickly and without warning. These events can be frightening for adults, but they are traumatic for children if they don't know what to do.

During a disaster, your family may have to leave your home and daily routine. Children may become anxious, confused, or frightened. It is important to give children guidance that will help them reduce their fears.

Children and Their Response to Disaster

Children depend on daily routines: They wake up, eat breakfast, go to school, play with friends. When emergencies or disasters interrupt this routine, children may become anxious.

In a disaster, they'll look to you and other adults for help. How you react to an emergency gives them clues on how to act. If you react with alarm, a child may become more scared.

They see our fear as proof that the danger is real. If you seem overcome with a sense of loss, a child may feel their losses more strongly.

Children's fears also may stem from their imagination, and you should take these feelings seriously. A child who feels afraid is afraid. Your words and actions can provide reassurance. When talking with your child, be sure to present a realistic picture that is both honest and manageable.

Feelings of fear are healthy and natural for adults and children. But as an adult, you need to keep control of the situation. When you're sure that danger has passed, concentrate on your child's emotional needs by asking the child what's uppermost in his or her mind.

Having children participate in the family's recovery activities will help them feel that their life will return to "normal." Your response during this time may have a lasting impact.

Source: American Red Cross. *Preparing and getting trained: Children.* http://www.redcross.org/portal/site/en/menuitem.d8aaecf214c576bf971e4cfe43181aa0/?vgnextoid=e4a20c45f663b110VgnVCM10000089f0870aRCRD&vgnextfmt=def.

Following disasters, children who have been affected directly or indirectly through a family member are more likely to exhibit a decline in school performance. One of the primary causes of this adverse affect is a decrease in attention and concentration. Changes in sleeping situations, nutrition, and routines can cause decreased alertness or exhaustion, which contributes to the poorer performance levels. Children may worry about or constantly revisit the disaster event, or may be suffering from psychological trauma, both of which affect their ability to learn and process information.

Psychological Vulnerabilities

All disaster victims face the risk of psychological stress and trauma. Children, however, face an increased risk due to their strong dependence upon caregivers, and their inability to fully comprehend the situation occurring around them. Children often maintain assumptions about their own safety that are shattered by disaster events, and they witness fear, injury, or loss of their primary caregivers. The effects of disaster events are therefore magnified in the minds of children (see Sidebar 1.8 and Figure 1.6).

SIDEBAR 1.8 TSUNAMI'S IMPACT ON CHILD SURVIVORS

Following the tsunami of December 2004, Save the Children asked over 500 parents and caregivers in Aceh Province, Indonesia to describe how their children's attitudes and behaviors changed as a result of the tsunami. The following answers were the most common:

- Children cannot sleep and are afraid to close their eyes at night.
- They don't want to go near the ocean.
- Some are afraid to go back to schools that were damaged.
- Many have lost their self-confidence.
- Some become upset or cry when they hear loud noises.
- Many have bad dreams.

Parents said their children's worst fears were that the tsunami would happen again and that they would be separated from their parents. In order to support recovery, Save the Children has developed education and recreation programs, as well as children's clubs, to help in restoring predictability and normalcy. Structured and supervised activities that give children a chance to express their fears and share their concerns with other children are providing a healing environment as well. Save the Children is also supporting parents to address their own fears and help their children begin recovery.

Source: Save the Children. 2005. *Policy brief—Protecting children in emergencies*. http://www.savethechildren.org/publications/policy-briefs/policy_brief_final_1.pdf.

The U.S. government Agency for Healthcare Research and Quality writes (Figure 1.7):

> The psychological effects of disaster on children are neither uniform nor universal in nature. Important factors in the psychological effect of a disaster on children include the nature of the disaster itself, the level of exposure to the disaster, the extent to which the children

FIGURE 1.6 Mass casualty and fatality incidents like the Asian Tsunami of 2004 can have very devastating and long-term impacts, especially on children.

and those around them are personally affected, and individual characteristics of each child. Children are still undergoing psychological development at the time of disaster. Their developmental stage characterizes their response and is responsible for the wide degree of variability in adjustment to traumatic events. (AHRQ, 2006)

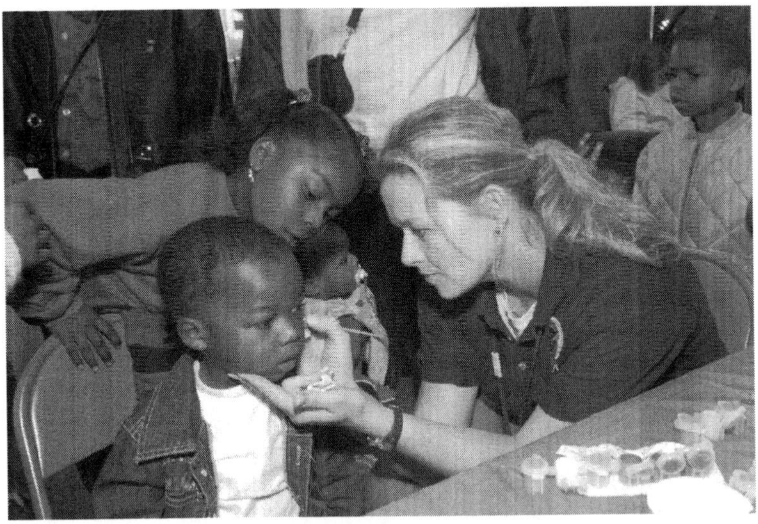

FIGURE 1.7 McComb, Mississippi, December 17, 2005. Donna Althof, the FEMA DRC coordinator, paints a candy cane on the face of a Hurricane Katrina evacuee. The Disaster Recovery Center (DRC) in McComb held a Christmas party for the children of Hurricane Katrina evacuees who are working with the McComb DRC. (Patsy Lynch/FEMA)

Safety and Security Vulnerabilities

Children involved in disaster situations can become highly vulnerable with regards to their physical safety and security. Child predators who wish to exploit vulnerable disaster-affected children often find they have much easier access to victims than they normally would in situations wherein there is lower individual supervision and a highly distracted police force. Evacuation and shelter situations can place convicted or otherwise unkown sex offenders and criminals in close quarters with children.

Children affected by disasters can also fall prey to the influences of peer pressure or depression. Child disaster victims often exhibit greater risk-taking behavior in terms of drug and alcohol abuse and sexual experimentation. They also may fail to show symptoms of depression, or these symptoms may go unnoticed in light of the surrounding chaos, leading to impulse actions such as suicide or violence.

Finally, studies have shown that domestic violence increases significantly in the aftermath of a disaster when parents become overwhelmed with the frightening reality of their situation. Children are often the victims of this violence, which occurs at a time when protective social services are overwhelmed with a caseload far greater than what they managed prior to the disaster (Figure 1.8).

FIGURE 1.8 Domestic violence, abuse, and child predators are some of the considerations planners need to address to ensure the safety and protection of children.

What Are the Special Emergency Response Needs of Children?

Planners need an explicit understanding of the needs of both children and the individuals, services, and products upon which children depend, in order to address those needs in the emergency operations plan. These needs fall into several areas of concern. Within each area of concern, needs may be placed into the four separate functions associated with the emergency management cycle: mitigation, preparedness, response, and recovery.

Most planners understand that the needs of children are extensive even in nondisaster situations. In times of disaster, these everyday needs not only persist, but also grow exponentially in light of new factors arising out of the consequences of the disaster itself, and the changing nature of the circumstances surrounding each child's care.

As defined by the United Nations, the needs of children fall under three general categories:

- Physical protection
- Psychosocial protection
- Cognitive protection

Physical protection includes those needs related to the security and physical (bodily) safety of the child. Children become more vulnerable in disaster situations, when traditional systems of protection from exploitation and child predation break down or become weakened. General health problems, accompanied by new disaster-related health problems and injuries, grow in number and severity quickly. The basic physical needs of all people, including shelter, nutrition, hygiene, sleep, recreation, and others, are less flexible among children, and must be addressed by only those trained in the particulars of each as they relate to younger, smaller, developing bodies.

Psychosocial protection aims to ensure that the psychological and social development of the child is neither harmed nor stunted—both of which typically occur among children during disasters to a degree far exceeding that of adults. The social and psychological development of children can be interrupted or altered by a disaster situation when the child's life and routine are likewise disrupted. In the aftermath of disasters, the psyche of children becomes fragile due to an almost absolute dependence upon individuals and systems whose strength and permanence have been called into question. Many children will have witnessed or experienced themselves the devastation of the disaster that causes psychological trauma even in adults.

Cognitive protection refers to those processes relating to the child's ability to perceive, process, and retain information. Childhood is a period of intense cognitive development, guided by school, parents, social networks, and experiences. Disasters can disrupt these processes for weeks, months, or even years. Children whose cognitive development has been negatively impacted by a disaster may quickly fall behind their peers, and suffer learning deficiencies that plague them for life.

Many of the individual needs of children fall into two, or even all three, of these categories. For instance, while a quality education most directly addresses a child's cognitive development, the social benefits of an education cannot be denied, nor can the physical health and development that are gained by maintaining a daily routine with other children and teachers in the protective environment of a classroom. And for each of these needs, there are degrees and particulars of need that will change with the age of the child, and with any special needs of children with special physical, social, or psychological conditions.

CASE STUDY: Psychological Effects of Disasters on Children

Two myths are potential barriers to recognizing children's responses to disaster and must be rejected: (1) that children are innately resilient and will recover rapidly, even from severe trauma; and (2) that children, especially young children, are not affected by disaster unless they are disturbed by their parents' responses. Both of these beliefs are false. A wealth of evidence indicates that children experience the effects of disaster doubly. Even very young children are directly affected by experiences of death, destruction, terror, personal physical assault, and by experiencing the absence or powerlessness of their parents. They are also indirectly affected through identification with the effects of the disaster on their parents and other trusted adults (such as teachers) and by their parents' reactions to the disaster.

Another barrier to recognizing children's responses to disaster is the tendency of parents to misinterpret their children's reactions. To parents who are already under stress, a child's withdrawal, regression, or misconduct may be understood as willful. Or, parents may not wish to be reminded of their own trauma or, seeking some small evidences that their life is again back in control, may have a need to see everything as "all right." In either case, they may ignore or deny evidence of their children's distress. The child, in turn, may feel ignored, not validated, not nurtured. This may have long-term consequences for the child's development. In the short run, feeling insecure, the child may inhibit expression of his or her own feelings, lest he or she distress and drive away the parents even more [Figure 1.9].

FIGURE 1.9 **Orlando, Florida, May 24, 2005. FEMA-funded crisis counseling grant produces "Heroes of the Storm," a twenty-minute puppet show. Developed by the Florida Department of Children and Families, it helps children deal with distress and trauma that may have been brought on by last year's hurricanes. (Ed Edahl/FEMA)**

Most children respond sensibly and appropriately to disaster, especially if they experience the protection, support, and stability of their parents and other trusted adults. However, like adults, they may respond to disaster with a wide range of symptoms. Their responses are generally similar to those of adults, although they may appear in more direct, less disguised form.

Among preschool children (ages 1–5), anxiety symptoms may appear in generalized form as fears about separation, fears of strangers, fears of "monsters" or animals, or sleep disturbances. The child may also avoid specific situations or environments, which may or may not have obvious links to the disaster. The child may appear preoccupied with words or symbols that may or may not be associated with the disaster in obvious ways or may engage in compulsively repetitive play which represents part of the disaster experience. The child may show a limited expression of emotion or a constricted pattern of play may appear. He or she may withdraw socially or may lose previously acquired developmental skills (e.g., toilet training).

Older children (ages 6–11 or so) may engage in repetitious play in which the child reenacts parts of the disaster or in repeated retelling of the story of the disaster. The child may express (openly or subtly) concerns about safety and preoccupation with danger. Sleep disturbances, irritability, or aggressive behavior and angry outbursts may appear. The child may pay close attention to his or her parents' worries or seem to worry excessively about family members and friends. School avoidance (possibly in the form of somatic symptoms) may appear. The child may show separation anxiety with primary caretakers, "magical" explanations to fill in gaps in understanding, and other behaviors usually characteristic of much younger children. Other changes in behavior, mood, and personality, obvious anxiety and fearfulness, withdrawal, loss of interest in activities, and "spacey" or distractible behavior may appear.

As children approach adolescence, their responses become increasingly like adult responses. Greater levels of aggressive behaviors, defiance of parents, delinquency, substance abuse, and risk-taking behaviors may be evident. School performance may decline. Wishes for revenge may be expressed. Adolescents are especially unlikely to seek out counseling.

Children of all ages are strongly affected by the responses of their parents or other caretakers to disaster. Children are especially vulnerable to feeling abandoned when they are separated from or lose their parents. "Protecting" children by sending them away from the scene of the disaster, thus separating them from their loved ones, adds the trauma of separation to the trauma of disaster.

SYMPTOMS SHOWN BY SCHOOL-AGED CHILDREN

- Depression
- Withdrawal
- Generalized fear, including nightmares, highly specific phobias of stimuli associated with the disaster
- Defiance
- Aggressiveness, "acting out"
- Resentfulness, suspiciousness, irritability
- Disorganized, "agitated" behavior
- Somatic complaints: headaches, gastrointestinal disturbances, general aches and pains. These may be revealed by a pattern of repeated school absences.
- Difficulties with concentration
- Intrusive memories and thoughts and sensations, which may be especially likely to appear when the child is bored or at rest or when falling asleep
- Repetitive dreams
- Loss of a sense of control and of responsibility
- Loss of a sense of a future

- Loss of a sense of individuality and identity
- Loss of a sense of reasonable expectations with respect to interpersonal interactions
- Loss of a realistic sense of when he or she is vulnerable or in danger
- Feelings of shame
- Ritual re-enactments of aspects of the disaster in play or drawing or story telling. In part, this can be understood as an attempt at mastery. Drawings may have images of trauma and bizarre expressions of unconscious imagery, with many elaborations and repetitions.
- Kinesthetic (bodily) re-enactments of aspects of the disaster; repetitive gestures or responses to stress reenacting those of the disaster
- Omen formation: the child comes to believe that certain "signs" preceding the disaster were warnings and that he or she should be alert for future signs of disaster
- Regression: Bed wetting, soiling, clinging, heightened separation anxiety.
- Post Traumatic Stress Disorder syndromes much like those of adults, although possibly with less amnesia, avoidance, and numbing evident.

For an adult, although the effects of disaster may be profound and lasting, they take place in an already formed personality. For children, the effects are magnified by the fact that the child's personality is still developing. The child has to construct his or her identity within a framework of the psychological damage done by the disaster. When the symptoms produced by disaster are not treated, or when the disaster is ongoing, either because of the destruction wrought (e.g., by an earthquake) or because the source of trauma is itself chronic (e.g., war or relocation to a refugee camp), the consequences are even graver. The child grows up with fear and anxiety, with the experience of destruction or cruelty or violence, with separations from home and family. Childhood itself, with its normal play, love, and affection, is lost. Longer-term responses of children who have been chronically traumatized may include a defensive desensitization. They seem cold, insensitive, lacking in emotion in daily life. Violence may come to be seen as the norm, legitimate. A sense of a meaningful future is lost.

Source: Ehrenreich, J. H. 2001. *A guidebook to psychosocial intervention.* Mental Health Workers Without Borders. http://www.mhwwb.org/Coping With Disaster.pdf. With permission.

CASE STUDY: Special Psychological Needs of Children Following Disasters

For the most part, the same principles that apply to adults apply to children, with appropriate adaptations for their age (i.e., use language appropriate to the child's age; be concrete). The various child-specific reactions to disaster discussed earlier suggest several additional principles for work with children:

- Children are affected both directly by the disaster and indirectly, by observing and being affected by their parents' reactions. Unless there are strong reasons to the contrary, such as an abusive parent-child relation or the physical or psychological unavailability of the parents, involving children together with their parents should be a major part of treatment.
- Encouraging parents to discuss what happened in the disaster with their child, to recognize and accept and understand their child's reactions and to communicate openly about their own reactions, is helpful.
- A barrier to identifying children in need of services may be the parents' ignoring or denying signs of distress in their children or parents or

attributing regressive behaviors such as bed wetting or acting out behaviors as "willful." Parents should be educated about these issues and case finding should be pursued through other routes (e.g., schools) as well.

- Parents may benefit from education with regard to appropriate responses to particular behaviors and to the benefits of specific treatments, as well. For instance (a) Regressive behaviors, such as bed wetting, should be accepted initially. The child should be comforted without demands. He or she should not be shamed or criticized or punished. Later, normal expectations can be gradually resumed. (b) Behavioral interventions (systems of rewarding desired behaviors, with limit setting on undesirable behaviors) are the most useful responses to inappropriate behaviors. (c) Physical comforting may be useful in reducing anxiety levels among children. One study has shown that regular back and neck massages may be helpful. (d) Children need reassurance and permission to express their own feelings without fear of being judged.
- Children may have special concrete needs—toys, bedding, special foods, availability of age appropriate activities (play groups, school, chores). Parents also benefit when these are provided, since they help the parents cope with the demands their children place on them. On-going childcare services, to enable parents to return to work or to deal with the practicalities of a return to normal function, are also needed.
- Separation of children from their parents should be avoided, if at all possible. When it is absolutely necessary (for the child's safety or because of the inability of the parents to care for the child), efforts should be made to ensure that the child is accompanied by other familiar and important figures in their life, such as a grandparent, older sibling or teacher.

- Children are especially prone to drawing inaccurate conclusions about the cause of the disaster, their own actions and the normality of their current feelings. For example, they may believe that they are somehow to blame for what happened. Exploration and correction of these ideas is part of treatment.
- Younger children (up to ten or eleven, at least) may not be able to use language effectively to describe their feelings or to work through their reactions. Drawing, play with puppets, role playing or writing which is not specifically focused on the disaster (e.g., poetry, stories) may be a useful way of enabling a fuller exploration of responses.
- Children should be given time to experience and express their feelings, but as soon as possible, a return to the structure of household routines should be pursued.
- Schools play a key role. They provide a safe haven for children during the day and serve as locations for case finding and for intervention and. [*sic*] By providing a structured environment for the child, they help the child regulate his or her reactions. A rapid return of children to school and monitoring of attendance and of unusual symptoms is helpful. (It is not unusual for children to want to be with their parents immediately following a disaster, however. Childcare services may be needed). When children return to school after a disaster, they should not be immediately rushed back to ordinary school routines. Instead, they should be given time to talk about the event and express their feelings about it (without forcing those who do not wish to talk to do so). In-school sessions with entire classes or groups of students may be helpful. The school can also hold meetings with parents to discuss children's responses and provide

education for parents in how to respond to children after a disaster.
- Children, like adults, benefit from feeling a sense of control over frightening situations. Involving children in age-appropriate and situation-appropriate tasks that are relevant to relief efforts (e.g., collecting supplies for disaster victims or taking on responsibilities such as caring for younger children in a shelter) is helpful both to the child and to other victims of the disaster.
- The repetitive graphic images of the disaster shown on television can generate anxiety. Exposure to television accounts of the disaster should be limited. An adult should be present to monitor and protect the child from overwhelming graphic images and to talk about what the child is watching.

Source: Ehrenreich, J. H. 2001. *A guidebook to psychosocial intervention.* Mental Health Workers Without Borders. http://www.mhwwb.org/Coping With Disaster.pdf. With permission.

Save the Children has developed psychosocial programs that help children and caregivers to cope with the emotional and psychological impacts of disasters. According to the Save the Children website:

> After major US disasters strike, Save the Children seeks to address these issues by offering community-based recovery and resilience-building programs for children and their caregivers. These workshops—also known as psychosocial programs because they address children's personal, emotional and social needs—use cooperative games and structured play, expressive and art activities to help children:
>
> - Rebuild a sense of safety and normalcy
> - Express their thoughts and feelings about their experiences
> - Strengthen resilience, or coping skills
> - Build positive relationships with peers and caregivers (Save the Children, Recovery and Resilience Building programs)

Over 30,000 children and 1,400 caregivers participated in Save the Children psychosocial programs in the aftermath of Hurricane Katrina. (Save the Children, 2007)

In 2009, Save the Children launched a nationwide initiative to establish Disaster-Resilient Communities for Children in four Texas cities (see Sidebar 1.9). One component of this initiative is the Resilient and Ready Program, "an hour long workshop designed to educate children (grades K–6) and build resiliency when faced with various forms of disasters, including earthquakes, floods and wildfires. The workshop combines cooperative games with disaster education to provide a fun, yet educational way for children to learn about preparedness" (Save the Children, 2009). More information concerning this initiative is provided in Chapters 3 and 4.

SIDEBAR 1.9 DISASTER-RESILIENT COMMUNITIES FOR CHILDREN

Using a nationally applicable framework that embraces community-based approaches, Save the Children works with emergency planners, emergency responders, schools, childcare leaders, caregivers and children to assess communities' strengths and address critical gaps in emergency planning for children's comprehensive needs. Based on a highly successful one-year pilot project in Tulsa, Oklahoma, Save the Children's *Disaster Resilient Communities for Children* initiative engages community stakeholders in implementing best practices of emergency planning to help to safeguard children in at-risk communities. With the support of locally engaged businesses and organizations, Save the Children hopes to replicate this program's success and make major metropolitan areas in Texas (Austin, Dallas, Houston and San Antonio) national leaders in disaster resilience and preparedness for children and families.

Source: Save the Children. 2009. Disaster resilient communities for children: Concept note. August.

A number of organizations have developed guidance for parents on how they can help their children cope with disasters (see Sidebar 1.10).

SIDEBAR 1.10 TEN TIPS TO HELP CHILDREN COPE WITH DISASTER

Children are often deeply affected by what they see and hear during and after an emergency. During major disasters, children across the country may be frightened by media reports of the destruction, even if their families were not in harm's way.

Concerned about the emotional well being of their children, many parents, teachers, grandparents and caregivers look for advice on how to respond to questions from children about disasters.

The following ten tips are based on Save the Children's years of experience responding to emergencies and crises in the United States and internationally and can be used as a guide for adults to support children through times of crisis.

1. Hug your children often and comfort them.
2. Listen to children carefully and give them opportunities to talk about what happened.
3. Limit TV time—news & pictures can be frightening.
4. Watch for changes in your children's behavior. If your child continues to display disruptions in eating, sleeping or daily activities, or if you as the caregiver feel uncomfortable or concerned, seek assistance from a mental health professional.
5. Be patient and understanding—your children might still be upset or frightened.
6. Give your children extra time and attention.
7. Use positive behavior and language around your children.
8. Take care of yourself and do healthy things to relax. Try to get enough rest.
9. Help your children return to school, normal activities and routines.
10. Encourage children to volunteer and help others.

Source: Save the Children, http://www.savethechildren.org/countries/usa/us-emergency-programs/us-preparedness/ten-tips.html.

Family Unity

Maintaining family unity in the face of a disaster is critical to protecting the physical and emotional security of a child (see Sidebar 1.11 and Figure 1.10). Children can be separated from their families for many reasons, including:

- During an evacuation before or after an event occurs
- At school or child care when an event occurs
- Being treated at a hospital or medical clinic when an event occurs
- Attending school or summer camp or on a school trip out of town when an event occurs
- Visiting friends or relatives away from home when an event occurs
- At the store, at the movies, or visiting a friend's house when an event occurs

The key factor is to develop protocols and procedures before the next disaster strikes for identifying children separated from their families for whatever reason and reuniting them with their families as quickly and as carefully as possible.

SIDEBAR 1.11 BEING SEPARATED FROM YOUR FAMILY

Save the Children reports:

Few things are more frightening for children or more threatening to their safety and well-being than being lost and alone, separated from family and community in the middle of a conflict or natural disaster. Yet, as a result of war or other emergencies, hundreds of thousands of children around the world suffer this terrible experience. Over the last decade, more than 1 million children have been orphaned or separated from their families by armed conflict. Children who become separated from their families are more vulnerable to illness, exploitation, recruitment, and abuse. Without family support and protection, separated children are even more vulnerable to these threats and have fewer resources to help them rebuild their lives. Unless there is early intervention, there is a risk that children will never find their families again, and, for very young children in particular, their survival may be threatened.

Source: Save the Children. 2005b. *Policy brief—Protecting children in emergencies*. http://www.savethechildren.org/publications/policy-briefs/policy_brief_final_1.pdf.

Separation is especially an issue during an evacuation or forced displacement. Nearly 5,200 children were separated from their

FIGURE 1.10 **New Orleans, Louisiana, August 30, 2008. A mother with her four children evacuating New Orleans checks in at the New Orleans Airport terminal, showing her driver's license and giving all the information needed to board the plane. (Jacinta Quesada/FEMA)**

families in the aftermath of Hurricane Katrina, and it took nearly seven months to reunite all of these children with their families (see Sidebar 1.12).

SIDEBAR 1.12 REUNITING FAMILIES IN HURRICANE KATRINA

According to the National Center for Missing and Exploited Children:

On August 29, 2005, Hurricane Katrina slammed into the Gulf Coast. The furious storm led to incredible property damage, destroyed infrastructure, downed power lines, destroyed roads, and caused the unprecedented evacuation of 411,000 people to 48 states. Many families were separated. Within hours, the U.S. Department of Justice requested NCMEC establish a hotline to handle calls about both adults and children. Thirty Team Adam Consultants were deployed to Alabama, Louisiana, Mississippi, and Texas to help locate displaced children and reunite them with their families. As a result of NCMEC's efforts, in conjunction with local and state agencies, the last of the 5,192 children reported missing or displaced as a result of Hurricanes Katrina and Rita was reunited with her mother and siblings in Houston, Texas, in March 2006.

Source: National Center for Missing and Exploited Children. http://www.missingkids.com/en_US/publications/NC170.pdf. With permission.

In the aftermath of Hurricane Katrina, the Centers for Disease Control and Prevention (CDC) published a protocol to identify and protect displaced children (see Sidebar 1.13).

SIDEBAR 1.13 CENTERS FOR DISEASE CONTROL AND PREVENTION

Protocol to Rapidly Identify and Protect Displaced Children

- Survey all children in your shelter to identify children who are not with their legal guardians—these children have a high probability of being listed as missing by family members; find out where they are sleeping in the shelter; and the name and age of the person who is supervising them. A survey for identifying displaced child evacuees is available online at http://www.health.ok.gov/bt/.
- Place a hospital-style identification bracelet (or a picture identification card, ideally) on the child and a matching one on the supervising adult(s). Check frequently to make sure that the wristband matches that of the adult(s) seen with the child in the shelter.
- The names of all children identified through the survey as not being with their legal guardians should be considered at high-risk and immediately reported to the National Center of Missing and Exploited Children (NCMEC) at 1-888-544-5475. The NCMEC can then crosscheck them with the names of children who have been reported missing.
- After the "high risk" children have been reported, a complete list of children's names in the clinic or shelter should be sent to the NCMEC in case adults and/or children have provided incorrect information about their relationship and status.

- Children who are not with their legal guardians (i.e., prior to the hurricane) should undergo a safety and well-being assessment (taking into consideration an assessment of the relationship between the child and accompanying adult), ideally performed by a physician with pediatric experience.
- If NCMEC informs you that the child has been reported as missing, locate the child and facilitate reunification of the child and his/her legal guardian.

Source: Centers for Disease Control and Prevention. 2005. *CDC health advisory: Instructions for identifying and protecting displaced children*. September 28. http://www2a.cdc.gov/HAN/ArchiveSys/ViewMsgV.asp?AlertNum=00236.

In 2008, the National Commission on Children and Disasters was established by an act of Congress to examine the needs of children in disasters and to identify ways that government and nongovernmental organizations could work to effectively address those needs (see Sidebar 1.14). In October 2009, the commission released an interim report on its findings to date. A summary of the report's findings and recommendations can be found in Appendix A of this book. A copy of the commission's interim report can be found at http://www.childrenanddisasters.acf.hhs.gov/20091014_508IR_partII.pdf. The commission is scheduled to release its final report on October 14, 2010.

One significant finding in the commission's interim report concerned the issue of case management to address the unique needs of children and families after a disaster. The reports states:

> The Commission supports the U.S. Government Accountability Office (GAO) reports' recommendation for the development of a federal disaster case management program and suggests that it be holistic in scope, flexible and sensitive to cultural and economic differences in communities, while placing a priority on serving the needs of families with children. Disaster case management should be led by a single Federal agency which will coordinate, among all relevant agencies and organizations, disaster case management and ensure there is a) adequate understanding of the health, education and human services needs of children and

families, b) involvement of voluntary agencies that provide disaster case management, and c) access to funding that supports all aspects of disaster case management, including direct services. Disaster preparedness funding must be provided for infrastructure and capacity building to support a disaster case management program, in advance of a disaster, and to contract for the rapid deployment of case managers into disaster affected areas.

The purpose of disaster case management is to rapidly return children and families who have survived a disaster to a state of self-sufficiency. The program should develop a consistent set of comprehensive program evaluation tools that regularly measure and monitor success based upon tangible positive outcomes for families (especially those most in need), rather than case managers simply making referrals. The program evaluation should also include guidelines for assessing and monitoring recovery milestones for children. All individuals within a Presidentially-declared disaster area should be eligible to receive disaster case management services. (National Commission on Children and Disasters, 2009)

SIDEBAR 1.14 NATIONAL COMMISSION ON CHILDREN AND DISASTERS

Background

The National Commission on Children and Disasters ("the Commission") was established pursuant to the Kids in Disasters Well-being, Safety and Health Act of 2007 as provided in Division G, Title VI of the Consolidated Appropriations Act of 2008 (Public Law (P.L.) 110–161). The Commission's status as an independent Federal Advisory Committee was clarified in Division A, Section 157 (b) of the Consolidated Security, Disaster Assistance, and Continuing Appropriations Act, 2009 (P.L. 110–329).

The Commission shall conduct a comprehensive study to independently examine and assess the needs of children (0–18 years of age) in relation to the preparation for, response to and recovery from all emergencies, hazards and disasters, by building upon the evaluations of other entities and avoiding unnecessary duplication by reviewing the findings, conclusions and recommendations of these entities. In addition to this *Interim Report*, the Commission will submit a *Final Report* to the President and Congress no later than October 14, 2010.

The Commission shall report specific findings, conclusions and recommendations relating to: 1) child physical health, mental health, and trauma; 2) child care in all settings; child welfare; 3) elementary and secondary education; 4) sheltering, temporary housing and affordable housing; 5) transportation; 6) juvenile justice; 7) evacuation; 8) relevant activities in emergency management; and 9) the need for planning and establishing a national resource center on children and disasters. The Commission shall also report on coordination of resources and services, administrative actions, policies, regulations, and legislative changes as the Commission considers appropriate (P.L. 110–161).

The Commission is bipartisan, consisting of 10 members appointed by the President and Congressional leaders. Commission members represent a variety of disciplines, including pediatrics, state and local emergency management, emergency medical services, non-governmental organizations dedicated to children, and state elected office. The Commission organized four subcommittees comprised of Commissioners and subject matter experts: 1) Education, Child Welfare and Juvenile Justice; 2) Evacuation, Transportation and Housing; 3) Human Services Recovery; and 4) Pediatric Medical Care. The Commission meets publicly on a quarterly basis and subcommittees meet monthly to address their specific focus areas.

Source: National Commission on Children and Disasters. 2009. *Interim report*. October 14. http://www.childrenanddisasters.acf.hhs.gov/20091014_508IR_partII.pdf.

FEMA has recently begun to address the unique needs of children in disasters. A training course concerning children in disasters is now offered online and as an instructor-led course by FEMA. In congressional testimony in August 2009, FEMA Administrator Craig Fugate announced the establishment of a children's working group to "provide an immediate forum for promoting the needs of children across the agency" (Fugate, 2009) (see Sidebar 1.15 and Figure 1.11).

SIDEBAR 1.15 FEMA'S CHILDREN'S WORKING GROUP: EXCERPT FROM TESTIMONY BY FEMA ADMINISTRATOR CRAIG FUGATE BEFORE THE U.S. SENATE

Moving Forward: New Approaches for Protecting the Needs of Children

In addition to its work on the Commission, Save the Children also recently issued a report calling for immediate federal action to better protect our community's children in times of disaster. The report makes several recommendations, including the establishment of an Office for Children's Advocacy at FEMA. I am pleased to announce that in response to this report and as a result of ongoing discussions with the Commission, FEMA is creating a Children's Working Group.

The purpose of the working group is to create a centralized platform—across all of FEMA's directorates—to ensure that the needs of children are incorporated into all of our disaster preparedness, response, and recovery efforts. Representatives from virtually all aspects of the agency will serve on the working group, which will be chaired by a senior member of the FEMA leadership team. The group will not only serve to create a common operating picture across FEMA, it will also improve our capacity to work collaboratively across the Federal government and with State and local partners in support of children's needs. This new team will advocate for children's issues at every stage of the planning process, rather than having the special needs of our most precious community members addressed as an afterthought.

More specifically, the Children's Working Group will focus on the following key areas:

- Child-specific guidance for evacuation, sheltering, and relocation;
- Tracking and reunification of families;
- Coordinated case management support;
- Enhanced preparedness for child care centers and schools as well as for children in child welfare and juvenile justice systems;

- Enhanced national planning, including incorporation of children into national planning scenarios and exercises;
- Incorporation of children's needs into grant guidance;
- Improved recovery coordination across the Federal government and with State, tribal and local partners in support of children's education, health and housing;
- Consideration as to how the Federal family can help ensure child care centers are able to rebuild and restore services more quickly following a disaster; and
- Increased public awareness efforts to educate families and protect children during disasters.

In short, the establishment of the Children's Working Group will provide an immediate forum for promoting the needs of children across the agency. It will allow us to move forward quickly in evaluating the recommendations of both the National Commission on Children and Disasters and non-governmental groups such as Save the Children.

It is our intent that the Children's Working Group will help identify and facilitate how best to integrate the special needs of children into all of our planning efforts without isolating children's issues from community issues at large.

This working group represents a new way of tackling and focusing on this issue, one that is aimed at integrating children's planning throughout the agency, coordinating among the federal family, and across the Nation. We are optimistic that this approach will create real, lasting change when it comes to our planning for, and treatment of, children's needs during disasters.

Source: Fugate, C. 2009. Testimony before the U.S. Senate, Committee on Homeland Security and Governmental Affairs, Ad Hoc Subcommittee on Disaster Recovery. In *Focus on children in disasters: Evacuation planning and mental health recovery*. Washington, DC, August 4. http://hsgac.senate.gov/public/index.cfm?FuseAction=Files.View&FileStore_id=ac143d9, c760-47d6-bc46-0a9845b74116.

Conclusion

You now have an understanding of three of the unique needs of children in disasters. Physical security is important for protecting children from harm and ensuring that appropriate medical care is available for children injured in disasters. A child's emotional

FIGURE 1.11 **Washington, DC, December 10, 2009—FEMA Administrator Craig Fugate testifies on addressing the needs of children in disasters before the Senate Committee on Homeland Security and Government Affairs, Ad Hoc Subcommittee on Disaster Recovery. The main purpose of the hearing is to evaluate the interim report from the National Commission on Children and Disasters. Specifically, the subcommittee is asking that Fugate address: (1) FEMA's coordination with HHS in developing strategies to address the needs of children in disasters; (2) its partnership with the National Commission; and (3) what FEMA is doing to address the concerns raised in the National Commission's interim report. (Bill Koplitz/FEMA)**

stability can be easily disrupted by a disaster event, and care must be taken in identifying the symptoms associated with a child traumatized by a disaster event. Programs are available that can help children and caregivers to cope with disasters after the event occurs, and to learn to be prepared to cope prior to when the next disaster strikes. Family unity is critical to the overall security children feel in their everyday life and especially in a disaster. Steps must be taken before the next disaster to reduce the chances that families will be separated and ensure that, if they are separated, the families are reunited in a timely and careful manner.

References

Agency for Healthcare Research and Quality (AHRQ). 2006. *Pediatric terrorism and disaster preparedness: A resource for pediatricians*. U.S. Department of Health and Human Services. http://www.ahrq.gov/research/pedprep/pedresource.pdf.

American Academy of Pediatrics. 2002. *Disaster preparedness initiatives.* American Academy of Pediatrics. http://www.aap.org/advocacy/releases/disaster_preparedness.htm.

American Red Cross. *Preparing and getting trained: Children.* http://www.redcross.org/portal/site/en/menuitem.d8aaecf214c576bf971e4cfe43181aa0/?vgnextoid=e4a20c45f663b110VgnVCM10000089f0870aRCRD&vgnextfmt=def.

Centers for Disease Control and Prevention. 2005. *CDC health advisory: Instructions for identifying and protecting displaced children.* September 28. http://www2a.cdc.gov/HAN/ArchiveSys/ViewMsgV.asp?AlertNum=00236.

Ehrenreich, J. H. 2001. *A guidebook to psychosocial intervention.* Mental Health Workers Without Borders. http://www.mhwwb.org/CopingWithDisaster.pdf.

Fugate, C. 2009. Testimony before the U.S. Senate, Committee on Homeland Security and Governmental Affairs, Ad Hoc Subcommittee on Disaster Recovery. In *Focus on children in disasters: Evacuation planning and mental health recovery.* Washington, DC, August 4. http://hsgac.senate.gov/public/index.cfm?FuseAction=Files.View&FileStore_id=ac143d9,c760-47d6-bc46-0a9845b74116.

Greenman, J. 2005. *What happened to my world? Helping children cope with natural disaster catastrophe.* Watertown, MA: Comfort for Kids. http://www.mercycorps.org/sites/default/files/file1134070665.pdf.

Krug, S. 2006. Testimony of Steven Krug, MD, FAAP on behalf of the American Academy of Pediatrics. Homeland Security Subcommittee on Emergency Preparedness, Science and Technology. In *Emergency care crisis: A nation unprepared for public health disasters.* July 26.

Mailman School of Public Health. 2003. *Pediatric preparedness for disasters and terrorism: A national consensus conference.* National Center for Disaster Preparedness, Columbia University. http://www.ncdp.mailman.columbia.edu/files/pediatric_preparedness.pdf.

National Center for Missing and Exploited Children. http://www.missingkids.com/en_US/publications/NC170.pdf.

National Commission on Children and Disasters. 2009. Interim report. October 14. http://www.childrenanddisasters.acf.hhs.gov/20091014_508IR_partII.pdf.

Needle, S. No date. *A disaster preparedness plan for pediatricians.* American Academy of Pediatrics: Mississippi Chapter. http://practice.aap.org/disasterpreptool.aspx.

Save the Children. 2005a. *Building disaster resilient communities for children. A guide for local leaders, emergency managers and child advocates.* http://www.apco911.org/new/commcenter911/downloads/Building%20Disaster%20Resilient%20Communities%20for%20Children%20Guide.pdf.

Save the Children. 2005b. *Policy brief—Protecting children in emergencies.* http://www.savethechildren.org/publications/policy-briefs/policy_brief_final_1.pdf.

Save the Children. 2009. Disaster resilient communities for children: Concept note. August.

Save the Children. Recovery and resilience building programs. http://www.savethechildren.org/programs/us-programs/recovery-resilience.html.

Save the Children. Safe spaces—A signature program. http://www.savethechildren.org/programs/us-programs/safe-spaces-us.html.

U.S. Census Bureau. USA quickfacts from the US Census Bureau. http://quickfacts.census.gov/qfd/states/00000.html.

Chapter 2 Child Infrastructure

Introduction

In Chapter 1 we learned that children have unique needs in disasters. We learned that children need protection from physical harm, psychosocial distress, family separation, and denial of access to quality education. And we learned that routine is critical to the physical and emotional well-being of a child, and a disaster can disrupt a child's routine and have severe impacts for that child. Much of a child's everyday routine is shaped by family, friends, and caregivers and is based in schools and child care centers. A child's infrastructure includes:

- Parents, grandparents, guardians, foster parents, siblings
- Schools
- Child care providers and caregivers
- Critical community infrastructure
- Child social services
- Classmates and friends

The goal of this chapter is to describe the role of the emergency manager in planning for these components of a child's

FIGURE 2.1 Chapman, Kansas, June 12, 2008. The middle school is left in a mangled heap after a June 11 F-3 tornado ripped through town. The tornado also leveled the school administration building and the high school and blew out windows and stripped the roof from the elementary school. (Anita Westervelt/FEMA)

infrastructure, helping him or her prepare for disasters and to determine the benefits of including the child infrastructure in the community's emergency operations plan (Figure 2.1).

This chapter includes the following sections:

- Families
- Schools
- Child care providers and caregivers
- Critical community infrastructure
- Child social services

Families

Families come in all shapes and sizes, and it is important that emergency managers recognize and acknowledge the various legal and societal definitions of a family. In our society today children live in families that are headed by:

- Two parents
- Single parent

- Grandparent(s)
- Guardian(s)
- Foster parent(s)
- Sibling(s)
- Homeless/street children

Whatever the family unit, the first means for accounting for children in disasters is through the family. Family leaders will make the decision to evacuate or not in the face of an impending disaster, to seek shelter, and to provide safety and care for their children. Families are responsible for much that occurs in a child's daily life, including the following unique children's needs that emergency managers should be aware of as they make plans to address the unique needs of children in disasters:

Child safety and security
- Guardianship
- Accountability and tracking
- Family reunification
- Shelter safety
- Protection from discrimination based on age, gender, race, ability, etc.

Nutrition
- Age-appropriate diet
- Water
- Supplemental nutrition
- Nutrition for nursing mothers
- Hygienic nursing and feeding materials and supplies

Clothing and shelter
- Size- and gender-specific clothing
- A sense of "home" that does not change often
- A safe space to learn, play, and socialize
- Routine, sufficient sleep, in appropriate sleeping accommodations
- A sense of general stability and daily routine
- Environmental safety (smoking, alcohol, drugs, weapons, language)

Hygiene

- Infant, baby, child, and adolescent supplies (diapers, wipes, skin creams, oral care)
- Safe, child-appropriate bathing and washing facilities
- Basic hygiene information, guidance, and supervision

Evacuation and transportation

- Evacuation of schools and day care centers (Figure 2.2)
- Accountability (tracking) of children evacuated from child care and education facilities
- Transportation that accommodates the needs of infants and toddlers
- Family-centered evacuation
- Transportation within shelters
- Transportation to health/medical facilities

Emergency management education for children, parents, and caregivers

- Family preparedness and planning
- School and day care preparedness, planning, and exercise
- Community preparedness

FIGURE 2.2 Oklahoma City, Oklahoma, April 26, 1995. Search and rescue crew members pose in front of a memorial to the children in the day cares who were killed in the bombing. (Photo from FEMA News)

Families play a critical role in preparing children for dealing with a disaster event. There are numerous organizations that have developed family disaster planning and preparedness materials. Each of these plans revolves around four basic steps: create a family plan, create a family disaster kit, keep informed, and practice your family plan.

Presented on the following pages are:

- *Natural Disaster: Is Your Family Prepared?* developed by the National Center for Missing and Exploited Children (NCMEC) (Sidebar 2.1)
- American Red Cross family disaster planning tips (Figure 2.3)
- *4 Steps to Prepare Your Family for Disasters*, developed by the American Academy of Pediatrics (Figure 2.4)

Emergency managers should be aware that low- to moderate-income families may have difficulty creating a family disaster kit that includes several days' supply of food and water and a variety of tools. These families may not have the finances to create such kits. In addition, low- to moderate-income families and children may have difficulty staying informed, especially those families with non-English-speaking members and without access to non-English-speaking media outlets.

SIDEBAR 2.1 NATURAL DISASTER: IS YOUR FAMILY PREPARED?

The National Center for Missing and Exploited Children (NCMEC) reminds families that it's important to plan for your family's safety.

Families may become separated during the chaos of a natural disaster, especially when evacuation is required. NCMEC offers the following recommendations to all families potentially impacted by a natural disaster:

- Know where your kids are at all times.
- Stay together.
- Take photos of your children with you when evacuated.

- Give children identification information to carry with them, including the child's name, date of birth, address, phone numbers, etc. *If a child is too young or otherwise unable to speak for him- or herself, consider writing his/her name, date of birth, parents' names, home address, and telephone/cell numbers somewhere on the child's body in indelible marker.*
- E-mail digital photos of all family members to extended relatives and/or friends.
- Photocopy important documents and mail to a friend/relative in a safe location.
- Make a plan with your children, so they know what to do if your family becomes separated during an evacuation.

Source: National Center for Missing and Exploited Children (NCMEC). http://www.missingkids.com/missingkids/servlet/PageServlet?LanguageCountry=en_US&PageId=3252.

Understanding the demographic makeup of the community will help emergency managers in planning for a disaster. Mapping your community (GIS) to see where the households with kids and foster children are located is a good idea.

The City of New Orleans has established a city-assisted evacuation plan to help those residents who do not have the means to evacuate on their own. A key component of this plan is helping those residents with special medical needs. Individuals with special medical needs report to one location for evacuation, and residents without special medical needs report to another location and are evacuated separately. The city has developed procedures so that if an adult with special medical needs reports for evacuation with children who have no special medical needs, this family unit will not be separated.

Schools

Schools play a critical role in a child's life and are particularly important in helping a child reestablish his or her routine in the aftermath of a disaster. Students returning home to their old school or displaced students attending new schools in a new community

Be Red Cross Ready

Get a kit. Make a plan. Be informed.

It's important to prepare for possible disasters and other emergencies. Natural and human-caused disasters can strike suddenly, at any time and anywhere. There are three actions everyone can take that can help make a difference ...

Be Red Cross Ready Checklist

- ❑ I know what emergencies or disasters are most likely to occur in my community.
- ❑ I have a family disaster plan and have practiced it.
- ❑ I have an emergency preparedness kit.
- ❑ At least one member of my household is trained in first aid and CPR/AED.
- ❑ I have taken action to help my community prepare.

Get a kit

At a minimum, have the basic supplies listed below. Keep supplies in an easy-to-carry emergency preparedness kit that you can use at home or take with you in case you must evacuate.

• Water—one gallon per person, per day (3-day supply for evacuation, 2-week supply for home) • Food—non-perishable, easy-to-prepare items (3-day supply for evacuation, 2-week supply for home) • Flashlight • Battery-powered or hand-crank radio (NOAA Weather Radio, if possible) • Extra batteries • First aid kit • Medications (7-day supply) and medical items • Multi-purpose tool • Sanitation and personal hygiene items • Copies of personal documents (medication list and pertinent medical information, proof of address, deed/lease to home, passports, birth certificates, insurance policies) • Cell phone with chargers • Family and emergency contact information • Extra cash • Emergency blanket • Map(s) of the area

Consider the needs of all family members and add supplies to your kit. Suggested items to help meet additional needs are:
• Medical supplies (hearing aids with extra batteries, glasses, contact lenses, syringes, cane) • Baby supplies (bottles, formula, baby food, diapers) • Games and activities for children • Pet supplies (collar, leash, ID, food, carrier, bowl) • Two-way radios • Extra set of car keys and house keys • Manual can opener

Additional supplies to keep at home or in your kit based on the types of disasters common to your area:
• Whistle • N95 or surgical masks • Matches • Rain gear • Towels • Work gloves • Tools/supplies for securing your home • Extra clothing, hat and sturdy shoes • Plastic sheeting • Duct tape • Scissors • Household liquid bleach • Entertainment items • Blankets or sleeping bags

Make a plan

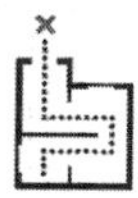

- ❑ Meet with your family or household members.
- ❑ Discuss how to prepare and respond to emergencies that are most likely to happen where you live, learn, work and play.
- ❑ Identify responsibilities for each member of your household and plan to work together as a team.
- ❑ If a family member is in the military, plan how you would respond if they were deployed.

Plan what to do in case you are separated during an emergency

- ❑ Choose two places to meet:
  - Right outside your home in case of a sudden emergency, such as a fire
  - Outside your neighborhood, in case you cannot return home or are asked to evacuate
- ❑ Choose an out-of-area emergency contact person. It may be easier to text or call long distance if local phone lines are overloaded or out of service. Everyone should have emergency contact information in writing or programmed into their cell phones.

Plan what to do if you have to evacuate

- ❑ Decide where you would go and what route you would take to get there. You may choose to go to a hotel/motel, stay with friends or relatives in a safe location or go to an evacuation shelter if necessary.
- ❑ Practice evacuating your home twice a year. Drive your planned evacuation route and plot alternate routes on your map in case roads are impassable.
- ❑ Plan ahead for your pets. Keep a phone list of pet-friendly hotels/motels and animal shelters that are along your evacuation routes.

Be informed

Learn what disasters or emergencies may occur in your area. These events can range from those affecting only you and your family, like a home fire or medical emergency, to those affecting your entire community, like an earthquake or flood.

- ❑ Identify how local authorities will notify you during a disaster and how you will get information, whether through local radio, TV or NOAA Weather Radio stations or channels.
- ❑ Know the difference between different weather alerts such as watches and warnings and what actions to take in each.
- ❑ Know what actions to take to protect yourself during disasters that may occur in areas where you travel or have moved recently. For example, if you travel to a place where earthquakes are common and you are not familiar with them, make sure you know what to do to protect yourself should one occur.
- ❑ When a major disaster occurs, your community can change in an instant. Loved ones may be hurt and emergency response is likely to be delayed. Make sure that at least one member of your household is trained in first aid and CPR and knows how to use an automated external defibrillator (AED). This training is useful in many emergency situations.
- ❑ Share what you have learned with your family, household and neighbors and encourage them to be informed.

Emergency Contact Cards for All Household Members

Get your cards online at **http://www.redcross.org /prepare/ ECCard.pdf.**

- ❑ Print one card for each family member.
- ❑ Write the contact information for each household member, such as work, school and cell phone numbers.
- ❑ Fold the card so it fits in your pocket, wallet or purse.
- ❑ Carry the card with you so it is available in the event of a disaster or other emergency.

Let Your Family Know You're Safe

Tell your loved ones about the American Red Cross Safe and Well Web site available through RedCross.org. This Internet-based tool should be integrated into your emergency communications plan. People within a disaster-affected area can register themselves as "safe and well" and concerned family and friends who know the person's phone number or address can search for messages posted by those who self-register. If you don't have Internet access, call 1-866-GET-INFO to register yourself and your family.

American Red Cross

For more information on disaster and emergency preparedness, visit RedCross.org.

FIGURE 2.3 American Red Cross family disaster planning tips. These can be found at http://www.redcross.org/www-files/Documents/pdf/Preparedness/checklists/Be_Red_Cross_Ready.pdf. ©2010 The American National Red Cross. All Rights Reserved. With permission.

4 Steps To Prepare Your Family for Disasters

This guide will help you and your family prepare for a disaster. Keep this sheet in a special place so you will always know where to find it. Get the family together now to start following the 4 steps to safety readiness!

1 FIND OUT WHAT THE DISASTER RISKS ARE IN YOUR AREA

Find Out From Your Local Emergency Management Office, Health Department, Or American Red Cross Chapter:

- What types of disasters are likely to happen and how to prepare for each.
- What your community's warning signals sound like and what to do if you hear them.
- How to help the elderly and people with special needs.

FAMILY readiness kit
PREPARING TO HANDLE DISASTERS

2 CREATE A FAMILY DISASTER PLAN
Hold A Family Meeting: Keep It Simple And Work As A Team.

What To Tell Children

It is important to educate children about disasters, without overly alarming them. Use the following guidelines:

Tell children that a disaster is something that could hurt people or cause damage. Explain that nature sometimes provides "too much of a good thing"– fire, rain, and wind.

Explain how important it is to make a Family Disaster Plan.

Teach children:
- How to call for help.
- When to call each emergency number.
- To call the family contact if separated.
- To keep personal identification information in their possession at all times.

Plan

- Talk about the dangers of the disaster(s) with your family.
- Have a plan in case you are separated. (A) Choose a place outside your neighborhood in case you cannot go home. (B) Choose someone out of town to be your family contact. Each family member and any babysitter must know the address and phone for A and B.
- Fill out the local emergency phone numbers and child identification cards. Fill out an Emergency Information Form (EIF) for each child with special health care needs (see www.aap.org/advocacy/emergprep.html).
- Become familiar with the specifics of your child's child care or school disaster plans as you could be separated from your child during a disaster.
- Plan what to do if you are asked to evacuate.
- Plan several escape routes.
- Plan how to take care of your pets.

Evacuation

If you are told to evacuate, take these steps:
- Leave right away if told to do so.
- Listen to your battery-powered radio for instructions from local officials.
- Wear protective clothing and shoes.
- Shut off water, gas, and electricity if told to do so.
- Leave a note telling when you left and where you are going.
- Call your family contact to tell him or her where you are going.
- Take your Family Emergency Supplies (listed on next page).
- Lock your home.
- Use routes suggested by officials.

FIGURE 2.4 4 Steps to Prepare Your Family for Disasters, developed by the American Academy of Pediatrics. This document can be found at http://www.aap.org/family/frk/fourstepsFRK.pdf.

require the following to continue their education with minimal interruption and to get into a routine:

Education
- Uninterrupted educational routines and academic progression
- The opportunity to perform homework and other out-of-school studies

3 COMPLETE THIS CHECKLIST

- ☐ Put emergency phone numbers by each phone.
- ☐ Show everyone how and when to turn off the utilities.
- ☐ Make sure you have enough insurance coverage (for example: flood, fire, earthquake, wind).
- ☐ Do a home hazard hunt for items that can move, fall, break or cause a fire.
- ☐ Stock enough emergency supplies to last 7 days (see list at bottom right).
- ☐ Take a Red Cross first aid and CPR class.
- ☐ Plan home escape routes—2 from each room.
- ☐ Find safe places in your home for each type of disaster.
- ☐ Make 2 copies of important documents and keep the originals in a safe deposit box. Keep 1 copy on hand and give the second to your out-of-town contact.

PRACTICE AND MAINTAIN YOUR PLAN 4

Every Month --------
Test your smoke alarms.

Every 6 Months ------
Go over the Family Disaster Plan and do escape drills. Quiz children. Replace stored food and water.

Every Year -----------
Replace the batteries in smoke alarms (unless your smoke alarm uses long-life batteries).

NEIGHBORS HELPING NEIGHBORS

Meet with neighbors to plan how you can work together during a disaster.

- Talk about who has special skills (medical, technical).
- Make plans for child care in case parents can't get home.

UTILITIES

Do the following so you will be ready if told to turn off your utilities:

- Find the main electric fuse box, water service main, and natural gas main.
- Learn how and when to turn these off and teach family members.
- Keep a wrench and flashlight near gas and water shut-off valves.
- If you turn the gas off, you will need a professional to turn it back on.

IMPORTANT DOCUMENTS

Make two copies and keep the originals of the following in a safe deposit box or waterproof container:

- Wills, insurance policies, contracts, deeds, investments.
- Passports, social security cards, immunization records, EIF.
- Bank account numbers/credit card account numbers.
- Inventory of valuable household goods.
- Family records and photos (eg, birth and marriage certificates).
- Documentation to assist in identifying children who may be separated from their parents (eg, photos, adoption records, birth certificates).

EMERGENCY SUPPLIES LIST

- Signal flare
- Map of the area and important phone numbers
- Special items for infants and the elderly (diapers, formula, medication)
- Three gallons of water per person
- Seven day supply of ready-to-eat canned or packaged food
- Manual can opener
- Paper cups, plates, and plastic utensils
- Blankets or sleeping bags
- Toiletries (10-day supply of prescription medications, hand sanitizer)
- Cell phone batteries and/or phone charger
- A change of clothing, rain gear, and sturdy shoes for each family member

Put the following supplies in an easy-to-carry waterproof container:

- Battery-powered radio, flashlight, and extra batteries
- First aid kit and manual and prescription medications
- Credit card and cash
- Personal identification
- An extra set of car keys
- An extra pair of eyeglasses
- Matches in a waterproof container

Visit the US Department of Homeland Security Web site (www.ready.gov) and the AAP Children, Terrorism and Disasters Web site (www.aap.org/terrorism), including a Family Readiness Kit (www.aap.org/family/frk/frkit.htm), for more information.

FIGURE 2.4 (Continued)

- The availability of credentialed, trustworthy teachers
- The availability of educational materials
- The availability of space to hold classes
- Education for traumatized, disaster-affected, or relocated children

Schools are more than just buildings, although the buildings are often critical elements in a disaster when they serve as shelters. The teachers, counselors, and even school nurses play vital roles in a child's infrastructure (see Sidebar 2.2 and Figure 2.5).

SIDEBAR 2.2 SCHOOLS AND CHILDREN

Schools play a key role. They provide a safe haven for children during the day and serve as locations for case finding and for intervention. By providing a structured environment for the child, they help the child regulate his or her reactions. A rapid return of children to school and monitoring of attendance and of unusual symptoms is helpful. (It is not unusual for children to want to be with their parents immediately following a disaster, however. Childcare services may be needed). When children return to school after a disaster, they should not be immediately rushed back to ordinary school routines. Instead, they should be given time to talk about the event and express their feelings about it (without forcing those who do not wish to talk to do so). In-school sessions with entire classes or groups of students may be helpful. The school can also hold meetings with parents to discuss children's responses and provide education for parents in how to respond to children after a disaster.

Source: Ehrenreich, J. H. 2001. *A guidebook to psychosocial intervention*. Mental Health Workers Without Borders. http://www.bittersand-cream.com/index.php?p=1_6. With permission.

FIGURE 2.5 FEMA, Biloxi, Mississippi, August 15, 2006. New busses are now transporting children at Popp's Ferry Elementary after hundreds were destroyed by Hurricane Katrina. (Michelle Miller-Freeck/FEMA)

Predisaster, teachers and counselors can help shape a child's perception of what impact a disaster can have on them and how a child can cope with these impacts. Teachers and school administrators are responsible for the physical safety of children when they are in school and must establish school evacuation and shutdown procedures and conduct regular drills with children. The school administrators must communicate to the parents and guardians of their children how the school will function should a disaster event occur during a school day and how and when parents and guardians can remove the children from the school. Emergency managers must also be aware of school evacuation and shutdown plans and procedures and should work closely with the school system in designing, implementing, and exercising these plans.

Postdisaster, the emotional and psychological needs of teachers and counselors must also be considered (see Sidebar 2.3). Teachers and counselors are also impacted by disasters, and they may need assistance in dealing with the stresses caused by a disaster. In the aftermath of Hurricane Katrina, Save the Children developed Journey of Hope to address the emotional and psychological needs of teachers, counselors, and caregivers impacted by the storm (see Sidebar 2.4)

SIDEBAR 2.3 SUPPORT TEACHERS AND OTHER SCHOOL STAFF

Emergency Managers should "provide staff members with information on the symptoms of children's stress reactions and guidance on how to handle class discussions and answer children's question. As indicated, offer to help conduct a group discussion. Reinforce that teachers should pay attention to their own needs and not feel compelled to do anything they are not comfortable doing. Suggest that administrators provide time for staff to share their feelings and reactions on a voluntary basis as well as help staff develop support groups. In addition, teachers who had property damage or personal injury to themselves or family members may need leave time to attend to their needs."

Source: Save the Children. 2007. *The unique needs of children in emergencies: A guide for the inclusion of children in emergency operations plans*. September. http://www.savethechildren.org/publications/emergencies/Children-in-Emergencies-Planning-Guide.pdf.

SIDEBAR 2.4 JOURNEY OF HOPE

The *Journey of Hope* is a one-day workshop (available in 2hr, 4hr, & 6hr versions) designed to support teachers, administrators, parents and childcare providers in efforts to process recent events, cope with current challenges, and realize healthier futures.

Background

While Save the Children typically focuses on programs for children, support for the caregivers of children (teachers, administrators and parents) has emerged as an urgent unmet need on the Gulf Coast. School staff members have reported feeling overwhelmed by new curriculum standards, resource needs in the face of budget shortfalls, uncertainty about the future, and a workload that leaves little time and space to process grief, loss and anxiety. Unaddressed, the ongoing stress can potentially lead to burnout, interpersonal conflicts, and anger and frustration in the classroom. Facing the challenges of daily living in new environments without familiar communities and usual supports, teachers and parents are likely experiencing similar struggles as they try to meet the needs of their children and families. Addressing their own needs for self-care and strengthening community cohesion increases the capacity of caregivers to be fully present and attentive to the needs of children.

Project Description

Journey of Hope provides the opportunity for teachers and parents to understand the journey of their own lives through and beyond the recent disaster. The model draws on the ideas and experiences of teachers, school social workers, administrators and others working for children's well-being. *Journey of Hope* gathers participants around a circle in order to build trust and a sense of community. Activities utilize creative methods including silent storytelling, music and cooperative games adapted for adults, as well as practical knowledge and skills for self-care. The workshop facilitates the creation of a safe space for teachers and other caregivers in:

- Building trust and community
- Understanding reactions to stress and enhancing skills for coping

- Collective processing of grief and loss
- Identifying and amplifying community strengths and assets
- Collaborative planning for future community-led action and support.

The aim is to provide space for individual and group reflection of their journey, and to develop a sustainable plan for strengthening the school and living community.

One final note, include school nurses in planning for disaster. School nurses should coordinate with local health departments and EMS units and if they are not part of the emergency plan now, they should be.

Source: Save the Children. *Journey of hope for caregivers.*

In 2007, Save the Children released a guide for emergency managers for including children's needs and issues in their emergency planning, entitled *The Unique Needs of Children in Emergencies: A Guide for Inclusion of Children in Emergency Operations Plans.* The guide provides recommendations for the full spectrum of individuals and organizations that should be involved in working with local emergency managers to enhance their emergency operations plans concerning children. A copy of this guide is included in Appendix G and can be accessed at http://www.savethechildren.org/publications/emergencies/Children-in-Emergencies-Planning-Guide.pdf.

This guide recommends that the superintendent of schools engage in a variety of activities to prepare schools and school children for disasters, including:

- Become involved with the community's emergency operations planning process.
- Utilize internal resources to network externally and assist in the district's emergency planning (e.g., school nurse's liaison with public health sector, school psychologist/social worker with local mental health resources).
- Establish predisaster agreements between schools and facilities to temporarily house children until they can be released to parents/guardians.
- Conduct shelter-in-place planning and drills at schools.

FIGURE 2.6 **Baton Rouge, Louisiana, January 17, 2006. This class is being conducted in a new modular building used as a temporary classroom at Audubon Elementary School. FEMA has funded these buildings in several school districts to accommodate students displaced by Hurricane Katrina to alleviate overcrowded conditions in the schools that welcomed the hurricane victims to their community. (Robert Kaufmann/FEMA)**

- Develop plans for contacting or notifying parents and guardians.
- Involve parents and guardians in school-based disaster planning efforts.
- Conduct disaster drills in schools.
- Plan with local community groups how to place children who have not been picked up after a local disaster.
- Develop plans for establishing instant classrooms (including staff, supplies, and appropriate curricula) within close proximity to shelter locations, in the event that schools are damaged, destroyed, or converted into community shelters [Figure 2.6].
- Ensure that all students' educational records are backed up in a safe, off-site location.
- Incorporate materials on the hazards that affect the community in regular curricula.
- Plan for the replacement of teachers and child care staff that will leave to deal with their own disaster consequences.
- Provide temporary replacements for educators who have been affected by the disaster.
- Assist educators in returning to work, and have a system in place to recruit and hire additional staff as needed.

- With the district social services office/coordinator, provide training for educators in supporting children facing stress and recognizing the signs of potentially more serious psychological problems, including anxiety, depression, behavioral problems, and posttraumatic stress disorder (PTSD), and appropriate responses and referrals.
- With the district social services office/coordinator, provide support for teachers facing stress.

(Save the Children, 2007)

Some students do not immediately return home and to their old school in the aftermath of a disaster. Just as in Hurricane Katrina, students and families may be displaced for months at a time from their homes and schools. In order to continue their education and development with as minimal an interruption as possible, displaced students are enrolled in the schools in the communities where they currently reside until they can return home. Efforts must be made by the new schools to welcome and accommodate displaced students and to help them adjust and cope with their new situation.

FIGURE 2.7 **Waverly, Iowa, December 2, 2009. Dignitaries look on as children break ground for the new Waverly-Shellrock School to replace the one that was damaged during the 2008 floods. Iowa Recovery Center Director Kay Phillips (far right) and FEMA Region VII Administrator Beth Freeman (second right) look on as the children take their first scoop of dirt. More than $10 million in FEMA public assistance grants are being used to fund the project. (Vincent Clark/FEMA)**

Child Care Providers and Caregivers

According to the National Association of Child Care Resource and Referral Agencies (NACCRRA, 2006b), "Child care is a fact of life for most American families with preschool and primary children today. Nearly two-thirds of children under the age of six, or 11.6 million children are routinely cared for by someone other than their working parents each day. Parents and employers depend on child care programs to protect the health, safety, and well being of children while employees are at work." (See the following case study.)

Children's needs in this area are summarized below:

Supervision, day care, and educational facilities

- Safe supervision to free up parents with outside (work, health, recovery) responsibilities (may be a surge beyond normal needs)
- A sense of routine that is safe, calm, nurturing, and normalizing
- A safe and productive developmental learning environment
- The ability to socialize with other children (and ample area to do so)
- Adequate treatment of special needs children
- Assistance for supervision, day care employees, teachers, and administrators
- Communication (for parents)
- Accountability of all children (before and after disasters)
- Protection from disasters when events occur, and the ability to respond afterward (training, supplies, evacuation procedures)
- Safe, resilient structures

According to the National Commission on Children and Disasters interim report,

> Following a disaster, child care is an essential human service necessary to protect the safety of children and support the stabilization of families. Childcare helps expedite recovery efforts by

ensuring that children are safe while parents visit damaged property, access public benefits, search for employment and housing, and make other efforts to rebuild their lives. Moreover, childcare recovery supports a community's economic recovery—if a community does not have access to childcare for its youngest children, families cannot return to work and the community cannot recover economically. Finally, research indicates that consistent, high-quality early education and child care improve the health and promote the cognitive development of young children, both of which can be negatively affected by a disaster.

Without repairing, rebuilding and reopening child care facilities that are damaged in disasters, communities may lose their capacity to provide child care services, which can stymie recovery by limiting the ability of parents to return to work and the ability of families to return to communities. Furthermore, research indicates that investment in the child care sector is effective in spurring economic development in both the short and long term. (National Commission on Children and Disaster, 2009)

CASE STUDY: Putting Child Care in the Picture: Why This Service Is a Critical Part of the Community Infrastructure

When Hurricane Katrina hit the Gulf Coast of Mississippi in August 2005, Chevron executives moved quickly to restart the Pascagoula refinery and get gas flowing again. They also took stock of other types of infrastructure, including an often-overlooked one: child care.

"After the hurricane, I understood how little I knew about how interconnected everything was, how everything could disappear overnight," says Steve Renfroe, a member of Chevron's leadership team. "A disaster of the magnitude of Katrina has the power to stop the economy, but how do you restart it? We used portable electric generators to generate the fuel we needed to restart the refineries. Child care is like that generator. It enables parents to go back to work—a key factor in getting the rest of the economy back up and running."

With more than 70 percent of the area's child care facilities damaged or destroyed, much work was needed.

Renfroe went to local, state, and federal authorities but found out that child care was not on the federal government's list of critical services, and thus not eligible for disaster recovery funds. So Chevron joined with local foundations, the nonprofit Save the Children, and Mississippi State University's Early Childhood Institute to rebuild the child care centers without government support.

Source: American Planning Association. 2007. Putting child care in the picture: Why this service is a critical part of community infrastructure. *Planning Magazine,* June. http://government.cce.cornell.edu/doc/pdf/Planning% 20Jun%202006.pdf.

According to the interim report by the National Commission on Children and Disasters (2009), "Child care providers must be prepared for disasters, not only to ensure children's safety and mental well-being in the face of danger, but also to facilitate recovery by providing support services to parents, employees, and employers in the aftermath of a disaster."

However, a lack of basic disaster preparedness requirements for child care providers is commonplace in states throughout our nation. In June 2009, Save the Children released a report, *The Disaster Decade*, which contained a report card on child care disaster planning requirements across fifty states and the District of Columbia. Among the key findings (National Commission on Children and Disasters, 2009):

- Only seven states have laws or regulations requiring licensed child care providers to have basic written emergency plans in place addressing evacuation, reunification, and accommodating children with special needs.
- Only twenty-one states require licensed child care facilities to have a designated site and evacuation route in the event of a disaster.
- Only fifteen states require licensed child care facilities to have a reunification plan for children and families in the event they become separated during an emergency.

A copy of *The Disaster Decade* report card can be accessed at http://www.savethechildren.org/publications/usa/disaster-decade-lessons.pdf. Additional facts from the report are presented in Sidebar 2.5.

SIDEBAR 2.5 THE DISASTER DECADE

Children in Schools or Child Care Are at Risk

There are 67 million children in American schools and child care facilities at any given point on a weekday. Children are most vulnerable when they are away from their families. If a disaster strikes, it's crucial that parents are able to quickly reunite with their children in a safe place. After Katrina, it took up to six months to reunify some children with their families. Of all 50 states and the District of Columbia, Save the Children found that:

- 14% of states meet all four basic emergency preparedness standards for licensed child care facilities and K–12 schools.
- 41% require all licensed child care facilities to have a written evacuation and relocation plan.
- 29% require all licensed child care facilities to have a written plan to notify parents during an emergency.
- 22% require a written plan for accommodating all children with special needs during an emergency evacuation and relocation.

Source: Save the Children. 2009. *The disaster decade*. June. http://www.savethechildren.org/publications/usa/disaster-decade-lessons.pdf.

The National Commission on Children and Disasters interim report (2009) made the following recommendations concerning child care and disasters:

- State child care regulatory agencies should include disaster planning, training and exercising requirements within the scope of the state's minimum health and safety standards for child care licensure or registration.
- Disaster plans for child care providers must, at a minimum, incorporate specific capabilities for shelter-in-place, evacuation, relocation, family reunification, staff training, continuity of operations, and accommodation of children with special needs. State and local emergency management planning activities must be expanded to include participation of child care administrators, regulatory agencies, and child care resource and referral agencies.

- Similarly, state child care administrators must develop state-wide child care disaster plans in coordination with emergency managers, child care regulatory agencies and child care resource and referral agencies.
- Model plans, guidance and technical assistance will aid disaster planning, and training, and exercising efforts of individual child care providers and encourage state and local planning collaborations.
- Congress could require state child care regulatory agencies to include disaster planning, training and exercising for child care providers and state-wide child care disaster plans that include guidelines for recovery, including temporary operating standards to be used in the aftermath of disasters.

NACCRRA (http://www.naccrra.org/disaster/docs/disaster_prep_ccc.pdf) has produced several guides for child care resource and referral (CCR&R) agencies and child care providers to

> help CCR&Rs prepare for disasters and help child care programs and providers also prepare for and respond to such events. Each year in the United States, about five million children experience some form of traumatic event; many of these children are in childcare programs served by CCR&Rs. The information is designed to help local resource and referral agencies as well as statewide networks. It also includes recommendations for local, state, and federal governments on how to minimize the negative impacts of disasters on child care services and capacity. And finally, it has as its goal, to ensure the impacts of disasters on children, America's most vulnerable citizens, are minimized during and in the weeks, months, and years after a disaster occurs.

(See Sidebar 2.6). These guides can be accessed on the NACCRRA website at http://www.naccrra.org/disaster/.

SIDEBAR 2.6 ROLE OF CHILD CARE RESOURCE AND REFERRAL AGENCIES (CCR&RS) IN DISASTERS

Community-based child care resource and referral agencies (CCR&Rs) have an important role to play when a disaster strikes a community or a region. During the last decade, the United States has experienced several different types of disasters. These disasters have brought in to sharp focus how important it is for CCR&Rs to prepare to assist parents, employers, and the childcare delivery system when a disaster occurs.

CCR&Rs' responsibilities in relationship to disasters are many. While they share some of these responsibilities with others, including parents, providers, and emergency response personnel, they are in a unique position to ensure a community's child care system is prepared for disasters and to support it if one or more occurs. These responsibilities include:

- Helping child care programs and individual providers prepare for potential disasters.
- Representing the childcare community in local, state, regional, and national disaster planning.
- Informing and helping parents before, during, and after disasters.
- Aiding in setting up temporary childcare arrangements for first responders and families after a disaster.
- Helping displaced providers become reemployed and recruiting providers to replace those lost.
- Helping child care providers protect their childcare businesses during and after disasters.
- Helping restore the quantity and quality of childcare in a community after a disaster.
- Coordinating charitable contributions to child care providers and programs following a disaster.
- Protecting CCR&R assets during disasters so the agency can continue to serve the community.

Source: National Association of Child Care Resource and Referral Agencies (NACCRRA). 2006a. *Is child care ready? A disaster planning guide for child resource and referral agencies*. http://www.naccrra.org/disaster/docs/Disaster_Guide_MECH.pdf.

The training guide developed for child care providers states (NACCRRA, *Disaster Preparation*):

At the end of the training the participants will be able to:

- Explain why child care centers should have a disaster plan
- List the types of disasters most likely to occur in their area
- Develop an emergency plan for their child care center
- Make and practice an evacuation plan for their program
- Perform other tasks related to preparing for a disaster

Critical Infrastructure

Emergency managers must consider schools and child care centers as critical infrastructure in their communities, much the way roads, bridges, and government facilities are considered critical infrastructure in a community.

Predisaster, it is important to understand where existing schools and child care centers are located and what risks (i.e., flood, earthquake, tornado, hazardous materials accident, etc.) may impact those facilities. Where possible, retrofits should be considered and conducted to make these facilities disaster resilient, especially if they also serve as disaster shelters. Consideration of hazard risks must also be included in any decision for the siting and licensing of new facilities.

Postdisaster, emergency managers and community decision makers must be sure to include schools and child care centers and the other infrastructure that support these facilities on their priority list of critical infrastructure to be brought back up online quickly and safely. When schools or child care centers are closed for extended periods, children suffer because of the disruption in their routine and the lack of access to education. Lost school days is an underreported impact in any community from a major disaster.

In addition, closed schools and child care centers can impact the economy of a community already affected by a disaster. Parents and guardians of preschool and school-age children can't go to work if their children are not in school or in a child care facility they trust is safe (see Sidebar 2.7).

SIDEBAR 2.7 INVESTING IN THE CHILD CARE INDUSTRY: AN ECONOMIC DEVELOPMENT STRATEGY FOR LOUISIANA

"Investing in the Child Care Industry: An Economic Development Strategy for Louisiana," was commissioned by the Louisiana Department of Social Services. It was conducted by Dr. Geoffrey Nagle of Tulane and Dr. Dek Terrell of LSU and is part of a larger research project at Cornell University.

Among the findings in that study are such facts as there are 12,701 child-care businesses in Louisiana, which employ 22,644 workers. By comparison, the oil and gas extraction industry employs 18,278 and hotels and motels employ 17,559 statewide, according to the study.

The study, which looked at licensed child-care facilities, Head Start/Early Head Start programs, family child-care homes and in-home child care, noted that these businesses serve 149,849 children and generate more than $657 million in gross receipts.

"The child-care industry affects the economy in several ways," Overstreet explained of the study's results and what it means to the state. "First, it provides jobs for workers. Second, quality childcare affects parents' wages, since lack of care is a frequent reason for missing work or not working at all.

"Third, the child-care industry has a relatively good multiplier effect. Child-care businesses take in revenue but then make purchases and pay wages to workers who spend money."

The experts also point out that when businesses make purchases and their workers spend their paychecks, new jobs are created in other areas of the economy—so there is a multiplier effect involved in the money generated by child care.

"But perhaps the most significant economic impacts are in the future," Gioe stresses. "Research consistently shows that the first three years of life are the most critical for brain development and success in later life.

"Studies show that children who were enrolled in high-quality child-care programs earlier in life have higher graduation rates and employee productivity. They also are less likely to cost taxpayers money in remedial and special education, welfare or involvement in the criminal justice system."

Source: LSUAgCenter.com. 2005. *Be child care aware: Child care important industry, economic factor for state*. June. http://www.lsuagcenter.com/en/family_home/family/childcare/be_child_care_aware/Be+Child+Care+Aware+Child+Care+Important+Industry+Economic+Factor+For+State.htm.

Health and Hospital Infrastructure

Children have unique medical needs, as was discussed in Chapter 1. In order to grow in a healthy fashion, in normal circumstances or in the aftermath of a disaster, the following elements must be in place:

Health and hospital care

- Basic health screening and recognition
- Routine medical checkups (well visits) and preventive care
- Access to health information for parents
- Child-appropriate medicine and dosages
- Health record access, data collection, and medical tracking
- Access to medications and other necessary treatments (dialysis, diabetes, long-term prescriptions)
- Hospital surge capacity to accommodate child victims
- Pediatric hospital equipment and supplies
- Pediatricians and trained pediatric nursing staff
- Specialty pediatric care (pediatric burn units, pediatric trauma, etc.)

Emergency medical care and emergency response (Figure 2.8)

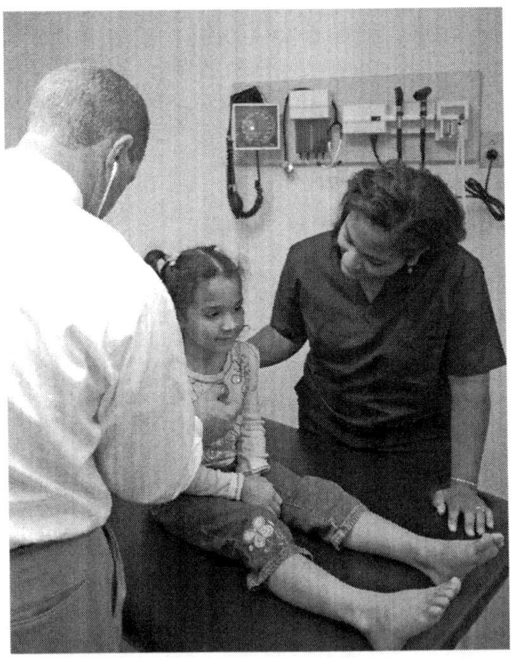

FIGURE 2.8 **Patient identification and tracking, pediatric-trained physicians and nurses, medications, and dosage are some of the considerations in child and infant emergency medical care and response.**

- Family-centered medical care
- Patient identification and tracking
- Medications, dosage information, vaccines, equipment, and supplies that are pediatric appropriate
- Trained technicians able to recognize special symptoms of children, and to apply the special medical response procedures on them as required
- Emergency management professionals in all disaster services (fire, police, EMS, and emergency management) trained in response procedures that account for the presence of children
- Special (heated, private) decontamination facilities for children in all situations (nonambulatory, parentless, infant, special needs)
- Ample warning

Psychological care

- Social integration (especially for displaced children)
- Psychological protection (including recognition)
- Psychological interventions
- Psychological treatment, therapy, or counseling
- Assistance for parents and caregivers
- Continuation of care for preexisting psychological conditions
- Child-specific grieving and memorial services

Social Services

Social services agencies play a key role in the lives of many children in a community. Understanding the roles and responsibilities of social services agencies to foster children, orphans, and other at-risk children is critical for emergency managers as they develop and refine their emergency plans. This is not only important for emergency managers working in communities that will be impacted by a disaster event, but also for emergency managers in communities that may host children who have been evacuated from a disaster area and are being cared for by a social services agency (see Sidebar 2.8).

SIDEBAR 2.8 GENERAL ACCOUNTING OFFICE REPORT ON CHILD WELFARE IN DISASTERS

In the absence of federal requirements that states develop child welfare disaster plans, many states have not done so. In addition, states that have developed disaster plans do not always address the dispersion of children and families. The lack of plans for dealing with the dispersion of children may result in confusion at a time when families are under strain and need services most. Without minimum requirements on what states should include in their child welfare disaster plans, some states may be unable to ensure the continuity of services within and across state lines for the children under their care.

To ensure continuity of services within or across state lines for the children under state care, Congress should consider requiring that states develop and submit child welfare disaster plans for HHS review.

To better assist states in developing child welfare disaster plans, we are recommending that the Secretary of Health and Human Services ensure that the department's child welfare disaster planning guidance address the dispersion of children and families within and across state lines. This guidance should include information on

- Preserving child welfare records,
- Identifying children who may be dispersed,
- Identifying new child welfare cases and providing services,
- Coordinating services and sharing information with other states, and
- Placing children from other states.

Finally, we are recommending that the Secretary develop and provide training on child welfare disaster planning to all states.

Source: General Accounting Office. 2006. *Child welfare: Federal action needed to ensure states have plans to safeguard children in the child welfare system displaced by disasters*. General Accounting Office Report GAO-06-944. July.

In the aftermath of Hurricane Katrina, over forty states across the country received federal disaster assistance from FEMA and other agencies to help pay for hosting Katrina evacuees that were displaced to their community. Emergency managers in these host communities worked closely with social services agencies to help displaced children in their care. Emergency managers should consult with their city or county attorney's office about the myriad legal issues involved in working with displaced children (see Sidebars 2.9 and 2.10).

SIDEBAR 2.9 LEGAL SYSTEM

Engaging the legal system in the community is one way emergency managers can appropriately deal with legal issues regarding at-risk children in disasters. The legal system could:

- Determine all legal considerations concerning the care and treatment of minor children (including unaccompanied minor children), such as consent, guardianship, decontamination consent, records privacy and photographs of unidentified children
- Appoint lawyers to serve as guardians ad litem for children orphaned or those who have lost a custodial parent
- Include all relevant domestic courts (e.g., family, probate, juvenile) in the planning process to consider children's best interests.

Source: Save the Children. 2007. The unique needs of children in emergencies: A guide for the inclusion of children in emergency operations plans. September. http://www.savethechildren.org/publications/emergencies/Children-in-Emergencies-Planning-Guide.pdf.

SIDEBAR 2.10 LEGAL CONSIDERATIONS FOR WORKING WITH CHILDREN IN DISASTERS

The following are legal questions and issues that may arise during a disaster. Having policies and procedures in place prior to an event should be considered.

- For unaccompanied children during a disaster, consent is not needed to treat for a life or limb-threatening situation. Is parental consent needed to treat a child victim with minor injuries? With psychological injuries?
- Is parental consent required to decontaminate an unaccompanied child? What if child is asymptomatic? What if child is refusing?

- What medical or social information can be released and to whom during a disaster?
- Check HIPAA rules and your legal counsel concerning the unidentified patient locator protocols, such as posting Polaroid photographs of unidentified children.
- Who can children be released to and if not the parent or caregiver, what permission or information is needed? What is your protocol for releasing children if no legal guardian or parent can be found or if no permission document is provided?

Source: New York City Department of Health and Mental Hygiene (NYC Health). 2006. *Hospital guidelines for pediatrics in disasters*. Centers for Bioterrorism Preparedness Program Pediatric Task Force.

Conclusion

You now have an understanding of what the elements are that make the infrastructure that supports and nourishes a child's daily life. Family (in its many forms), schools, child care providers and caregivers, critical community infrastructure, social services, and classmates and friends all play a role in the daily life of a child. A disaster can disrupt and displace these child support systems and negatively impact the physical and emotional well-being of a child. In building an effective community emergency plan, emergency managers must carefully consider the interdependences among these various child infrastructure elements and work in concert with school officials, child care providers, and resource and referral agencies, social services, and the legal system to ensure that these support systems are protected and can be brought back online quickly and safely in the aftermath of a disaster.

References

American Academy of Pediatrics. *4 steps to prepare your family for disasters*. http://www.aap.org/family/frk/fourstepsFRK.pdf.

American Planning Association. 2007. Putting child care in the picture: Why this service is a critical part of community infrastructure. P*lanning Magazine*, June. http://government.cce.cornell.edu/doc/pdf/Planning%20Jun%202006.pdf.

American Red Cross. *Family disaster planning.* http://www.redcross.org/www-files/Documents/pdf/Preparedness/checklists/Be_Red_Cross_Ready.pdf.

Ehrenreich, J. H. 2001. *A guidebook to psychosocial intervention.* Mental Health Workers Without Borders. http://www.mhwwb.org/CopingWithDisaster.pdf.

General Accounting Office. 2006. *Child welfare: Federal action needed to ensure states have plans to safeguard children in the child welfare system displaced by disasters.* General Accounting Office Report GAO-06-944. July.

Harvard Educational Review. 2005. Katrina and Rita: What can the United States learn from international experiences with education in displacement? http://www.hepg.org/her/abstract/1.

LSUAgCenter.com. 2005. *Be child care aware: Child care important industry, economic factor for state.* June. http://www.lsuagcenter.com/en/family_home/family/childcare/be_child_care_aware/Be+Child+Care+Aware+Child+Care+Important+Industry+Economic+Factor+For+State.htm.

National Association of Child Care Resource and Referral Agencies (NACCRRA). 2006a. *Is child care ready? A disaster planning guide for child resource and referral agencies.* http://www.naccrra.org/disaster/docs/Disaster_Guide_MECH.pdf.

National Association of Child Care Resource and Referral Agencies (NACCRRA). 2006b. *Disaster preparation: A training guide for child care centers.* http://www.naccrra.org/disaster/docs/disaster_prep_ccc.pdf.

National Center for Missing and Exploited Children (NCMEC). *Natural disaster: Is your family prepared?* http://www.missingkids.com/missingkids/servlet/PageServlet?LanguageCountry=en_US&PageId=3252.

National Commission on Children and Disasters. 2009. Interim report. October 14. http://www.childrenanddisasters.acf.hhs.gov/20091014_508IR_partII.pdf.

New York City Department of Health and Mental Hygiene (NYC Health). 2006. *Hospital guidelines for pediatrics in disasters.* Centers for Bioterrorism Preparedness Program Pediatric Task Force.

Save the Children. 2007. *The unique needs of children in emergencies: A guide for the inclusion of children in emergency operations plans.* September. http://www.savethechildren.org/publications/emergencies/Children-in-Emergencies-Planning-Guide.pdf.

Save the Children. 2009. *The disaster decade: Lessons unlearned for the U.S.*, 4. Westport, CT: Save the Children U.S. Programs. http://www.savethechildren.org/publications/usa/disaster-decade-lessons.pdf.

Save the Children. 2005. *Journey of hope for caregivers.*

Chapter 3

Mitigation

Introduction

Disasters are a reality of living in the natural world. Over the last decade, the social and economic costs of disasters to the United States and throughout the world have grown significantly. Each disaster takes a toll on individuals, and especially children's sense of safety and security and their emotional well-being. A key to reducing these impacts on children is to adopt and implement mitigation measures that will make their homes and their communities more resilient from disasters. Most practitioners agree that the primary intent of mitigation is to ensure that fewer communities and individuals become victims of disasters. The goal of mitigation is to create economically secure, socially stable, better built, and more environmentally sound communities that are out of harm's way.

Reducing the impacts of future disasters is the key to successful mitigation practices. The result is less disruption to the community and a quicker return to routine. Routine is very important to children for their physical and emotional well-being and for their education. Mitigation measures that reduce future disaster impacts on homes, schools, and child care facilities are critical to maintaining a child's everyday routine.

The most common mitigation techniques include:

- Hazard identification and planning
- Design, construction, and retrofit
- Land use planning
- Financial incentives
- Structural controls

This chapter will primarily focus on the various mitigation practices that can be implemented to ensure that the infrastructure that supports children safety and security is resilient. Practical case studies that demonstrate successful mitigation programs are also provided to demonstrate how different organizations and communities have addressed different types of hazards.

Community Infrastructure and Children

Children rely on a diversity of infrastructure within their communities in their everyday activities, including:

- Facilities (i.e., school buildings, child care centers, recreation centers, government buildings)
- Transportation networks (i.e., roads, bridges, transit systems, school buses)
- Public utilities (i.e., electricity, gas, water, sanitation)

All of these systems are at risk in any disaster. The degree of risk often varies with the hazard. For example, an earthquake could have a significant impact on all of these systems within a community, while a tornado could impact just a single structure, such as a school or a home. A flood might have a variable impact on more than one system. However, there are so many dependencies between the infrastructure systems that the impact a disaster has on any one system has a ripple impact on other systems. For example, if the roads are washed out from a flood, the school buses will not be able to transport children to school, or if an earthquake destroys a wastewater treatment plant, schools or hospitals could be closed for a time because there isn't potable water.

Mitigating Community Infrastructure for Children

Hazards Identification and Planning

This is the most obvious tool for mitigation. You can't mitigate a hazard if you don't know what it is or how it might impact a part of the children's community infrastructure. The most essential part of any mitigation strategy or plan is an analysis of what the hazards are in a particular area. The resources for hazards identification are numerous. The federal government has extensive programs that map virtually every hazard, and these products are available to communities. FEMA's National Flood Insurance Program (NFIP) provides detailed flood maps and studies, and the U.S. Geological Survey (USGS) provides extensive earthquake and landslide studies and maps. Many state agencies have refined the products for hazard identification. For example, special soil stability studies and geological investigations, which are required in some parts of California, further refine this analysis. Knowing your hazards, understanding the impacts a disaster will have on the systems, and then creating a plan to mitigate those impacts is crucial to reducing the impacts of disasters on children.

For that reason, it is recommended that every community should have a community hazard mitigation plan that identifies existing hazard risks in the community and proposes a strategy for mitigating these risks. This mitigation plan is best developed with all elements of the community being included in the process: elected officials, education and academic representatives, nonprofit and voluntary organizations, business leaders, environmental and union representatives, special advocacy groups, and interested citizens. This plan then becomes a road map for seeking support for predisaster mitigation funding and then, in the event of a disaster, funding for postdisaster hazard mitigation grants. The community plan will be implemented in coordination with the emergency management organization within the community. Emergency managers should review their community hazard mitigation plan to determine how existing community risks may impact the critical infrastructure that directly or indirectly supports the needs of children.

The results of this review should be used to reconsider the priorities for mitigation projects currently included in the mitigation

FIGURE 3.1 Raleigh, North Carolina, October 17, 2003. The FEMA mitigation booth at the North Carolina State Fair has materials to help teach mitigation to children as well as adults affected by Hurricane Isabel. (Photo by Mark Wolfe/FEMA News Photo)

strategy in a community hazard mitigation plan. Consideration should be given to designing and implementing mitigation measures that will reduce the impacts of future disasters on those elements of the community's critical infrastructure that directly or indirectly impact the child infrastructure in the community (Figure 3.1).

CASE STUDY: Tulsa Partners Program for Preparing Child Care Centers and Family Home Child Care Sites

Preparedness and continuity planning can help child care providers and their children survive disasters, large or small, with safe, secure, and continuous care.

The two projects described below were designed to help busy child care providers with their disaster planning. Thirteen children care centers and family homes (which have the capacity to provide care to almost 1,200 children) participated in two main training workshops scheduled one month apart.

The Tulsa Child Care Resource Center (CCRC) delivered NACCRRA's "Is Child Care Ready" curriculum, specific to both centers and family homes in the first session, then over the next month providers were challenged to develop and/or improve an emergency management plan specific to their facility. To support this project, Tulsa Partners identified and trained more than a dozen volunteers, representing the CCRC and underwriters from a private partner, State Farm Insurance, to support centers and homes in developing their plans.

A month later the group returned for a second session that offered more detailed information and focused on resolving any planning problems. The providers were enthusiastic and thoughtful about planning to manage emergencies in ways that kept their children safe, and shared their insight with other providers. Sponsors and partners set up information booths, with free breakfast and giveaways, including Tulsa-area Wal-Mart stores provided each participating facility with a large rolling tub filled with emergency supplies, plus $25 gift certificates for additional supplies; and a national manufacturer Midland Radio Corporation donated NOAA weather radios.

- **"Is Child Care Ready":** Emergency planning

  The Tulsa CCRC is a local nonprofit that provides, among other services, training and advocacy for child care providers in four Northeastern Oklahoma counties. NACCRRA includes 800 local CCRCs, provides training and advocacy on a national level, and has developed an extensive curriculum to guide emergency operations planning for child care facilities. This curriculum served as the basis for the child care center and family home child care site training.

- **"Open for Business®":** Child care assessments & business continuity planning

  In the first session, emergency management professionals drew upon the Open for Business® planning system developed by the Institute for Business & Home Safety to teach providers about the importance of business continuity planning, how to conduct "hazard hunt" assessments of their facilities, and ways to reduce risks through low-cost improvements such as wind-resistant windows. Additional suggested improvements included: Tornado Safe Rooms, NOAA weather radios, smoke alarms, and backup generators.

The Open for Business® and NACCRRA curricula were combined to provide a complete planning process for emergency preparedness and business continuity. These plans identify ways the child care centers can continue communicating with emergency management professionals and other child-focused networks during and after a disaster.

Additionally, these plans identify an alternative safe site facilities might move their children to in the event they need to evacuate their site, how they would transport children, what they would need to continue operating there, how they would notify parents, and how they would reunite the children with their families.

The Tulsa CCRC used this training to develop plans for their own facility and is continuing to provide this two-part workshop training as a component of their ongoing education outreach to child care centers and family home child care sites. As of June 2008, twenty facilities have been trained through this program.

Source: Save the Children. 2008. *Including children in emergency planning: Giving children priority—before, during, and after disasters.*

Design, Construction, and Retrofit

The design and construction process provides one of the most cost-effective means of reducing risk in community infrastructure. This process is governed by building codes, architecture and design criteria, and soils and landscaping considerations. Code criteria that support mitigation apply to new construction, substantial renovation, or renovation to change the type or use of the building or to retrofit the facility. For virtually all of the community infrastructure systems that support children, especially facilities and transportation systems, there are multiple techniques that can be implemented to reduce the risk that these systems will face from a future disaster. Some case study examples of how these mitigation techniques have been applied to reduce children's vulnerability follow.

CASE STUDY: Mitigating the Tornado Hazard in Kansas Schools

Wichita, Kansas lies right in the heart of Tornado Alley— the area cutting across the center of the United States where tornadoes are most likely to strike. When strong tornadoes impact homes and buildings, the result is almost always disastrous. When they strike schools, where the children of the community may all be gathered at once, the physical and emotional loss can be confounded ten-fold. On May 3, 1999, that is exactly what happened.

Luckily, when Chisholm Life Special Education School for teenagers to young adults and Greiffenstein Special Education Center were severely damaged by a pack of tornadoes, schools were closed and no children were present. Although the county office of emergency management had conducted a hazard assessment in recognition of the tornado threat, and had identified areas of safe refuge within both structures—major damage still occurred in several of these identified areas where children would surely have congregated. The significance of these findings was not lost on community members, who recognized that they might not be as lucky the next time tornadoes strike.

Using all of the information gathered in the post-event investigation relating to the schools, the State of Kansas used funding from several Federal sources (including the Hazard Mitigation Grant Program and a supplemental appropriation from Congress) to identify and build additional protection measures for school children in the state. The Kansas Division of Emergency Management (KDEM) and the Kansas Hazard Mitigation Team (KHMT) decided to construct in-school tornado shelters with the funds and to ensure that shelters be included in any new school construction or renovation project.

In Wichita, 2 safe room projects were initiated within the public school district, which by design will serve approximately 7,800 of the District's 9,000 students. The facilities will also protect many more community members who use the facilities extensively for various activities including precinct voting, church worship services, and community outreach and recreation such as the Boy Scouts and Girl Scouts. The structural mitigation components have been accompanied by associated processes and procedures, such as:

- The creation of a shelter management team
- The creation of shelter maintenance procedures and schedules
- Shelter warning, training, and drill procedures and schedules
- Weather monitoring
- Shelter access inspections
- The creation of shelter activation procedures, including head count, shelter security, in-shelter monitoring of weather, and stand-down procedures

Sedgwick County Emergency Management continues to work closely with the Wichita Public School District to evaluate areas of refuge in the schools. Evaluators identify the schools' safest areas and make recommendations that instruct school administrators in the best methods for increasing occupant safety. Using this evaluation, the school district officials are able to determine the most appropriate and practical means of creating the shelter (which may include constructing an entirely new school, building an addition on to the existing structure, or retrofitting an identified area).

Today, all new approved shelter construction carried out in the Wichita program meets the criteria presented in the FEMA publication entitled *Design and Construction Guidance for Community Shelters.* In addition, all shelter construction projects are inspected by a trained team that assists in determining the best location for shelter areas, identifying areas that need improvement, and determining how to resolve any structural concerns.

Source: Haddow, G., and Bullock, J. 2006. *Introduction to emergency management.* 2nd ed. Burlington, MA: Elsevier.

CASE STUDY: Memories of Camille: School Survives Katrina

Ocean Springs, MS—Memories of Hurricane Camille's devastating impact on the Mississippi Gulf Coast in the summer of 1969 prompted Ocean Springs Middle School to take preventative measures prior to Hurricane Katrina.

Many long-time residents vividly remember how Camille's fury resulted in numerous deaths and widespread destruction, closing schools for weeks. Learning from experience, the school vowed to develop techniques to reduce the loss of life and property in future disasters.

The school installed permanent wind-resistant shutters on vulnerable classroom windows to help protect against strong winds charging in from the Gulf of Mexico. The Mississippi Emergency Management Agency applied to the Federal Emergency Management Agency's (FEMA) Hazard Mitigation Grant Program (HMGP) on behalf of the Ocean Springs Middle School, and was awarded $49,477 in funding for the hurricane mitigation project. FEMA paid 75 percent of the cost of the project, and the City of Ocean Springs funded the remainder.

The shutters performed exceptionally well when Hurricane Katrina made landfall on August 29, 2005, registering winds of up to 104 miles per hour in this Gulf Coast community.

The hurricane shutters shielded windows from windborne objects and also protected the contents inside the building. Without shutters, a window may be easily breeched by hurricane winds. This creates tremendous upward pressure that may cause major roof failure, exposing the interior of the building to the storm.

After Hurricane Katrina, Ocean Springs Middle School remained intact and operational, unlike many public buildings in the city that were severely damaged and uninhabitable. In fact, the school served as a disaster command center immediately following the storm and later as a shelter for families who had lost their homes.

According to David Baggett, the current principal of Ocean Springs Middle School, "Getting back to school is so important after a disaster because the students need stability when they have lost their homes. They need a place where they feel safe and secure." Mr. Baggett's own home was completely destroyed by Hurricane Katrina.

Other schools in the district were not as fortunate as Ocean Springs Middle School. Ocean Springs Elementary located just a mile away, experienced extensive damage because its windows were not protected.

Storm shutters are a cost-effective way to protect schools. They are designed to withstand the impact of hurricane-force winds and prevent window failure that could allow wind, rain, and debris to enter a building. Ocean Springs Middle School demonstrated that taking preventative safety measures not only provides teachers and students with an increased sense of security, but also ensures continuity of vital educational and social resources in the wake of a disaster.

Source: FEMA Mitigation Best Practices Portfolio. http://www.fema.gov/mitigationbp/brief.do?mitssId=2165.

CASE STUDY: Colton Schools Seismic Mitigation School Retrofit Program

San Bernardino County, CA—The Colton Unified School District, in San Bernardino County, Calif., combines traditional and year-round schedules, thereby having a high level of occupancy and use of facilities. Year-round life safety is a major focus of the school district's preparedness and mitigation program.

The county was seriously affected by the Landers and Big Bear earthquakes, which struck the area one hour apart in 1992. Both earthquakes caused damage to buildings and interrupted school schedules.

These events—plus the realization that there is ongoing potential for hazards and damage to facilities in the seismically active area (near the San Andreas Fault)—prompted the county's Office of Education to apply for a hazard mitigation grant from FEMA. Funds are for non-structural mitigation for all school districts in the county.

The Colton Unified School District's consultant recommended mitigation solutions that would exceed life-safety standards. The first non-structural mitigation projects were done in kitchens of three schools where stoves, freezers and refrigerators were secured to prevent tipping during earthquakes. Mitigation plans also called for installation of computer hold-downs, and securing mobile carts and filing cabinets.

Funds for this project were made available from FEMA's Hazard Mitigation Grant Program, and were obtained by the San Bernardino County Office of Education for the Colton school district's non-structural mitigation effort. Non-structural retrofit projects have been demonstrated to be cost-effective mitigation. For the District's project, the benefit/cost analysis shows a ratio of savings from future events to the cost of mitigation of at least one-to-one.

The position of the county schools office and Colton school district is that hazards can and do repeat themselves, that non-structural mitigation done to lessen effects of these hazards can greatly reduce damage and life-threatening affects of hazards, and that non-structural mitigation can last for the life of facilities.

Source: FEMA Mitigation Best Practices Portfolio. http://www.fema.gov/mitigationbp/brief.do?mitssId=208.

Land Use Planning

Mitigation programs are most successful when undertaken at the local level, where most decisions about development are made. The strategies for land use planning offer many options for effecting infrastructure mitigation, including acquisition, easements, storm water management, annexation, environmental review, and floodplain management plans.

Land use planning was one of the earliest tools used to encourage mitigation. In 1968 Congress passed the National Flood Insurance Act that established the National Flood Insurance Program (NFIP). This act required local governments to pass a floodplain management ordinance in return for federally backed, low-cost flood insurance being available to the community. This act started one of the largest federal mapping efforts because the government promised local governments that it would provide them with the technical tools to determine where the floodplains were in their communities so they could locate schools, hospitals, and other critical facilities away from these areas. Moving structures or a system out of harm's way through property acquisition or relocation is clearly one of the most effective land-use planning tools, but it is also the most costly. However, the case studies that follow show how communities found innovative means to accomplish relocation and other mitigation projects.

CASE STUDY: The Castaic School District

Castaic Union School District, located in southern California, is a case study that demonstrates the threat from multiple hazards. After the 1994 Northridge Earthquake, Castaic Union School District conducted a study of the earthquake-related risks that threatened their elementary and middle schools, and administration buildings. The assessment revealed that earthquake-related structural damage was not the only risk the school District faced.

The District maintained and operated 63 buildings (77,000 square feet of usable space) in Northern Los Angeles County that consisted of a mix of permanent and portable structures with construction dates as far back as 1917. These structures service approximately 1,200 students and 115 staff. The San Andreas and San Gabriel fault systems, two of the most active faults in the country, pass through the area in which the District is located. In addition, the U.S. Geological Survey has concluded that significant new earthquake activity may occur along both the San Andreas and San Gabriel systems.

These factors led the Castaic Union School District to conclude in their study that the probability of a large earthquake affecting their facilities was high. They also learned however, that the risk went well beyond possible damages caused by ground shaking. Along with the expected seismic damage, the study revealed two additional threats: flooding from the Castaic Dam and fire or explosion from a rupture in nearby oil pipelines.

The District's risk assessment study indicated that the school buildings were located within the inundation area of the Castaic Dam (located only 1.7 miles upstream). If the dam were to fail, the school buildings and their occupants would be inundated with catastrophic flooding. The 2,200-acre reservoir above the dam could release nearly 105 billion gallons of water, inundating the area below the dam with 50 feet of water.

In 1992, the California Department of Water Resources (DWR) re-examined the seismic performance of the dam. Based on the analyses, the DWR considers the dam to meet all current safety requirements, and able to resist failure due to the maximum credible earthquake. However, the district's risk assessment concluded the probability the Castaic Dam will fail is never zero.

Along with the threat posed by the Castaic Dam, the study also revealed that the buildings were at high risk of damage from both fire and explosion should nearby pipelines fail. Two high pressure crude oil pipelines currently cross the campus (a 1925 gas-welded pipeline, and a 1964 modern arc-welded steel pipeline), both of which could rupture during ground shaking or ground displacement in earthquakes. An analysis of the lines and the fault conditions near the District indicated a 35% chance of failure somewhere in the Castaic area as a result of any large earthquake.

This information caused alarm about the safety of the District's facilities. In the event of a pipeline failure, a fire or explosion could result from the ignition of the released oil, putting both facilities and people at great risk. Additionally, the ability to prevent a nearby fire from spreading would be limited by the decreased reliability of water lines and hydrants, as well as the increased demands on emergency fire services after an earthquake.

Using the results of the District's risk analysis, it was determined that the potential economic costs from either a dam failure or oil pipeline break following an earthquake were enormous. The first potential cost to the School District would be incurred from both building and content damage. Replacement of the school buildings would cost an estimated $7.7 million. Second, if such an earthquake occurred, alternative school facilities would have to be located and rented at an estimated cost of over $500,000 per year. Third, the community would have to absorb the costs of losing the educational services provided by the District in the time period between the actual loss of the facilities and the relocation to temporary facilities. The School District calculated the cost of the lost public services based on the operating expenses required to provide the services. The daily cost of lost educational services was estimated at $28,601.

In addition to these direct and indirect financial losses, the risk of earthquake-related casualties in the District's facilities was determined to be significant. In an earthquake-induced dam failure, the predicted speed of inundation on the campus caused the risk of casualties to be very high. When calculating this risk, a casualty rate of 250 individuals was determined based on the average hourly rate of campus usage in a typical week.

However, in the event of a dam failure during school hours, the loss of life could be as high as 1200 students and 115 faculty members. In an earthquake-induced potential pipeline failure, the District calculated a casualty rate of 9 individuals and injury rate of 45 individuals. Once again, the actual number of casualties increases dramatically if the earthquake and pipeline failure occurs during school hours.

Through the cost–benefit analysis, the District determined that the most feasible method to reduce their risks would be to condemn the structures on the old, high-risk site and relocate the campus to a low-risk area. Given the nature and severity of the potential hazards, mitigation options other than relocation were judged infeasible.

Once the decision had been made to relocate, the District went to work to identify an alternative site for the school facilities. The selected location for the campus was completely out of the dam inundation area and far removed from the high-pressure oil pipelines. Thus, the risk posed by the dam and oil pipelines hazards would be eliminated.

While the campus would still be within an active earthquake fault area, the new campus building would be constructed to fully conform to 1995 building code provisions, thus making them more resistant to seismic damage than the buildings being replaced.

The District then agreed to turn the land over to the Newhall County Water District as soon as the relocation effort was underway. The old school property is located above two active wells, which the water district can use to supply their customers in Castaic. In doing so, they changed the property deed to restrict human habitation and development, and to return the site to natural open space.

The Castaic School District financed the relocation effort through a combination of grant money from FEMA and the sale of bonds. The District applied for and received a $7.2 million grant through FEMA's Hazard Mitigation Grant Program for the market value of the property, including the existing structures and infrastructure. The district used this funding, plus $20 million generated by school bonds, to rebuild the elementary school, district office and middle school; and to relocate the elementary school students into temporary buildings during the construction of the new facilities. The new middle school opened in the fall of 1996, and plans call for the new elementary school to open in August 1997.

Source: Haddow, G., and Bullock, J. 2003. *Introduction to emergency management*. Burlington, MA: Elsevier.

CASE STUDY: Relocated Road Prevents Washouts, Promotes Safety

Oxford County, ME—One of Maine's most pristine rivers, the Saco River, runs through the bucolic region of southwestern Maine. Bisected by the Saco River is the small Maine village of Hiram. Here, alongside the Saco runs River Road and its long history of flooding.

The town had received Federal Emergency Management Agency (FEMA) grant funds in the past to help prevent future flood damages to the road. But the section of the road that had been mitigated lies at a sharp bend in the river, and the scour effect on the riverbank had placed the entire road in jeopardy. The chronic problem of road washouts had a negative effect on neighbors, schools, businesses, municipal, and utility services; it divided the town into two, causing a major inconvenience and potential safety hazard.

The town decided to fix the problem once and for all. In order to do so, the town wanted to move part of the road back from the riverbank. However, the first major issue would be the costs associated with the project. Historically a farming center, today it is a bedroom community of Portland. The town of 1,406 residents has neither industry nor lakefront property, leaving the town with a very limited tax base.

The second issue was that the location that the town hoped to move the road to was private property. Fortunately, the property owner was civic minded and donated an easement to the town at no cost. This opened the door for the town to apply for another grant through FEMA's Hazard Mitigation Grant Program (HMGP).

The town applied for an HMGP grant through a flooding disaster (DR-1371-ME) declared on May 16, 2001. In April 2002, the town was awarded a grant to fund the moving of the road and the stabilization of the riverbank. FEMA's Hazard Mitigation Grant Program (HMGP) provides grants to states, Indian tribes, and local governments for long-term hazard mitigation projects following a major disaster declaration. Under this program FEMA pays up to 75 percent of the project cost. Either the state or the applicant covers the remaining 25 percent.

The project consisted of moving 1,825 feet of road approximately 20 feet west of the river. This improvement altered the angle of the slope to a 2:1 ratio and protected the slope with riprap and native vegetation. An added benefit was that the town also was able to remove a sharp curve and a knoll and fill a dip in the road.

The total cost of the project was $538,000 of which the town paid the total local share of $134,000. The direct cost benefit to the town is $755,610 in mitigated financial loss.

As of February 2009, the project is 100 percent complete, and Hiram town officials report that River Road has had no more flooding problems.

Source: FEMA Mitigation Best Practices Portfolio. http://www.fema.gov/mitigationbp/brief.do?mitssId=6549.

CASE STUDY: Mitigation Project Gets an 'A' Plus

Harris County, TX—The prediction of rain was not welcomed at Klein High School prior to 2003. Due to the expansion of the campus and the rapid development of the surrounding areas, storm drains were heavily taxed. Heavy rain often flooded some of the school's buildings. After sandbagging for several years, Klein Independent School District (ISD) sought a better solution.

"We used to have these cute little Home Depot type plastic storage units right outside entry doors, and we had a good stock of sandbags," said Donald Blue, Director of Capital Projects for Klein ISD. "Every time we got a good rain, we'd put a little sandbag down around the doors. Students had to step over them, and of course we couldn't put handicap accessible ramps over the sandbags."

Klein ISD retained an engineering firm to perform a study and make recommendations. A storm water drainage project was proposed.

The Drainage Project was initiated in April 2003 and completed in January 2006 at a cost of $970,113. Klein ISD received a $727,580 grant from the Federal Emergency Management Agency (FEMA) through its Hazard Mitigation Grant Program (HMGP).

Phase I of the project consisted of three parts. First, the removal and relocation of existing facilities at the practice field and excavating a storm water detention pond located on the practice field. The detention pond is two feet deep, and the excavated dirt was used to create a berm around the practice field.

The second part was the installation of Tide Flex Check Valves (backflow) to the school's existing storm sewer system to ensure that potential off campus storm water cannot flow back through the system and flood the campus.

Last came the removal and replacement of approximately 400 square yards of asphalt pavement to install

400 linear feet of 12-inch gravity flow storm water pipe from the gymnasium to an existing drainage ditch.

Phase II of the storm water drainage improvements was the installation of a 54-inch gravity pipe, buried 15 feet deep. Since the improvements, Klein ISD has not had any problems.

Source: FEMA Mitigation Best Practices Portfolio. http://www.fema.gov/mitigationbp/brief.do?mitssId=5107.

Financial Incentives

This is one of the emerging areas for promoting mitigation. Among the approaches being used by localities to reduce risk are creation of special tax assessments, passage of tax increases or bonds to pay for mitigation, relocation assistance, and targeting of federal community development or renewal grant funds for mitigation.

The economic effects of repetitive flooding led the citizens of Napa, California, and Tulsa, Oklahoma, to pass small tax increases to pay for flood mitigation activities. In both cases, the tax had minimal effect on the community citizens but had a major effect in reducing the potential economic losses from future floods. Berkeley, California, has passed more than ten different bond issues to support seismic retrofitting of public buildings, schools, and private residences.

Funding from the Community Development Block Grant (CDBG), a Housing and Urban Development (HUD) program, has been used extensively to support local efforts at property acquisition and relocation. These funds have been used to meet the nonfederal match on other federal funding, which has often been a stumbling block to local mitigation. Other federal programs of the Small Business Administration (SBA) and the Economic Development Administration provide financial incentives for mitigation.

Other emerging areas of financial tools include special assessment districts, impact fees, and transfer of development rights. All these tools provide either incentives or penalties to developers as a means of promoting good risk reduction development practices.

CASE STUDY: Using Grants to Help Convert Overhead Electrical Lines to Underground

Independence, MO—For the City of Independence, removing power lines from utility poles and burying them underground is not just a matter of aesthetics; it's also good business. Through mitigation grants, Independence Power and Light (IPL) buried power lines from distribution line poles to residential structures, proving that this tactic enhances power reliability, reduces property loss, and lessens risk to human life—and it saves money.

Continuously reinstalling downed power lines, which resulted from several storms that toppled trees and snapped branches, did not make financial sense for the municipally owned company. As replacement costs continued to escalate—along with the risk to life and property damages—reversing the "reinstalling" trend became a priority [Figure 3.2].

"We are not offering customers a service by repeating what we did three or four decades ago. We have to

FIGURE 3.2 **For the City of Independence, Missouri, removing power lines from utility poles and burying them underground became both a viable economic and safety mitigation strategy.**

quit pouring money into [downed power lines in] storm after storm and start finding ways to benefit customers and reduce future damages," said Jack Looney, district engineering planner supervisor at Independence Power and Light. "We can do that through underground utility services."

The ice storm of 2002 crippled the area, leaving over 2,000 of IPL's 47,000 residential customers without power and some of who suffered utility-related property damages. For most, the average electrical outage was six days. Storm damages exceeded $1.4 million. Transmission and distribution lines were down; one lineman was fatally injured while repairing services.

"It's not the ice on the lines that causes the most damage, but the weight of ice on adjacent trees that fall and force power lines down," Looney said.

The storm was declared a Federal disaster, and mitigation funds became available through the Federal Emergency Management Agency (FEMA) Hazard Mitigation Grant Program (HMGP). HMGP provides funding to State and local governments to implement long-term hazard mitigation measures and recover from major disaster declarations. FEMA can fund up to 75 percent of the eligible cost of each project.

"By converting overhead electric services underground, our goal is to reduce our customers' vulnerability to danger, restore power for more customers in a shorter period and reduce the expense of repairing services as well as property damages, additional crews and other overhead services," Looney explained. "Reinstalling overhead lines following a major ice storm as 2002 is a 14-day event. It takes about seven days to repair the main distribution system and the rest of the time is spent putting services back up."

Teaming with Missouri's State Emergency Management Agency (SEMA), IPL sought mitigation grants to facilitate the underground conversion of service distribution lines to 1,200 high-risk residential customers. IPL set out to prove that moving utility lines underground is good mitigation.

Success of the grant application primarily rests on complying with FEMA guidelines—the project must conform to the State Hazard Mitigation Plan, provide beneficial impact upon the designated disaster area, conform to environmental regulations, solve a problem independently and be cost effective.

Source: FEMA Mitigation Best Practices Portfolio. http://www.fema.gov/mitigationbp/brief.do?mitssId=6371.

CASE STUDY: Light Fixtures and Earthquakes: Protecting School Children

Los Angeles, CA—The Los Angeles Unified School District (LAUSD) is second in size only to the New York City School District. At present, the District is composed of over 900 schools, serving over 800,000 students, and employing 57,000 full-time and 24,000 part-time staff. The LAUSD provides public education services to a 708 square mile area including the cities of Los Angeles, Bell, Carson, Cudahay, Gardenia, Huntington Park, Lomita, Maywood, San Fernando, South Gate, Vernon, and West Hollywood; portions of 18 other cities; and the unincorporated areas of Los Angeles County.

At the time of the 1994 Northridge Earthquake, the LAUSD facilities were illuminated with suspended ceilings and imbedded pendant lighting systems. These lights tend to fall from the ceiling when impacted by strong seismic motion. Hundreds of lighting units fell onto desks in the classrooms when the earthquake hit.

Fortunately, the earthquake occurred early in the morning when the schools were closed. As a result of this experience the LAUSD, with the support of FEMA, decided to undertake the seismic retrofitting or replacement of pendant lights to increase life safety, reduce the earthquake injury risk, and to meet current building code standards.

In the Northridge Earthquake, 5,500 buildings owned by LAUSD were damaged with total damages currently estimated at $134 million. Under Section 406 of the

Stafford Act, FEMA funded $3.1 million for damaged, unbraced pendant ceiling and lights. In addition, $45 million were obligated to mitigate unbraced pendant ceiling and light systems of the same design that were not damaged.

The reinforcement and/or replacement of the unbraced pendant lights in the Los Angeles Unified School District will reduce the high risk of injury to the more than 800,000 school children during the next earthquake event.

Source: FEMA Mitigation Best Practices Portfolio. http://www.fema.gov/mitigationbp/brief.do?mitssId=226.

Structural Controls

Structural controls are controversial as a mitigation tool. Structural controls usually have been used to protect existing developments or systems that may be in an area that is hazardous. In doing so, they can have both positive and negative effects on the areas they are not protecting. In addition, as the name implies, they are used to control the hazard, not reduce it. The most common form of structural control is the levee. But there are other structural controls, such as culverts, that are extremely useful and, usually, cost-effective to address hazards that impact community infrastructure systems, especially roads.

CASE STUDY: Culvert Upgrade: Prevents Flooding, Provides Safety

Sullivan County, NH—You would hardly notice the Quabbinnight Brook as it passes under Sugar River Drive in the City of Claremont, NH on a sunny day. But during heavy rain, storm water often backed up at an undersized culvert under the road, resulting in massive flooding on the upstream side of Sugar River Drive.

Engineering studies showed that the culvert, a six foot corrugated metal pipe, did not have the capacity to carry a 25-year storm event. The culvert had already failed and the flow of the brook was no longer contained. The flooding caused deterioration of the roadway embankment and would eventually result in embankment failure.

The Claremont Department of Public Works continually patched the roadway above the culvert. Yet, it continued to sink two to three inches after patching, indicating a loss of bedding material around the failed culvert.

Flooding of Sugar River Drive isolated more than 150 households, more than 600 people, the Sullivan County Nursing Home, and the County House of Correction from the city. Emergency personnel, including fire, police, and ambulance services, would face a 25-minute detour through a neighboring town, but only if the alternate road was passable. School busses, heavy construction, and farm equipment also accessed Sugar River Drive.

The solution to the problem was to replace the failed culvert with a concrete box culvert.

The new, larger, box culvert is 12 by 5 by 40 feet with wing walls.

The project was funded by the Federal Emergency Management Agency (FEMA) Hazard Mitigation Grant Program (HMGP), which provides grants to states, Indian tribes, and local governments for long-term hazard mitigation projects following a major disaster declaration. Under this program FEMA pays up to 75 percent of the project cost. Either the state or the applicant covers the remaining 25 percent.

The project was completed in the spring of 2006. The total cost for the Sugar River Drive project was $150,000. FEMA's share was $112,500, and the local match was $37,500.

Claremont officials report no more flooding problems on Sugar River Drive as of February 2009.

Source: FEMA Mitigation Best Practices Portfolio. http://www.fema.gov/mitigationbp/brief.do?mitssId=6510.

Mitigating the Home

The destruction of a home can have a devastating impact on a child. The community hazard mitigation plan should include identification of those high-risk residential neighborhoods in a community and should provide recommendations on how to mitigate the risks in these areas. Mitigation measures may include acquiring and relocating houses, elevating houses, constructing a "safe room" in houses, installing storm shutters to protect windows or putting protective film over the windows, and using hurricane clamps to keep the roof from coming off in high winds.

Low- to moderate-income neighborhoods are often hardest hit by disasters because of their location in a high-risk area and the types of construction often found in these neighborhoods. Community leaders and emergency managers should pay special attention to these areas and give them priority in implementing mitigation measures designed to protect children's homes. Supporting individuals to undertake mitigation measures on their homes is most successful when financial incentives are made available from local sources, both governmental and private loans. The following case studies illustrate two examples of such programs.

CASE STUDY: Kennebunk Acquisition, Demolition, and Elevation

York County, ME—Sitting on the banks of the Mousam River in Kennebunk, Maine on a lazy summer's day, you could never imagine the torrent that repeatedly floods the Intervale neighborhood. But during heavy rains, storm water often overflows the riverbanks and floods 18 houses; 12 of these houses are along the river, and six are inland across Intervale Road.

This neighborhood has a history of flooding that goes back to 1953 with six reported events. None of the properties had flood insurance. Forty-two residents are directly affected, but the downstream effect from the flooding of this neighborhood is much greater, causing pollution from septic, oil, gas, asbestos, etc. It has had a ripple effect on neighbors, schools, businesses, and municipal and utility services.

The Town of Kennebunk decided after much town and neighborhood input that the only viable solution was to remove the willing homeowners from the floodplain either through buyouts or elevations.

The plan of action was for the town to apply for a Hazard Mitigation Grant Program (HMGP) grant through the Federal Emergency Management Agency (FEMA). The grant provides funds to states, Indian tribes, and local governments for long-term hazard mitigation projects following a major disaster declaration. Under this program FEMA pays up to 75 percent of the project cost. Either the state or the applicant covers the remaining 25 percent.

The grant was applied for in September 2007 and awarded in December 2007. The grant was for the acquisition and demolition of three houses and the elevation of eight houses. The demolished houses were burned down as both a training exercise for new fire recruits and as an opportunity to test the mutual aid abilities of area fire departments in a safe environment.

The cost of the project was $1,503,875 the town paid the total local share of $375,969. The project is 98 percent complete except for some final landscaping.

Now that the work is done, the Intervale neighborhood is once again an idyllic 1960s enclave of families and neighbors with a couple of new pocket parks that even have access to the Mousam River, which affords a variety of recreational opportunities.

Kennebunk officials report no more flooding problems in this neighborhood as of February 2009.

Source: FEMA Mitigation Best Practices Portfolio. http://www.fema.gov/mitigationbp/brief.do?mitssId=6537.

CASE STUDY: Tulsa Safe Room Program

Tulsa, Oklahoma lies in the heart of Tornado Alley. Tornadoes with major damage have hit Tulsa on average of every four or five years. Most recently, the May 3, 1999, tornadoes killed 44 people and decimated communities through Oklahoma. As a result of these storms, the President declared a major disaster. Oklahoma was provided the opportunity to take advantage of new construction technology to mitigate the effects of tornadoes.

The concept of safe room construction was developed and pilot tested in 1998 by the Wind Engineering Research Center of Texas Tech University with financial support from the Federal Emergency Management Agency (FEMA). Safe rooms are anchored and armored rooms that provide shelter during tornadoes, even above ground.

Tulsa proposed to FEMA that it use its Hazard Mitigation Grant Program (HMGP) funding provided through the President's declaration, to provide grants to homeowners to build safe rooms in their homes.

Under their Project Impact designation, Tulsa brought together a coalition of partners including FEMA, Oklahoma State Emergency Management, Home Builders of Greater Tulsa, Tulsa Public Works, State Farm Insurance and other community partners.

This coalition then agreed on building and construction standards, permitting, certification and compliance procedures and public education and awareness programs.

This coalition set as their goal a tornado safe room in every newly constructed and existing home by the year 2020.

This program was supported through a variety of public and private funding but the major key to its success was the partnership of the building and construction community.

Tulsa builders embraced the safe room concept and quickly made it a positive marketing tool for their business. The city continued to encourage growth of the program by providing certain financial incentives. Eleven major Tulsa builders launched the first safe room subdivision in a new upscale residential area of Tulsa. It is believed to be the first safe room subdivision in Oklahoma, and perhaps the first in the Nation financed entirely by private builders.

The program continues to expand not just within Tulsa and Oklahoma, but also to other States and communities in tornado alley. Within Tulsa, wheel chair accessible safe rooms have been designed and built. The next step is building safe rooms in public buildings and schools. The technology is there but the societal questions of size, access and quantity of space and related issues are still being worked on.

The Tulsa safe room project provides an excellent example of taking advantage of the opportunity afforded in the post disaster climate. Its success provides an even better example of how building coalitions, particularly with the private sector ensures sustainability of the mitigation program.

Source: Haddow, G., and Bullock, J. 2006. *Introduction to emergency management*. 2nd ed. Burlington, MA: Elsevier.

Hazard Mitigation Resources

FEMA is responsible for most of the programs of the federal government that support mitigation; this section focuses on these programs. The Small Business Administration, Economic Development Administration (EDA), and HUD have policies that support mitigation. The PATH program at HUD supports incorporating mitigation into public housing. The Environmental Protection Agency (EPA) has several programs in floodplain management and in 2002 initiated a new pilot program for national watersheds. The National Earthquake Hazards Reduction Program includes several other federal agencies and provided significant technical assistance for earthquake mitigation; however, the predominant federal agency involved in disaster mitigation is FEMA. FEMA's programs include the Hazard Mitigation Grant Program (HMGP), the Predisaster Mitigation (PDM) Program, and the Flood Mitigation Assistance (FMA) Program.

The **Hazard Mitigation Grant Program** (HMGP) is the largest source of funding for state and local mitigation activities. This program provides grants to state and local governments to implement long-term hazard mitigation programs after the president has declared a major disaster. HMGP projects must reduce the risk, and the benefits of the project must exceed the costs.

Examples of activities supported by HMGP include the following:

- Acquisition of property on a voluntary basis and commitment to open use of the property
- Retrofitting of structures and lifelines

- Elevation of structures
- Vegetation management programs
- Building code enforcement
- Localized flood control projects
- Public education and awareness

The **Flood Mitigation Assistance** (FMA) Program, according to FEMA, "was created as part of the National Flood Insurance Reform Act (NFIRA) of 1994 (42 U.S.C. 4101) with the goal of reducing or eliminating claims under the National Flood Insurance Program (NFIP). FEMA provides FMA funds to assist States and communities implement measures that reduce or eliminate the long-term risk of flood damage to buildings, manufactured homes, and other structures insurable under the National Flood Insurance Program" (www.fema.gov).

The **Predisaster Mitigation** (PDM) Grant Program, according to FEMA, "provides funds to states, territories, Indian tribal governments, communities, and universities for hazard mitigation planning and the implementation of mitigation projects prior to a disaster event. Funding these plans and projects reduces overall risks to the population and structures, while also reducing reliance on funding from actual disaster declarations. PDM grants are to be awarded on a competitive basis and without reference to state allocations, quotas, or other formula-based allocation of funds" (www.fema.gov).

Communities should also consider creating a local funding source that could be used to match federal, state, and private sector funding for hazard mitigation projects. Communities such as Tulsa, Oklahoma, and Napa, California, have established consistent local funding sources that have helped pay for extensive hazard mitigation projects and programs that have made these communities models for disaster resilience.

Conclusion

Children's ability to cope in the face of disaster is directly tied to the resiliency of their community and their community's infrastructure. During Hurricane Katrina, over 290,000 children were displaced from their schools across the Gulf Coast region, disrupting the routine of the school environment that is so important for child resiliency. Mitigation is the key to community resiliency and securing a safer environment for children. But implementing mitigation measures in the home or in the community requires sustained action and champions within a community. Successful mitigation involves (1) building a partnership among all elements of the community, both public and private; (2) using this partnership to identifying community hazards; (3) identifying mitigation actions to address the hazards; (4) setting priorities for taking those mitigation actions; and (5) securing the resources to implement the mitigation priorities. Throughout the chapter we have used case studies to demonstrate how communities have implemented mitigation measures for a variety of hazards in diverse projects and made their communities safer for their citizens and their children. The challenge is to take their experiences and create new ones in the thousands of communities whose children face a new disaster each day.

References

FEMA Mitigation Best Practices Portfolio. http://www.fema.gov/mitigationbp/brief.do?mitssId=208.

FEMA Mitigation Best Practices Portfolio. http://www.fema.gov/mitigationbp/brief.do?mitssId=226.

FEMA Mitigation Best Practices Portfolio. http://www.fema.gov/mitigationbp/brief.do?mitssId=2165.

FEMA Mitigation Best Practices Portfolio. http://www.fema.gov/mitigationbp/brief.do?mitssId=5107.

FEMA Mitigation Best Practices Portfolio. http://www.fema.gov/mitigationbp/brief.do?mitssId=6371.

FEMA Mitigation Best Practices Portfolio. http://www.fema.gov/mitigationbp/brief.do?mitssId=6510.

FEMA Mitigation Best Practices Portfolio. http://www.fema.gov/mitigationbp/brief.do?mitssId=6537.

FEMA Mitigation Best Practices Portfolio. http://www.fema.gov/mitigationbp/brief.do?mitssId=6549.

Haddow, G., and Bullock, J. 2003. *Introduction to emergency management.* Burlington, MA: Elsevier.

Haddow, G., and Bullock, J. 2006. *Introduction to emergency management.* 2nd ed. Burlington, MA: Elsevier.

Save the Children. 2008. *Including children in emergency planning: Giving children priority—before, during, and after disasters.*

Chapter 4
Preparedness

Introduction

There are numerous steps that can be taken by a community to prepare children for disasters and to ensure that those facilities that support children have the appropriate emergency plans. Emergency managers must work closely with community stakeholders, school officials, child care providers, and emergency shelter managers to ensure that the needs of children are addressed in their emergency operations plans.

The first part of this chapter is dedicated to identifying those actions that emergency managers should consider when revising and refining their existing emergency operations plans to reflect the unique needs of children in disasters. The second part of the chapter identifies specific steps that all stakeholders involved in disasters at the community level should consider. Throughout the chapter examples of plan formats, checklists, case studies, lessons learned, and other support materials will be presented (see Sidebar 4.1 and Figure 4.1).

SIDEBAR 4.1 PREPARING TO HELP CHILDREN IN DISASTERS

With proper planning and guidance, emergency management agencies can minimize the risk faced by the community's children. Children, families and those tasked with the care of children (teachers, childcare centers, etc.), can all take action before disasters occur to prepare for and mitigate their effects. Response and child-stewardship organizations that are most likely to assume the role of protecting children in the immediate aftermath of a disastrous event can be equipped for and provided with proper training to manage the specific needs of this special population. And the community can plan for the specific needs that children will have in the longer-term recovery phase, when these vulnerable lives are gradually brought back to normalcy.

Source: Save the Children. 2007. The *unique needs of children in emergencies: A guide for the inclusion of children in emergency operations plans*. September. http://www.savethechildren.org/publications/emergencies/Children-in-Emergencies-Planning-Guide.pdf.

FIGURE 4.1 **Fargo, North Dakota, March 27, 2009. Two young volunteers fill sandbags in the Fargo Dome in Fargo, North Dakota. The sandbags are used to protect levees surrounding Fargo. The Red River was expected to crest on Saturday at over 41 feet. (Patsy Lynch/FEMA)**

Learning Objectives

At the conclusion of the chapter, the participants will be able to:

- Evaluate their community's emergency operations plan (EOP) against a checklist in *The Unique Needs of Children in Emergencies*
- Determine which local organizations should be on a planning team to develop an annex to the community's EOP relating to the unique needs of children or to revise the EOP to integrate those needs
- Discuss the factors that lead to resiliency among children faced with disaster
- Explain the requirement for emergency operations planning for schools and child care centers
- Recognize the details that indicate that a shelter plan has taken into account the unique needs of children

Preparedness Actions

In Chapter 2, twelve areas of need were identified concerning children in disasters:

- Child safety and security
- Nutrition
- Clothing and shelter
- Hygiene
- Evacuation and transportation
- Health and hospital care
- Emergency medical care and emergency response
- Supervision, day care, and educational facilities
- Education
- Psychological care
- Emergency Management education for children, parents, and caregivers
- Other needs

Within each area of need, there are actions that may be taken by individuals, agencies, and organizations to meet those needs. These needs fall into four general categories, each a component of the comprehensive emergency management cycle: mitigation, preparedness, response, and recovery. (Note: Presented in this chapter are the mitigation and preparedness actions. Response and recovery actions will be presented in Chapter 5.) It is only after a planning team has determined the needs of children that exist in their community that they can begin to determine what actions may be taken (and what actions are feasible) to address the needs and to reduce the vulnerability of children. The following lists provide examples of actions that may be considered by the planning team when developing an annex to meet the needs of children in emergencies. This list is by no means prescriptive or complete.

Area 1: Child Safety and Security

Mitigation and Preparedness

- Develop and enact/install systems that provide early warning and immediate response assistance to facilities in the care of children (schools, day care centers, recreational programs)
- Conduct regular hazard safety inspections of child care facilities and schools, and provide structural and non-structural mitigation advice and assistance as required
- Develop guardianship protocols to guide the care of children separated from their parents at shelters, schools, or day care centers
- Develop plans for placement of children during disaster and terrorist events in case of injured or deceased family members
- Develop a list of all local staff who have already received criminal background checks, and who would be cleared to work with children for both security and other purposes (e.g., teachers, day care center staff, recreational department staff, coaches, etc.)
- Develop plans for quickly and accurately checking the background of and establishing the credentials for all responders, relief providers, and volunteers (spontaneous and affiliated) who will be working directly with disaster-affected children (in shelters, emergency medical services, psychosocial care, and other areas) (one example is the

Health Resources and Services Administration [HRSA] Emergency System for Advance Registration of Volunteer Health Professionals)

- Develop systems for identifying responders certified to work with children (such as a badging system)
- Develop an accountability system to track the movement and location of children within hospitals (injured children, the children of injured parents, and abandoned or separated children), within community shelters, within evacuation efforts, sheltered-in-place at congregation points (e.g., day care, school), and elsewhere as required
- Develop systems, protocols, and points of contact for sharing information on children between the office of emergency management and facilities in the care of children
- Develop a system to provide concerned parents with information regarding the whereabouts and safety of their children
- Develop systems and policies that protect all children from discrimination based on their age, gender, race, or ability
- Provide training to police, fire department officials, and other emergency service professionals who will be charged with ensuring the safety and security of children about the unique vulnerabilities of children affected by disasters
- Include child safety and security issues in all drills and exercises
- Develop systems that will ensure that security exists for unattended/unsupervised adolescents in shelters, schools, day care centers, and other facilities in the care of children

Area 2: Nutrition

Mitigation and Preparedness

- Develop and assign a child emergency nutrition specialist position
- Ensure that facilities in the care of children are stocked with at least a forty-eight-hour supply of emergency food, water, and nutritional supplements that are appropriate for

the ages and condition of the children likely to be located at the facility

- Ensure that shelters are stocked with emergency food, water, and nutritional supplements appropriate for children of all ages, and with the feeding implements for children of all ages (including bottle-fed infants and infants on introductory solid food diets)
- Ensure that all facilities in the care of children, and all shelter locations, are equipped with the nutritional supplements required by children and pregnant mothers (e.g., fluoride drops, iron and calcium supplements)
- Develop emergency feeding protocols for children, and provide them to all facilities that may act as a shelter to children in a disaster area
- Develop a list of sources or providers of child-specific food items in the community, and a system to deliver appropriate and ample stocks of these items to facilities that are likely to need them in an emergency situation
- Ensure that nursing mothers have a place to safely collect and securely store breast milk, ensuring that mix-ups cannot occur
- Ensure that mothers of bottle-fed children have the equipment and facilities to clean (and sterilize) feeding implements, if necessary

Area 3: Clothing and Shelter

Mitigation and Preparedness

- Supply shelters with bedding supplies that are appropriate for infants and toddlers (bassinets and cribs, individual sleeping pads, and the necessary sheets and blankets)
- Ensure that facilities and supplies are available to wash children's clothing and bedding (e.g., sensitive skin pediatric detergents)
- Establish predisaster agreements between facilities in the care of children and mass care organizations that dictate what shelters children will be brought to in emergencies, and likely needs of those children

- Provide mass care organizations with training on the particulars of sheltered children and their needs
- Develop policies for the guardianship of children and responsibilities of parents within shelters
- Develop systems to ensure that clothes for children are distributed to the appropriate shelter locations
- Assist all facilities in the care of children with planning for shelter-in-place scenarios

Area 4: Hygiene

Mitigation and Preparedness

- Establish child-safe storage for cleaning and disinfecting equipment in shelter locations and other locations where children may congregate following disasters
- Establish hand hygiene procedures and stockpile adequate amounts of soap, sinks, and paper towels
- Develop protocols for diapering
- Develop protocols for cleaning of toys and other shared implements (such as toilets, changing stations, feeding areas, etc.)
- Stockpile adequate supplies of cleaning and disinfecting solutions and materials

Area 5: Evacuation and Transportation (Figure 4.2)

Mitigation and Preparedness

- Confirm and log the availability of vehicles suitable for the transport of children and able to withstand many of the consequences of disasters (snow, water, heat, etc.) within the community
- Provide guidance or assistance to facilities in the care of children about evacuation planning and procedures
- Map all facilities where large numbers of children are likely to congregate, and develop plans to safely evacuate them in the event of a rapid-onset emergency
- Ensure that vehicles equipped to transport children are available for evacuation and transportation during the

FIGURE 4.2 **Mobile, Alabama, May 3, 2006. Mobile County school children, before their tour of the Hurricane Hunter research aircraft, listen to a presentation by FEMA Deputy Federal Coordinating Officer (DFCO) Jesse Munoz. National Weather Service and NOAA Hurricane Hunter aircraft and crew promote hurricane awareness and preparedness. (George Armstrong/FEMA)**

disaster response and recovery phases (including child restraint devices)

- Plan to transport injured children to hospital facilities outside the immediate affected area, including routes, destinations, vehicles, and safety devices (e.g., car seats)
- Orient all evacuation and disaster transportation personnel about the special safety and security needs of children

Area 6: Health and Hospital Care

Mitigation and Preparedness

- Develop a list, including contact information and specialty, of all pediatricians in the community (including those who live in the community but work elsewhere, or who are retired)
- Ensure all pediatricians and pediatric hospitals develop and maintain continuity of operations plans (COOPs)

- Include pediatric health care facilities (e.g., children's hospitals, pediatric emergency departments, and pediatricians' offices) in all aspects of emergency planning and preparation
- Include a detailed pediatric component in any Web-based or other hospital resource availability networks
- Provide training to ensure that general emergency practitioners are able to recognize and respond to the needs of an ill or injured child at all levels of care—from the prehospital setting, to the emergency department care, to definitive inpatient medical and surgical care
- Ensure preparedness in all hospitals for a surge in pediatric patients
- Ensure that all facilities to be used for the shelter of children are equipped with general over-the-counter medicine for children (pain reliever, antihistamines, allergy creams and liquids, teething relief, antifungal creams, etc.) and child-appropriate first aid supplies
- Encourage parents to keep backup copies of children's health records in a safe, secure location in case their physician's records are destroyed

Area 7: Emergency Medical Care and Emergency Response

Mitigation and Preparedness

- Equip emergency response personnel and vehicles with adequate supplies of child-safe and child-dosed antibiotics, antidotes, and vaccines (e.g., pediatric resuscitation equipment, Broselow tape)
- Purchase pediatric emergency response supplies, equipment, and pharmaceuticals sufficient for a mass-casualty incident involving children
- Maintain pediatric emergency supplies, validating expiration dates regularly
- Develop procedures for managing pediatric emergencies at all facilities where care is likely to occur (in the field, shelters, clinics, hospitals)

- Purchase special child-appropriate decontamination showers (children are subject to hypothermia much faster and can suffer psychological trauma from unnecessary exposure) that are appropriate for children of all ages (including infants), parentless children, nonambulatory children, and special needs children
- Provide training to emergency services (police, fire, EMS, emergency management) on pediatric emergency care, including pediatric triage, recognition of the different vital signs, symptoms, and other indications exhibited by children, pediatric prehospital care, and other treatment issues, including those of special needs children
- Provide pediatric emergency care informational resources at emergency response facilities (shelters, emergency services offices)
- Establish agreements with pediatricians to provide emergency care in the event of a disaster event where pediatric emergency care physicians are overwhelmed
- Include disaster medical and emergency management issues (including children or actors posing as children) in communitywide drills and exercises
- Develop regional mutual assistance agreements to accommodate pediatric victims (with children's hospitals, for example)
- Incorporate poison control centers into emergency medical procedures as a resource and central clearinghouse for toxicological information (including antidotes and contamination procedures that may need to be broadcast to the public in biological or chemical emergencies)
- Equip children's hospitals with equipment and supplies capable of managing a surge in pediatric patients
- Establish agreements with organizations and agencies (government and nongovernmental) who will address the special needs of children following a disaster in the community
- Establish government liaison position for children in disasters issues
- Establish an emergency operations center (EOC) coordinator for children in emergencies

- Establish a children-in-emergencies recovery coordinator
- Form and foster community partnerships that help to manage children's issues in disaster response and recovery

Area 8: Supervision, Day Care, and Educational Facilities

Mitigation and Preparedness

- Assess emergency management needs relevant to children's issues at all facilities in the care of children
- Ensure that all facilities in the care of children conduct COOP planning, are prepared for the sudden loss of community services, and that all staff are trained in child CPR, EMS, and the particulars of evacuating or sheltering the children within their care
- Conduct shelter-in-place planning and drills at schools, day care centers, and facilities and locations where children congregate
- Inventory all day care space available both within the community and in surrounding communities, noting the number of filled and empty slots
- Develop policies and plans for the ongoing care of children who are separated from their parents and are unable to be quickly reunited, including transportation, supervision, shelter, care, and nutrition
- Develop plans for establishing instant day care centers in the event that the day care infrastructure in the community is damaged or destroyed
- Plan for the staffing, operation, and equipment of day care centers to be established at community emergency shelters
- Develop plans for contacting or notifying parents/guardians of children within the care of the school or center
- Develop protocols for the timely reunification of families
- Establish systems for and conduct predisaster identification of children (e.g., name tags, other forms of ID), especially for those who are not verbal, or who cannot give their own name, a parent's name, or other critical information

- Integrate schools and day care facilities into local disaster plans, with special attention paid to evacuation, transportation, and reunification of children with parents, and incorporate the incident command system at these facilities
- Conduct disaster exercises and drills in partnership with emergency services
- Involve parents in school- or day care–based disaster planning efforts
- Plan for the replacement of teachers and day care staff that will leave to deal with their own disaster consequences
- Mitigate known disaster vulnerabilities at schools, day care centers, camps, sporting venues, and all other facilities where children congregate

Area 9: Education

Mitigation and Preparedness

- Ensure shelters can be stocked with arts and crafts and other creative supplies for children
- Find out how to locate or create Safe Spaces kits for shelters
- Develop plans for establishing instant classrooms, including staff, supplies, and appropriate curricula, within close proximity of shelter locations, in the event that schools are damaged, destroyed, or converted into community shelters
- Plan for the replacement of teachers and day care staff that will leave to deal with their own disaster consequences
- Develop plans for the replacement of damaged or destroyed educational materials
- Ensure that all students' educational records are backed up in a safe, off-site location

Area 10: Psychological Care

Mitigation and Preparedness

- Incorporate materials on the hazards that affect the community in regular curricula
- Provide training for educators and day care providers in the psychological care and recovery of children with disaster-related psychiatric illnesses (e.g., posttraumatic

stress disorder [PTSD], anxiety, depression, behavioral problems), including trigger and symptom recognition, interventions, and treatment

- Establish procedures for the mobilization of a family information and support center
- Enhance preexisting children's mental health infrastructure as necessary to handle the surge of need likely to follow a disaster
- Train pediatricians to be able to identify psychological symptoms, perform mental health triage, initiate brief supportive interventions, and make appropriate interventions when necessary

Area 11: Emergency Management Education for Children, Parents, and Caregivers

Mitigation and Preparedness

- Provide families with guidance on home disaster preparedness, and encourage families to develop family disaster plans
- Educate families on methods to mitigate the disaster risks to children
- Conduct disaster drills in schools, day care facilities, and all other facilities where children congregate
- Prepare and provide emergency preparedness and response guidance for families of children with special health care and other needs
- Inform parents about the immediate and long-term effects of disasters on children to help them identify if their children are suffering from the effects of a disaster
- Include training on the assessment and care of children and in the usage of pediatric equipment in conjunction with other disaster training programs, in order to highlight the unique psychological, developmental, and physiological concerns of children and their unique vulnerabilities
- Provide pediatric disaster-related education to supplemental response groups (e.g., school staff, day care personnel, community response organizations, civic organizations, specialty medical services, family practices, hospices, youth organizations)

- Include sufficient proportions of pediatric victims and child-related scenarios in all regional disaster drills, and actively involve the major pediatric care providers within the community (e.g., children's hospitals, pediatric societies, day care centers, schools)
- Partner pediatricians with schools, child care centers, and other locations where children spend their time to assist them in developing adequate emergency plans and stockpiling appropriate disaster supplies
- Educate children about disaster response, including what to do if they are separated from their parents or if they require rescue

Area 12: Other Needs

Mitigation and Preparedness

- Determine all legal considerations concerning the care and treatment of minor children, including unaccompanied minor children, such as consent, guardianship, decontamination consent, records privacy, and photographs (of unidentified children)
- Conduct drills with federal, state, and regional/local emergency managers that include exclusively pediatric victims or a majority of pediatric victims in various circumstances (e.g., in schools, day care facilities, school buses, etc.) to adequately test the capacity of the system to handle pediatric patients
- Communication (translation services)
- Family and parental support
- Pregnant and lactating mothers
- Transient children
- Illegal children or children of illegal alien parents

Emergency Operations Plans

Emergency managers should review their current emergency operations plans (EOP) to identify what changes needed to be made to ensure that the unique needs of children are addressed in these plans. This process will require involving numerous new stakeholders who will bring valuable information concerning the programs and facilities that support children in the community. Emergency managers must carefully consider the assumptions that their EOP is built on and understand the role they play in making their EOP child friendly.

The Save the Children guide *The Unique Needs of Children in Emergencies: A Guide for the Inclusion of Children in Emergency Operations Plans* states: "The planning team for the development of the Children in Emergencies document should be drawn from various groups that have a role or stake in the emergency response needs of children. The list below is by no means to be considered all-inclusive. Nor is it necessary for every community to involve all of these positions in its effort—the key to forming a planning team is for the planning coordinator to ensure that membership represent an accurate cross section of the organizations involved in the jurisdiction's emergency response effort as it relates to children, parents, guardians and pregnant women" (Save the Children, 2007) (see Sidebar 4.2).

SIDEBAR 4.2 POSSIBLE PLANNING TEAM MEMBERS (AGENCIES, ORGANIZATIONS, AND INDIVIDUALS)

- The Office of the Chief Executive
- Emergency Services (law enforcement, fire/rescue and EMS)
- Emergency dispatchers
- Public health and safety officials
- · Social service agencies and volunteer organizations (including a children's services agency)
- Area hospitals (children's and general)
- Urgent care providers
- Suppliers of equipment and materials for the educational, health, hygienic and nutritional needs of children
- Pediatricians
- Educational administrators/Superintendent of schools
- Teachers' organization leaders

- Childcare association representatives
- Public Information Officer (PIO)
- Local media
- Jurisdiction's legal counsel
- Emergency managers and agency representatives from neighboring jurisdictions (to establish mutual aid agreements)
- State and/or Federal representatives, as appropriate
- Mass care coordinator and mass care facility managers
- Parent and guardian organization representatives
- Other organizations or agencies involved in the care of children or child/family recreation (e.g., community recreation department, childcare licensing agency)
- Organizations managing transient populations that include children (hotel associations, tourism boards)
- Mental health agencies
- Poison control centers
- Social service agencies
- Local Emergency Management Planning Committee (LEPC) members
- Faith-based groups and churches
- School nurses
- Courts (as needed)
- Community zoning officials

Source: Save the Children. 2007. *The unique needs of children in emergencies: A guide for the inclusion of children in emergency operations plans*. September. http://www.savethechildren.org/publications/emergencies/Children-in-Emergencies-Planning-Guide.pdf.

The Save the Children report recommends: "Once the planning team has been established, the team should begin by assessing all of the information that is available as a result of the Basic EOP development, including (most importantly) the hazard risk assessment, the base map of the community and the inventory of emergency management resources available both within and outside the community" (Save the Children, 2007) (see Sidebar 4.3).

SIDEBAR 4.3 INFORMATION COLLECTION

The planning team may need to gather information that provides them with insight into the following:

- Statutory authorities (laws, regulations, statutes and other legal information) relating to the emergency care of children in the community
- Base map of the community, upon which all childcare facilities are located (e.g. schools, childcare centers)
- Population and demographic information for all children in the community
- Number of special needs children in the community and information regarding the kinds of need and the facilities available to attend to those needs
- Community school system information, including:
  - Name, address, and contact information for each school
  - Number and age of students in each school
  - Each school's status as a community shelter (or shelter for neighboring community)
- Childcare information, including:
  - List of community childcare facilities, including business names, addresses and contact information for each facility
  - Capacity of each facility
  - Viability of each facility to provide emergency shelter
  - Number of children enrolled in each facility
- Hospital and health care information
  - Name, address and contact information for each
  - Number of pediatric beds in each facility
  - Number of pediatric physicians in the hospital system
  - Hospitals in neighboring jurisdictions willing to accept pediatric casualty overflow (including all information above)
  - Name and contact information for all private pediatricians in the community
- Mass care shelter information
  - Shelter administrator name
  - Shelter address and other pertinent information

- Shelter capacity for children
- Non-Governmental Organizations (NGO) information
- List of child-focused NGOs operating the community (disaster and non-disaster related)
- Contact information and area of focus

- Transportation information
  - Inventory of vehicles that would be used to transport children during an evacuation or following a disaster
  - Status of child-safety devices or capacities of the vehicles
  - Address and contact information for transportation providers
  - Probable evacuation routes and plans for facilities serving/housing children

- Resource Database
  - List of suppliers who can provide emergency supplies and equipment related to the care of children (diapers, wipes, formula, feeding implements, etc.), including address and contact information
  - Inventory and pricing information for relevant supplies and equipment

- Emergency management information
  - Equipment, supplies and facilities that meet the emergency needs of children
  - Information regarding emergency services staff training in pediatric emergency response
  - Available courses within and outside the community that focus on pediatric emergency management

- Psychosocial (emotional support) information
  - Name and contact information of community pediatric psychologists
  - Name and contact information of school social workers
  - Name and contact information of local experts on child development

- Hazard Information
  - Community risk as it relates to children, the facilities housing/serving them and neighborhoods where there are notably higher densities of children

- Mitigation options available to minimize the risk to children and facilities housing/serving them

Source: Save the Children. 2007. *The unique needs of children in emergencies: A guide for the inclusion of children in emergency operations plans*. September. http://www.savethechildren.org/publications/emergencies/Children-in-Emergencies-Planning-Guide.pdf.

All plans are based on a series of assumptions that inform the development of a plan. The Save the Children report identified several examples of assumptions upon which emergency managers could use to build their emergency operations plans for children in disasters. This list of assumptions is provided in Sidebar 4.4.

SIDEBAR 4.4 PLANNING ASSUMPTIONS FOR CHILDREN IN DISASTERS

The following list of assumptions is provided only to present examples of the kinds of assumptions that a planning team's efforts may be based on. For any given community these assumptions may or may not be true:

- Children whose parents or guardians are present will remain under parental guardianship or under the care of the legal guardians
- The location of the community's children during the school year and during regular school hours is predictable as determined by the department of education and the individual educational facilities
- Outside of regular school hours, the location of children is dictated primarily by families and social networks
- Parents' and guardians' primary concern during times of emergency or disaster will be to locate and collect their children
- Many providers of children's care, including childcare and home care employees, teachers, camp counselors and others, will be affected by major disasters themselves. Their primary concerns at this time may be the whereabouts and safety of their own families

- Institutions normally tasked with the daytime care of children, including schools, childcare centers and others, are likely to be closed during and following a major disaster
- In events where there are numerous injuries or fatalities sustained by children, local pediatric providers and institutions will be quickly overwhelmed
- In certain disasters, children will be required to shelter in place with their families, such as pandemic flu or bioterrorism
- In certain disasters, children will be required to shelter in place at daytime care facilities, including schools and childcare centers
- Transient children, including the children of tourists, travelers passing through the community, patrons of local businesses and others, may require additional help related to guardianship, especially when parents or guardians are not present
- All schools and many private childcare and educational facilities maintain internal emergency operations plans of their own to address the needs of children, although these plans are applicable only while children remain in their care
- Catastrophic disasters may overwhelm the capacity of local facilities to deal with pediatric needs, including medical care, emergency care, special diets, sheltering arrangements and supervision [Figure 4.3]
- Until children are moved from the grounds of a school or childcare facility or until assistance is requested from the office of emergency management, children will remain under the care of the school or childcare facility administration.

Source: Save the Children. 2007. *The unique needs of children in emergencies: A guide for the inclusion of children in emergency operations plans.* September. http://www.savethechildren.org/publications/emergencies/Children-in-Emergencies-Planning-Guide.pdf.

FIGURE 4.3 **Fargo, North Dakota, March 26, 2009. The Red Cross has set up shelters around the state of North Dakota in anticipation of evacuees who may have to leave their homes in areas that are flooded. (Patsy Lynch/FEMA)**

The Save the Children report identifies roles and responsibilities for the many stakeholders involved in working with children in disasters. These stakeholders include:

- Local emergency managers
- Children's issues coordinator
- Transportation
- Mass care
- Superintendent of schools
- Human services
- Fire
- EMS
- Hospitals
- Public health
- Mental health
- Social services
- Legal system

- Law enforcement
- Public information
- Community zoning officials
- Public works and utilities

Presented below is a sampling of some of the roles and responsibilities identified by Save the Children (2007) for several of the above-listed stakeholders. A full list of the roles and responsibilities for all stakeholders identified in the report is presented in the full copy of the report, included in Appendix G of this book.

Local Emergency Managers

- Form and foster community partnerships that help to manage children's issues in disaster response and recovery
- Mitigate known disaster vulnerabilities at schools, child care centers, camps, sporting venues, and all other facilities where children congregate
- Educate families on methods to mitigate the disaster risks to children
- Provide families with guidance on home disaster preparedness and encourage families to develop family disaster plans
- Develop a program to educate children about disaster response, including what to do if they are separated from their parents or guardians or if they require rescue
- Establish an emergency operations center (EOC) children's issues coordinator
- Develop systems, protocols, and points of contact for sharing information on children between the office of emergency management and facilities that care for children prior to incidents
- Develop systems, protocols, and points of contact for sharing information on children between the office of emergency management and facilities in the care of children with the children's issues coordinator
- Develop systems for identifying responders certified to work with children (such as a badging system)

- Include pediatric health care facilities (e.g., children's hospitals, pediatric emergency departments, and pediatricians' offices) in all aspects of emergency planning and preparation
- Assist child care facilities and schools in their efforts to develop on-site emergency operations plans
- Conduct drills with federal, state, and regional/local emergency managers that include pediatric victims or a majority of pediatric victims in various circumstances (e.g., in schools, child care facilities, school buses, etc.) to adequately test the capacity of the system to handle pediatric patients
- Include child safety and security issues in all drills and exercises

Children's Issues Coordinator (EOC)

- Enact badging, credentialing, and background check systems for anyone who will be working primarily with children
- Track all affected children, including those who are evacuated, sheltered at off-site locations, hospitalized, or sheltered in place
- Track all children who are sheltered in place and assist the sheltering facilities in providing for the needs of those children
- Develop an accountability system to identify and track the movement and location of children within an evacuation effort
- Map all facilities where large numbers of children are likely to congregate, and develop plans to safely evacuate them in the event of a rapid-onset emergency
- Track all evacuated children (in conjunction with the transportation coordinator) and provide a central repository of this information for concerned parents, guardians, and family members
- Ensure that the needs of special needs children are met during evacuations

Transportation

- Confirm and log the availability of vehicles suitable for the transport of children and able to withstand many of the consequences of disasters (snow, water, heat, etc.) within the community
- Ensure that vehicles equipped to transport children are available for evacuation and transportation during the disaster response and recovery phases (e.g., vehicles with child restraint devices)
- Provide orientation for all evacuation and disaster transportation personnel on the special safety and security needs of children
- Track all evacuated children (in conjunction with the children's care coordinator) and provide a central repository of this information for concerned parents, guardians, and family members
- Ensure that all individuals transporting children have passed background checks

Mass Care

- Develop an accountability system to identify and track the movement and location of children within community shelters and children sheltered in place at congregation points (e.g., child care, school)
- Develop systems that will ensure that security exists for unattended/unsupervised adolescents in shelters and other facilities that care for children in emergencies
- Ensure that shelters are stocked with or can obtain emergency food, water, and nutritional supplements appropriate for children of all ages and feeding implements for children of all ages (including bottle-fed infants and infants on introductory solid food diets)
- Establish predisaster agreements between facilities that care for children and mass care organizations that determine which shelters children will be brought to in emergencies
- Develop policies on the responsibilities of parents and guardians within shelters

- Establish child-safe storage for cleaning and disinfecting equipment in shelter locations and other locations where children may congregate following disasters
- Establish hand hygiene procedures, adequate sinks, and stockpiles of adequate amounts of soap and paper towels
- Establish routines for children in shelters to foster a safe, calm, nurturing, and normalizing environment
- Allow opportunities for children to play and socialize with other children

Human Services

- Inventory all child care space available both within the community and in surrounding communities, noting the number of filled and empty slots
- Develop plans for establishing instant/emergency child care centers in the event that the child care infrastructure in the community is damaged or destroyed
- Plan for the staffing, operation, and equipment of child care centers to be established at community emergency shelters
- Work with local law enforcement to develop protocols for the timely reunification of families
- Establish systems for and conduct predisaster identification of children (e.g., name tags, other forms of ID), especially for those who are not verbal or who cannot give their own names, a parent's or guardian's name, or other critical information
- Prepare and provide emergency preparedness and response guidance for families of children with special health care and other needs
- Establish child care facilities at all community shelters
- Perform an assessment of damages to registered child care and other children's infrastructure components
- Establish instant child care centers
- Assist shelters in establishing child care facilities for sheltered residents
- Assist families of children with special health care and other needs

- Coordinate with the EOC children's issues coordinator to report on the status of child care and other children's infrastructure to the EOC
- Assist child care facilities in forming partnerships to assist each other during a crisis

Fire

- Arrange for regular hazard safety inspections of child care facilities and schools and for the provision of structural and nonstructural mitigation advice and assistance as required
- Ensure that emergency vehicles are equipped with rescue equipment suitable for pediatric victims

Emergency Medical Services

- Create plans for transporting injured children to hospital facilities outside the immediately affected area, including routes, destinations, vehicles, and safety devices (e.g., car seats)
- Equip emergency response personnel and vehicles with adequate supplies of child-safe and child-dosed antibiotics, antidotes, and vaccines
- Purchase pediatric emergency response supplies, equipment, and pharmaceuticals sufficient for a mass-casualty incident involving children
- Purchase special decontamination showers that are appropriate for children of all ages (including infants), as well as children without parents or guardians, nonambulatory children, and special needs children
- Make every effort to keep families together within the emergency medical system
- Maintain pediatric pharmaceutical emergency supplies, validating expiration dates regularly
- Provide family-centered emergency care to families with children
- Document all care

Hospitals (See Sidebar 4.5 and Figure 4.4)

- Work with emergency medical services to develop an accountability system to identify and track the movement and location of children from the field to hospital release
- All pediatricians and pediatric hospitals should develop and maintain continuity of operations plans (COOPs)
- All hospitals should be prepared to handle a surge in pediatric patients
- Purchase pediatric emergency response supplies, equipment, and pharmaceuticals sufficient for a mass-casualty incident involving children
- Make every effort to keep families together within hospitals
- Prepare for pediatric patients (overflow) in general hospitals not accustomed to child patient issues
- Maintain pediatric pharmaceutical emergency supplies, validating expiration dates regularly in conjunction with public health

SIDEBAR 4.5 HOSPITALS AND HEALTH CARE FACILITIES

All health care facilities, not simply children's hospitals, must be prepared for a surge of critically ill children. Although EMS field efforts will attempt to match the survivors' needs with the nearest appropriate hospital, the most recent disaster literature suggest that up to 50 percent of survivors arriving at a hospital under a surge (mass casualty) scenario will arrive by other means. To accommodate a surge of pediatric patients, all hospitals should ensure that adequate, up-to-date stocks of pediatric supplies are on site.

"Currently, the United States has fewer than 300 children's hospitals, a fraction of all hospitals (five percent), and only 40 percent of emergency department hospitals have procedures regarding pediatric transfers. A surge of ill children may present considerable staffing challenges to non-pediatric designated hospitals.

Source: National Commission on Children and Disasters. 2009. Interim report. October 14. http://www.childrenanddisasters.acf.hhs.gov/20091014_508IR_partII.pdf.

FIGURE 4.4 **Surge capacity in disasters, among other emergency response and treatment capabilities, is an important function of hospital planning and preparedness.**

Public Health

- Develop an inventory, including contact information and specialty, of all pediatricians in the community (including those who live in the community but work elsewhere or who are retired)
- Include a detailed pediatric component in any Web- or community-based resource networks
- Develop procedures for managing pediatric emergencies at all facilities where care is likely to be provided (in the field, shelters, clinics, hospitals)
- Establish agreements with pediatricians to provide emergency care in the event of a disaster where pediatric emergency care physicians are overwhelmed
- Develop regional mutual assistance agreements to accommodate pediatric victims (with children's hospitals, for example)
- Address the pediatric medical needs of special needs children (dialysis, preexisting physical therapy, disability related)

- Provide on-site pediatric emergency and primary health care at emergency shelters
- Maintain pediatric pharmaceutical emergency supplies, validating expiration dates regularly in conjunction with hospitals
- Provide informational resources on pediatric emergency care at emergency response facilities (shelters, emergency services offices)
- Establish continuity of nurturing care for children (care by the same person for children between 0 and 18 months is considered important)

Mental Health

- Enhance preexisting children's mental health infrastructure as necessary to handle the surge of need likely to follow a disaster
- Train pediatricians to be able to identify psychological symptoms, perform mental health triage, initiate brief supportive interventions, and make appropriate interventions or referrals when necessary
- Provide psychological counseling and care to children during evacuation
- Mobilize pediatric psychiatric specialists to assist in the recognition and treatment of pediatric psychiatric trauma and illness
- Perform interventions to minimize pediatric psychological trauma, especially in shelter and school settings
- Incorporate age-appropriate psychosocial interventions into ongoing in-school recovery programs and curricula
- Ensure that children with preexisting mental health conditions are not excluded from eligibility for mental health care after a disaster or crisis
- Mobilize outreach support teams to go into the community (e.g., schools, child care centers, churches) to provide stress debriefing, triage, and long-term monitoring
- Conduct community memorial and grieving services geared toward children

- Identify parents and guardians who are having difficulty in coping with the event, and refer them to appropriate support networks (children's recovery depends a great deal upon the status of their parents or guardians)
- Conduct early interventions with all children in the affected area, especially school-based interventions where children are most comfortable
- Inform parents about the immediate and long-term effects of disasters on children to help them identify if their children are suffering from the effects of a disaster
- Ensure that psychological counseling and care are provided to children during evacuation

Social Services

- Develop guardianship protocols to guide the care of children separated from their parents at shelters, schools, or child care centers
- Develop plans for placement of children during disaster and terrorist events in case of injured or deceased family members
- Establish predisaster agreements between facilities that care for children and mass care organizations that dictate what shelters children will be brought to in emergencies and the likely needs of those children
- Develop policies and plans for the ongoing care of children who are separated from their parents and are unable to be quickly reunited, including transportation, supervision, shelter, care, and nutrition
- Assist all facilities that care for children with planning for shelter-in-place scenarios
- Identify, track, and address the needs of sheltered special needs children
- Establish safe play areas in all shelters that foster natural childhood development
- Provide communication assistance for children who require it (e.g., children who do not speak English, children with speech or sensory disabilities)

- Assist in the social integration of children, especially those who are separated from their families and friends or who are otherwise displaced
- Ensure that transient children (children of tourists, non-residents in facilities, including camps and boarding schools) are identified, tracked, and cared for

Legal System

- Determine all legal considerations concerning the care and treatment of minor children (including unaccompanied minor children), such as consent, guardianship, decontamination consent, records privacy, and photographs of unidentified children
- Appoint lawyers to serve as guardians *ad litem* for children orphaned or those who have lost a custodial parent
- Include all relevant domestic courts (e.g., family, probate, juvenile) in the planning process to consider children's best interests

Law Enforcement

- Develop a list of all local workers who have already passed criminal background checks and who would be cleared to work with children for both security and other purposes (e.g., teachers, child care center staff, recreational department staff, coaches, etc.)
- Develop plans for quickly and accurately checking the background of and establishing the credentials for all responders, relief providers, and volunteers (spontaneous and affiliated) who will be working directly with disaster-affected children in shelters, emergency medical services, psychosocial care, and other areas
- Perform security checks on staff and volunteers who wish to work with children in the response and recovery phases
- Provide security to children in shelters
- Work with the National Center for Missing and Exploited Children to reunite families

Public Information

- Develop a system to provide concerned parents or guardians with information regarding the whereabouts and safety of their children
- Warn all facilities that care for children, as required
- Provide parents/guardians postdisaster response and recovery information about the disaster needs of children and the facilities that are currently offering to meet those needs
- Advise parents, guardians, other caregivers, the media, and public officials about ways to help children cope during times of stress (anniversaries of the event, holidays, life changes, etc.) after a disaster
- Work with law enforcement/EOC children's issues coordinator
- Develop predisaster messages on how to help children cope with disaster-related stress and the disaster's effects

Community Zoning Officials

- Ensure zoning codes are adequate to protect current child-inhabited facilities
- Author new codes that prevent child-inhabited facilities from building in potentially unsafe areas (e.g., brownfield locations, near hazardous material facilities)

Public Works and Utilities

- Provide emergency support to families of children with special health care needs
- Develop a resource list of all large child care facilities to expedite return of utilities; this includes liaising with private utilities

All Responding Agencies

- Develop systems and policies that protect all children from discrimination based on their age, gender, race, ability, or other factors (Save the Children, 2007)

School Preparedness

According to the Agency for Healthcare Research and Quality (2009), "among so-called child congregate facilities (schools, daycare centers, camps, athletic programs), schools constitute the largest group. More than 50 million children attend the Nation's 115,000 schools daily, spending more than 70–80 percent of their waking hours at school. Consequently, schools serve as surrogate parents, having primary responsibility for providing all of the needs of children, including their meals, education, treatment of illness, and protection from harm" (see Sidebar 4.6).

SIDEBAR 4.6 FEMA EXERCISES AND PREPAREDNESS GRANTS

The National Commission on Children and Disasters recommends exercises include objectives that test capacities including, but not limited to, pediatric triage, pre-hospital treatment, surge capacity, transport of children and coordination with schools, childcare providers, and child welfare and juvenile justice systems.

The Commission is collaborating with the Department of Homeland Security (DHS) Grants Directorate to strengthen community preparedness planning by make children a priority in grants awarded through the Homeland Security Grant Program (HSGP). In addition, the Commission recommends critical supply lists and allowable costs and expenses include program activities, planning, training, exercising, equipment, food and basic medical supplies for children. The Commission recommends that DHS encourage grantees to make pediatric capabilities integral to base plans rather than as a subset of special needs populations. The Commission further recommends that HSGP grant guidance enhance and expand capabilities for improved preparedness of child congregate care systems, providers and facilities, especially school districts and childcare providers.

Source: National Commission on Children and Disasters. 2009. Interim report. October 14. http://www.childrenanddisasters.acf.hhs.gov/20091014_508IR_partII.pdf.

CASE STUDY: Student Tools for Emergency Planning (STEP) Program

In 2008, the Federal Emergency Preparedness Agency (FEMA) and state emergency preparedness agencies teamed up with New England schools to launch a pilot program for New England fourth grade students to teach basic emergency preparedness skills. The Student Tools for Emergency Preparedness program provides ready-to-teach preparedness lessons for teachers to empower students to encourage their families to make home emergency kits and communication plans.

In addition to the lesson plan, some schools also were provided with items for students to make their own starter kits, including a water bottle, snack bar, emergency whistle, Mylar blanket, and carrying bag.

The family plan promoted by the program encouraged students to agree with their families on an alternate meeting place outside of the home, designate a person to call in case of an emergency (often in a different state), and for each family member to carry around cards with those important facts as well as work and school numbers.

More information about the emergency preparedness kits and communications plans can be found at (Figure 4.5):

1. www.fema.gov/plan/prepare/supplykit.shtm
2. www.fema.gov/plan/prepare/commplan.shtm

"Despite the integral nature of school in the life, health, and protection of children, there has been remarkably little attention devoted to emergency preparedness in schools. While certain aspects of school-based emergency response (e.g., fire drills and evacuation) are universal, other equally important aspects of emergency response, including sheltering-in and lockdown protocols, exist in few schools and school districts across the Nation. Based on our review, no comprehensive national guidelines have been created with flexibility needed for any school—regardless of size—to adopt." (Agency for Healthcare Research and Quality, 2009)

FIGURE 4.5 **Boston, Massachusetts, April 28, 2010. Deputy Administrator Richard Serino talked Wednesday with Boston and North Providence, Rhode Island, schoolchildren involved in FEMA Region I's STEP Program pilot, an initiative that encourages emergency preparedness among New England's youth. Students told the deputy administrator about the disasters they learned to prepare for, their family meeting locations, and the contents of their emergency kits. (David Bibo/FEMA)**

The Agency for Healthcare Research and Quality report recommended that local leadership in the schools (i.e., school superintendent, school board/committee), the local emergency manager and first responders, and a planning committee comprised of "school administrators, school principals, guidance counselors or school psychologists, teachers, nurses, secretarial staff, custodial staff, and parents" should be assembled to build a school emergency response plan (Agency for Healthcare Research and Quality, 2009) (see Sidebar 4.7).

SIDEBAR 4.7 SPECIFIC STEPS TO CREATE A SCHOOL PLAN

Step 1. Plan regular meetings. The team creating the plan should schedule regular meetings with school leaders, school committee leaders, town safety officers, and public health authorities.

Step 2. Perform a needs assessment. Schools should conduct surveys to evaluate the knowledge, opinions, and needs of their school as perceived by the school staff. (Appendix B. Needs Assessment Surveys)

Step 3. Conduct a structured interview with each school principal. The planning team should survey all principals using an instrument that permits a streamlined interview, identifies the specific needs of each school building, outlines structural vulnerabilities, and recognizes the needs of special populations. (Appendix C. Principal Interview Questions)

Step 4. Conduct a site survey of every school in the district. Knowledgeable members of the planning team should conduct a careful walkthrough of each school in order to:

Learn its structural nuances,

Identify any obstacles to a comprehensive plan,

Evaluate (or identify) lockdown and sheltering-in sites, and

Evaluate nearby hazards such as chemical industries or nuclear power plants.

Step 5. Create and plan education and training modules for the school staff. The planning team should provide specific training modules on key aspects of emergency response and pediatrics, including specific training and tabletop exercises. Tabletop disaster exercises are moderator-guided classroom exercises in emergency response. These exercises can help familiarize staff with general response procedures and resolve perceived logistics challenges. Such training is often available from local, State, or Federal emergency response programs. (Appendix E. Tabletop Exercise Resources)

Step 6. Create two documents—an all-hazards Emergency Response Manual and a school-specific Emergency Response Handbook. It is essential that two documents are created and the information within is practical and easily accessible.

All-Hazards Emergency Response Manual. Using the information obtained from the needs assessment surveys and borrowing from existing emergency response plans (both within the school district and from outside districts), the planning team should construct a comprehensive, easily accessed, and easy-to-use manual. This all-hazards response manual, which specifies appropriate responses to particular emergencies, is a permanent document. Information provided in this manual should include:

- Articles and documents on general crisis management guidelines and checklists for crisis readiness.
- Forms that can be used to document various kinds of crises.
- Various scenarios for "tabletop" exercises.
- Articles related to trauma and grief in children. If the manual is placed on the Internet, a paper copy should also be available in case the Web is not accessible.

School-Specific Emergency Response Handbook. Using information gained from school-specific surveys and site walkthroughs, the planning team, in conjunction with the school crisis team, should create a school-specific handbook with guidelines for the individual school and its staff. This document will have information and checklists that may change with each school year. Preferably, this handbook is unbound, in a three ring binder, so that pages can be inserted and removed as necessary. For quick access, the manual should be clearly indexed and specific to the roles of the various people who need to respond quickly and effectively. A vertical "flip format" with tabs identifying the plan for each type of crisis and specific job descriptions for teachers, principals/crisis management, nurses, and administration can be used. Information provided in the school-specific handbook should include:

- A comprehensive form delineating various aspects of preparedness, reviewed annually by the school principal. There should be spaces for the names of those personnel responsible for particular duties and lists of supplies needed in an emergency. (Appendix F. Annual School Emergency Preparedness Summary Form)
- Protocols for evacuation, lockdown, and sheltering-in-place.

- A document that details building-specific accommodations.
- A map of individual school buildings.
- Contact numbers for town emergency responders and local support resources.

Step 7. Create a timeline for accomplishing each of the above tasks. The timeline for creating an Emergency Response plan can be highly variable, although a reasonable goal is completion in one academic year. Implementation may take longer, depending on the degree of changes needed, available budget, and approval of all recommendations.

Step 8. Inform parents of the plan. Each school should have a series of parent-teacher meetings, informing the parents of the plan and providing them opportunities to ask questions, raise concerns, clarify information, and offer input.

Step 9. Implement the plan. As plan implementation begins, conduct staff meetings to inform staff members of the plan details. The entire staff must know where they can access key information about specific emergencies, their individual responsibilities, the names and roles of crisis team members, and the lockdown and sheltering-in-place sites.

Step 10. Conduct practice drills. Conduct practice drills, particularly those that would require deployment of evacuation, lockdown, or sheltering-in-place procedures. Consider using tabletop disaster drills. Afterwards, encourage practice drills in conjunction with local emergency response teams to evaluate practicality and effectiveness of emergency response plans.

Step 11. Re-evaluate the plan annually, and revise if necessary. At the beginning of each school year, the crisis team of each school should review the plan and revise if necessary, based on any significant changes in staffing, school structure, or student body.

Source: Agency for Healthcare Research and Quality. 2009. *School-based emergency preparedness: A national analysis and recommended protocol*. Pub. 09-0013. Rockville, MD: AHRQ. http://www.ahrq.gov/prep/schoolprep/schoolprep.pdf.

CASE STUDY: The Brookline Schools Readiness Project: A Roadmap to Creating a Comprehensive School Emergency Response Plan

The Center for Biopreparedness at Children's Hospital Boston developed a comprehensive School Emergency Response Plan for the Brookline, MA schools. This effort first involved identifying the characteristics of the Brookline Schools (i.e. student population, facilities, times of operations, etc.). A review of existing school emergency plans from around the country was conducted. A survey was conducted of school district crisis teams (including principals), school nurses and teaching staff. Interviews and site visits were conducted.

Based on the data collected, unresolved challenges were noted in the after-school athletic programs, effective liaison with local emergency response teams and management of special populations. The project team developed a series of recommendations concerning evacuation/relocation, shelter-in-place and lockdown. A tabletop exercise was developed, an education and training materials for school nurses and an Emergency Response Manual and Handbook developed.

Source: Agency for Healthcare Research and Quality. 2009. *School-based emergency preparedness: A national analysis and recommended protocol.* Pub. 09-0013 Rockville, MD: AHRQ. http://www.ahrq.gov/prep/schoolprep/schoolprep.pdf.

SIDEBAR 4.8 REGISTRY INFORMATION FROM SCHOOLS, CHILDCARE CENTERS, AND OTHER FACILITIES THAT CARE FOR CHILDREN

Unlike registries of individuals, which are built through optional self-reporting, a registry for schools and childcare facilities is more easily and systematically conducted. Such a registry is composed of a database or spreadsheet that lists each school or childcare facility's name, address, telephone number and other vital information. Vital information could include the points of contact (with offhours contact information for at least 2 senior staff members), licensed capacity or census data, number of staff and any existing transportation capability by the facility using either regular or wheel chair assist vehicles.

The "licensed capacity" census figure is the "worst case" or maximum population at the facility that could require support at any given time. For childcare facilities, this maximum is set by the operating license, generally issued by the State. These facilities may have a smaller number of children on any given day but never more than the license allows. Schools, K–12, are required to report their official headcount to the state on a specified date, (typically in the fall term) to qualify for state funds and this is the number that should be used when planning. The availability of staff members should include food service, custodial workers, volunteers or other people who are generally expected to be on site each day when accounting for the total number of "adults" on site. Summer school programs should be also be identified to the emergency management agency by the school system since the size of the school population and the locations of the school sessions will probably differ from the regular term and the location could change from year–to-year.

If a particular school facility has anything exceptional that other schools do not have, it must be documented in the registry as well. Examples include a higher percentage of children with disabilities or language barriers or possibly a childcare facility within the regular school that supports a large number of infants. It is also important to note if the school is totally dedicated to children with a specific disability, such as a deaf or blind oriented school, since this could require additional or targeted resources.

Children/youth with behavioral or developmental challenges are sometimes adjudicated to residential treatment facilities and removed from parental custody. These individuals usually stay in the facilities at night and attend school or training activities during the day. Like schools, residential treatment facilities should register with emergency management and provide the same information as schools.

Source: Save the Children. 2007. *The unique needs of children in emergencies: A guide for the inclusion of children in emergency operations plans*. September. http://www.savethechildren.org/publications/emergencies/Children-in-Emergencies-Planning-Guide.pdf.

Child Care Facilities

Emergency managers must be aware of where the child care facilities are located in their community and help these facilities develop detailed emergency plans. To better understand how child care providers will function in a disaster, emergency managers should consider including child care providers in planning and conducting community disaster exercises.

The National Association of Child Care Resource and Referral Agencies (NACCRRA) has developed a guide for child care providers on disaster preparedness that provides instructions on preparedness and emergency planning and samples of plan outlines and checklists.

In its report entitled *Is Childcare Ready? A Disaster Planning Guide for Childcare Resource and Referral Agencies*, NACCRRA (2006) outlines "some general steps all childcare programs should take to reduce the impact of different types of disasters:

- Regularly monitor for possible threats and hazards.
- Regularly clean and check heating, cooling, gas and electrical systems. Check that they are in good working order.
- Provide one or more carbon monoxide detectors, as well as regular maintenance and checks of smoke detectors.
- Ensure fire extinguishers are properly charged, mounted, and easy to reach in case of fire.
- Be sure key staff knows how to use a fire extinguisher properly and other staff or family members are trained in proper use.
- Ensure there are no barriers that prevent safe exit from the home or facility.
- Consider buying a generator for back-up power. A licensed electrician must install a generator."

Examples of emergency planning and preparedness tips, forms, and guides for child care providers developed by NACCRRA are presented in the following pages (Sidebars 4.9–4.13).

SIDEBAR 4.9 NACCRRA PLANNING AND PREPAREDNESS TIPS

One of the first steps in disaster planning is to inspect the childcare facility or family childcare home for potential hazards in a disaster. Some of the types of hazards to look for include:

- Objects that could fall during an earthquake or tornado.
- Large items that could tip over during high winds, an earthquake, or similar event.
- Potential plumbing breaks during earthquakes and tornadoes.
- Materials that could easily ignite during a wildfire or other fire.
- Areas that will drain poorly during heavy rains and flooding.
- Windows or doors that are obstructed and from which adults and children could not evacuate during a fire or other disaster.

There are some actions all childcare facilities should take to prepare for any disaster. These include:

- Collecting and keeping information on staff and volunteers/
- Collecting and keeping information on the children and families enrolled/
- Stocking supplies needed to remain in the facility or to evacuate.
- Developing a key contacts and phone list.
- Carrying out a plan for protecting vital records.
- Developing an evacuation plan.
- Training staff and children on the evacuation plan and practicing the plan.
- Encouraging employees to have a family emergency plan.

Source: National Association of Child Care Resource and Referral Agencies (NACCRRA). 2006. *Is childcare ready? A disaster planning guide for childcare resource and referral agencies*. http://www.naccrra.org/disaster/.

SIDEBAR 4.10 PROTECTING VITAL RECORDS AND RESOURCES

Childcare programs need many different types of records to operate—information about children, employee records, child and adult food program records, parent charges and payments, and others. Today many programs store this information in computer files. Besides these records, most programs have insurance policies, rental agreements, building plans, floor plans, bank account records, supplier contacts, service agreements, copies of inventories and other important papers needed to run the program. If there is a disaster, paper copies of vital records and papers could be destroyed. Computers could be damaged or inaccessible if there is no electricity after the disaster occurs. Most programs would find it difficult to operate without access to critical records and documents.

Programs need to decide what information they need to continue to operate and how they will ensure it is available in different types of situations. For example, the program needs to consider:

- What information would they need to take with them during an evacuation?
- What information would they need to have access to if they have to operate from a remote site?
- The information they would need to support an insurance claim if their property, equipment, and supplies were lost or damaged as the result of a disaster.
- How they will back up their computer records so they will be available if the computers are damaged or destroyed.
- How they will back up their computers' basic operating systems and reload critical software, if necessary.

To ensure the records, documents, and computer files the program needs to operate will continue to be available in different types of situations, programs should:

- Keep a copy of all important records and papers in a waterproof, fireproof portable container.
- Make copies of all important documents, operating manuals, inventories, etc. and store them at an off-site location at least 50 miles from the program location.
- Backup all computer files regularly and send a copy electronically to a computer at least 50 miles from the program location.
- Keep a backup copy of the computer basic operating system, boot files, and critical software at a location away from the program site.
- Keep the program's inventory of equipment and supplies current; send an electronic copy or a printed copy to a remote site.

- Take photographs or videotapes of the program facilities, outdoor equipment, landscaping, indoor equipment, and supplies and store them at a remote location.
- Keep a copy of computer and Internet logon codes and passwords at a remote site.
- Keep a copy of a photo of each enrolled child at a remote location.

Source: National Association of Child Care Resource and Referral Agencies (NACCRRA). 2006. *Is childcare ready? A disaster planning guide for childcare resource and referral agencies*. http://www.naccrra.org/disaster/.

SIDEBAR 4.11 SAMPLE OUTLINE FOR A CHILDCARE PROGRAM EVACUATION PLAN

I. Who Can Direct an Evacuation?
- Local Official
- State Official
- Program Representative

II. How the Parents Will Be Notified
III. What the Children Will Be Told
IV. What Signal Will Be Given to Notify Everyone in the Facility?
- If Power Available
- If No Power Available
- Signal for Different Types of Disasters

V. How All Staff, Children, Volunteers and Others in Facility Will Be Accounted For
VI. How Children and Staff Will Be Transported
- Infants
- Toddlers
- Older Children
- Children or Staff with Special Needs

VII. Medications, Supplies, and Records Taken During Evacuation
VIII. Coordinating Actions with Community Public Safety and/or Emergency Management Officials

IX. Evacuation Site
- Near
- Within Area
- Outside Area

X. Person/s Responsible for Each Action

XI. Transportation Plan
- Program Vehicles
- Staff Vehicles
- Additional Vehicles from Volunteers and Neighbors
- Gas in Vehicles
- Keeping Vehicles in Workable Condition
- First-aid Kits in Vehicles

XII. Additional Information
- Location of Electricity Shut-off
- How to Shut Off Electricity
- Location of Gas Shut-off
- How to Shut Off Gas
- Location of Water Shut-off
- How to Shut Off Water
- Location of Air Vent Shut-off (if applicable)
- How to Shut Off Air Circulation System
- Location of Emergency Evacuation Kit
- Location of Additional Emergency Supplies
- Location of Cell Phone

Source: National Association of Child Care Resource and Referral Agencies (NACCRRA). 2006. *Is childcare ready? A disaster planning guide for childcare resource and referral agencies*. http://www.naccrra.org/disaster/.

SIDEBAR 4.12 LIST OF ITEMS FOR CHILDCARE PROGRAM DISASTER KIT

(Enough of each item for 72 hours.)

- One or more changes of clothing for each child
- Disposable diapers and pull-ups
- Wet wipes and tissues

- Water (1 gallon per child, 2 gallons per adult, additional for sanitation and flushing toilets). Date the water and replenish it at least once a year to keep it fresh. If the water has an expiration date it may have to be changed more often.
- Powdered or canned infant formula for each infant
- Powdered or canned milk
- Baby food for each older infant
- Non-perishable food items
- Non-electric can openers
- Supplies of critical medications for children and staff (insulin, epi-pens, etc.)
- Disposable cups, bowls, plates, and eating utensils
- Paper towels, toilet paper, and personal sanitation proucts
- Hand sanitizer and cleaning agents
- Blankets to keep children and staff warm
- Battery-operated radio with extra batteries (AM/FM, weather/TV-band)
- Flashlights with long-life batteries in each room and extra batteries and bulbs in each room
- First aid kits
- Extra games, books, drawing materials, etc. to keep children occupied
- A cell phone
- A facility phone that does not require electricity to operate
- Whistle to signal for help
- Dust and filter masks (available at hardware stores)
- Moist towelettes for sanitation
- Wrench or pliers to run off utilities
- Plastic sheeting and duct tape to seal off rooms
- Garbage bags and plastic ties for personal sanitation and disposable of diapers and pull-ups

Source: National Association of Child Care Resource and Referral Agencies (NACCRRA). 2006. *Is childcare ready? A disaster planning guide for childcare resource and referral agencies.* http://www.naccrra.org/disaster/.

SIDEBAR 4.13 CHECKLIST FOR IMPORTANT RECORDS AND DOCUMENTS

Have one or more duplicate copies of the following records—one copy at a nearby location and one out-of-the area.

Records or Document	Nearby Location	Distant Location
Children's records		
Employee records		
Child and Adult Food Program records		
Accounts receivable (fees, subsidy requests, etc.		
Insurance policies		
Rental agreements		
Building/floor plans		
Bank records		
Credit card information		
Supplier agreements		
Service agreements		
Inventory		
Tax records		
Other:		

Source: National Association of Child Care Resource and Referral Agencies (NACCRRA). 2006. *Is childcare ready? A disaster planning guide for childcare resource and referral agencies.* http://www.naccrra.org/disaster/.

Emergency Shelters

The managers of emergency shelters have not traditionally considered the needs of children in the setup and management of the shelters. Children will be present in shelters, and emergency managers should ensure that shelter managers have in place the means to account for all children, provide security, and have the resources and supplies available to meet the needs of children (Figure 4.6).

FIGURE 4.6 **New Orleans, Louisiana, May 21, 2006. Wali Armstead, FEMA public affairs officer, draws a crowd at his raffle of preparedness and first aid kits at the FEMA Family Preparedness Day in New Orleans. FEMA brought together many organizations to present emergency preparedness information and allow parents and children to gather emergency supplies and decide where they will find safe shelter for themselves and pets during dangerous storms. Many of the items that go into an emergency supply kit were provided free at the event during raffles, activities, and games. (Marvin Nauman/FEMA)**

Save the Children (2007) developed a set of requirements for shelter managers that include:

- Develop an accountability system to identify and track the movement and location of children within community shelters and children sheltered in place at congregation points (e.g., child care, school)
- Develop systems that will ensure that security exists for unattended/unsupervised adolescents in shelters and other facilities that care for children in emergencies
- Ensure that shelters are stocked with or can obtain emergency food, water, and nutritional supplements appropriate for children of all ages and feeding implements for children of all ages (including bottle-fed infants and infants on introductory solid food diets)
- Develop a list of sources or providers of child-specific food items in the community and a system to deliver appropriate

and ample stocks of these items to facilities that are likely to need them in an emergency situation

- Establish predisaster agreements between facilities that care for children and mass care organizations that determine which shelters children will be brought to in emergencies
- Develop policies on the responsibilities of parents and guardians within shelters
- Establish child-safe storage for cleaning and disinfecting equipment in shelter locations and other locations where children may congregate following disasters
- Establish hand hygiene procedures, adequate sinks, and stockpiles of adequate amounts of soap and paper towels
- Develop protocols for diapering in shelters
- Develop protocols for cleaning toys and other shared implements (such as toilets, changing stations, feeding areas, etc.)
- Provide secure transportation within the shelter and the medical care and resources systems (including appropriate official supervision of and accountability for unattended children)
- Track all child-specific information at activated community shelters and report to EOC as required
- Establish routines for children in shelters to foster a safe, calm, nurturing, and normalizing environment
- Allow opportunities for children to play and socialize with other children

Building Resiliency

There are steps that can be taken to help children build resiliency in order to better cope with the next disaster. Knowing what disaster may impact their lives and how they can be part of how their family deals with the next disaster instills confidence in a child and makes that child better prepared to face the next disaster. FEMA, the American Red Cross, and Save the Children have developed a variety of programs and activities designed to prepare children for the next disaster. Information is available from FEMA for Kids: http://www.fema.gov/kids/index.htm. The parents' and teachers' page has activities, curriculum, and safety information for use in the classroom or at home: http://www.fema.gov/kids/teacher.htm.

CASE STUDY: FEMA for Kids

In 2007 FEMA distributed activity books to public and private schoolchildren in Orleans, Jefferson, and St. Martin parishes, all of which were affected by Hurricane Katrina. One that was hit particularly hard by the disaster, Westwego Elementary, used the program to help students to get prepared if they have to face another disaster.

The books are primarily targeted at elementary school children, and they feature tasks such as how to make a family disaster plan, what to pack in a disaster kit, what to do in case of a fire, and more (Figure 4.7).

Materials can be viewed at the FEMA for Kids Website: www.fema.gov/kids. Free books, posters, videos, and

FIGURE 4.7 **Biloxi, Mississippi, June 11, 2009. Public Affairs Specialist Neily Chapman shows children some of the items to pack in a disaster kit during a FEMA in-the-classroom presentation at the Margaret S. Sherry Memorial Library. The FEMA in-the-classroom team made presentations at several libraries in Harrison County over the summer to help children learn how to prepare for hurricane season. (Jennifer Smits/FEMA)**

other educational materials are available to anyone who calls 1 (800) 480-2520, or goes to the website.

Contact Information
Website: www.fema.gov/kids
Phone: (800) 480-2529

American Red Cross: Children and Disasters*

Disasters may strike quickly and without warning. These events can be frightening for adults, but they are traumatic for children if they don't know what to do.

During a disaster, your family may have to leave your home and daily routine. Children may become anxious, confused, or frightened. It is important to give children guidance that will help them reduce their fears.

Children and Their Response to Disaster

Children depend on daily routines: they wake up, eat breakfast, go to school, and play with friends. When emergencies or disasters interrupt this routine, children may become anxious.

In a disaster, they'll look to you and other adults for help. How you react to an emergency gives them clues on how to act. If you react with alarm, a child may become more scared. They see our fear as proof that the danger is real. If you seem overcome with a sense of loss, a child may feel his or her losses more strongly.

Children's fears also may stem from their imagination, and you should take these feelings seriously. A child who feels afraid is afraid. Your words and actions can provide reassurance. When talking with your child, be sure to present a realistic picture that is both honest and manageable.

Feelings of fear are healthy and natural for adults and children. But as an adult, you need to keep control of the situation. When you're

---

* *Source:* "Helping Children Cope with Disaster," developed by the Federal Emergency Agency and the American Red Cross: http://www.redcross.org/portal/site/en/menuitem.d8aaecf214c576bf971e4cfe43181aa0/?vgnextoid=e4a20c45f663b110VgnVCM10000089f0870aRCRD&vgnextfmt=def.

sure that danger has passed, concentrate on your child's emotional needs by asking the child what's uppermost in his or her mind.

Having children participate in the family's recovery activities will help them feel that their lives will return to normal. Your response during this time may have a lasting impact.

Be aware that after a disaster, children are most afraid that:

- The event will happen again
- Someone will be injured or killed
- They will be separated from the family
- They will be left alone

Advice to Parents: Prepare for Disaster

You can create a family disaster plan and practice it so that everyone will remember what to do when a disaster does occur.

Contact your local emergency management or civil defense office or your local Red Cross chapter for materials that describe how your family can create a disaster plan (Figure 4.8).

FIGURE 4.8 **New Orleans, Louisiana, May 21, 2006. FEMA holds its first FEMA Family Preparedness Day in New Orleans, where FEMA brought together many organizations to present emergency preparedness information and allow parents and children to gather emergency supplies and decide where they will find safe shelter for themselves and pets during dangerous storms. Many of the items that go into an emergency supply kit were provided free at the event during raffles, activities, and games. (Marvin Nauman/FEMA)**

Everyone in the household, including children, should play a part in the family's response and recovery efforts.

Teach your child how to recognize danger signals. Make sure your child knows what smoke detectors, fire alarms, and local community warning systems (horns, sirens) sound like.

Explain how to call for help. Teach your child how and when to call for help. Check the telephone directory for local emergency phone numbers and post these phone numbers by all telephones. If you live in a 911 service area, tell your child to call 911. Even very young children can be taught how and when to call for emergency assistance.

Help your child memorize important family information. Children should memorize their family name, address, and phone number. They should also know where to meet in case of an emergency. Some children may not be old enough to memorize the information. They could carry a small index card that lists emergency information to give to an adult or babysitter.

After the Disaster: Time for Recovery

Immediately after the disaster, try to reduce your child's fear and anxiety.

Keep the family together. While you look for housing and assistance, you may want to leave your children with relatives or friends. Instead, keep the family together as much as possible and make children a part of what you are doing to get the family back on its feet. Children get anxious, and they will worry that their parents will not return.

Calmly and firmly explain the situation. As best as you can, tell children what you know about the disaster. Explain what will happen next. For example, say, "Tonight, we will all stay together in the shelter." Get down to the child's eye level and talk to him or her.

Encourage children to talk. Let children talk about the disaster and ask questions as much as they want. Encourage children to describe what they're feeling. Listen to what they say. If possible, include the entire family in the discussion.

Include children in recovery activities. Give children chores that are their responsibility. This will help children feel they are part of the recovery. Having a task will help them understand that everything will be all right.

You can help children cope by understanding what causes their anxieties and fears. Reassure them with firmness and love. Your children will realize that life will eventually return to normal. If a child does not respond to the above suggestions, seek help from a mental health specialist or a member of the clergy.

A complete list of printed children's materials available from the American Red Cross can be found on the publications section of their site. For information from the Department of Homeland Security, visit www.ready.gov/kids.

CASE STUDY: Life EMS Ambulance

In the summer of 2008 Life EMS Ambulance in Kalamazoo, Michigan, offered four separate sessions of Camp 911, a one-day summer camp that aims to teach children what to do to get immediate help in emergency situations and other ways to keep themselves safe.

Participants did not receive CPR certification, but they did get basic instructions in CPR and first aid, and they learned what rescuers and first responders do in emergency situations. The program also included segments on bike safety training and drug and alcohol prevention.

Students were able to try out the equipment that firefighters and emergency workers use, and practice CPR moves on a dummy. They learned how to call 911 and how to get low to the ground and escape from a burning trailer. Students also received healthy snacks, brochures, and DNA kits that included fingerprinting and hair sample kits provided by the American Heart Association.

Talking to Children about Disasters*

You should not worry that talking about disasters will make children fearful. On the contrary, children are usually more frightened by what is whispered or not mentioned aloud than by

* *Source:* American Red Cross. 2007. *Talking to children about disasters*. March. http://www.redcross.org/images/pdfs/code/Talking_to_Children_About_Disasters.pdf.

matter-of-fact discussion. Let children speak freely about what scares or puzzles them—for example, "What will happen to my puppy if we have to evacuate?" "If there's a flood and I'm at school, I won't be able to find you." Try to answer questions and address concerns with concrete, easy-to-follow information.

When helping children learn how to prepare for, respond safely during, and recover from a disaster, it is important to adapt your discussions, instructions, and practice drills to their skills and abilities. Be aware that young children can easily confuse messages such as "drop, cover, and hold on" (response during an earthquake) and "stop, drop, and roll" (response if your clothes catch on fire).

Tell children that a disaster is something that happens that could hurt people, cause damage, or cut off utilities, such as water, telephones, or electricity. Explain to them that nature sometimes provides "too much of a good thing"—fire, rain, wind, snow. Talk about typical effects of disasters that children can relate to, such as loss of electricity, water, and telephone service.

Give examples of several disasters that could happen in your community. Help children recognize the warning signs for each. Discussing disaster ahead of time reduces fear and anxiety and lets everyone know how to respond.

Be prepared to answer children's questions about scary things that they have heard about or seen on television, such as terrorist attacks. Give constructive information about how they can be prepared to protect themselves.

Teach children how and when to call for help. Teach them to call 911 or your local emergency telephone number. At home, post emergency telephone numbers by all phones and explain when to call each number. Include the work numbers and cell phone numbers of household members. Even very young children can be taught how and when to call for emergency assistance. If a child cannot read, make an emergency phone number chart with pictures or icons for 911, "daddy," and "mommy" that may help the child identify the correct number to call.

Tell children that in a disaster there are many people who can help them. Talk about ways that an emergency manager, American Red Cross volunteer, police officer, firefighter, teacher, neighbor, doctor, or utility worker might help after a disaster.

Teach children to call your out-of-town contact in case they are separated from the family and cannot reach family members in an emergency. Tell them, "If no one answers, leave a voice message if possible and then call the alternative contact." Help them memorize the telephone numbers, and write them down on a card that they can keep with them.

Quiz your children every six months so they will remember where to meet, what phone numbers to call, and safety rules.

Explain that when people know what to do and practice in advance, everyone is able to take care of themselves better in emergencies.

By including all members of your household—regardless of age—in disaster preparedness discussions, you will emphasize each person's importance as a member of the safety team.

CASE STUDY: Hurricane Preparedness Workshops

Early in 2006, New Orleans and The Gulf Coast were taking tentative first steps towards recovery and rebuilding in the wake of the devastation of Hurricane Katrina. As families and communities struggled to put their lives back together physically and emotionally they were facing the start of another long and frightening hurricane season. Save the Children Katrina Response through their work with children, families and caregivers saw how this added stress and uncertainty at such a vulnerable point in the areas recovery was having a negative impact on the children in the area.

In response to this need, the staff created a Hurricane Preparedness Workshop to bring to schools, camps and daycares. In a child centered and enjoyable format Save the Children sought to help children be prepared in the event of another hurricane. The mission of Save was not only to help children understand the value of a family plan and to encourage parents and guardians to create such a plan but to also develop a sense of competency in the face of any disaster.

To this end the one hour workshop not only included games surrounding the distribution of a "preparedness backpack" containing emergency supplies such as a flashlight, hygiene kit, whistle and emergency information card but activaties and materials designed to assist the child in developing skills and beliefs that would serve them well emotionally.

At the beginning of each workshop fun, physical activities took place around a parachute as a springboard for a discussion of things that help keep us safe. This enabled the children to begin thinking of people, places and things in their own lives that are available in frightening times. Each workshop also included the reading of a story tailored to the particular age group and geographic location of the children. Each story had as its central theme people, animals and in one case a navigational buoy that all faced the threat of a destructive hurricane and through planning and resourcefulness were able triumph.

Each backpack also contained a teddy bear, journal and crayons and pens. Each child was encouraged to use these items to calm themselves and record their feelings. Save the Children is aware that these workshops are only a beginning and through partnerships with educational and community agencies hope to expand this effort in both depth and breadth.

As of Oct. 27, 2006, 269 hurricane preparedness workshops have been conducted serving 5,374 kids. A total of 5,374 backpacks have been distributed.

Source: Save the Children. www.savethechildren.com

Lessons Learned: Pediatric Disaster Preparedness in the Wake of Katrina

RECOMMENDED ACTIONS

1. A summit conference should be convened to conduct a pediatric disaster readiness needs assessment. This conference should be attended by pediatric care experts and child

health advocates, including key stakeholder professional organizations (such as AAP, ACEP, American Academy of Family Physicians, Emergency Nurses Association, and so on), the HRSA/MCHB EMSC program, the leadership of EMS and public safety agencies, and relevant state and federal government authorities. This summit should examine the issues in pediatric disaster response and recovery exposed by Hurricane Katrina, the adverse outcomes caused by these deficiencies, and set an agenda for improving pediatric readiness.

2. An Office for Pediatric Disaster Preparedness should be created with the full participation and support of the leadership of pediatric, emergency medicine, and other healthcare provider professional organizations caring for children, the EMSC stakeholder community, federal policymakers, and other disaster relief organizations.
3. Existing resources on disaster preparedness should be reviewed and revised as necessary in the light of the most recent disasters and the deficiencies observed in disaster response and recovery efforts.
4. The Office of Disaster Preparedness should work with federal policy makers to involve state pediatric chapters, local healthcare professional societies, and pediatric primary and specialty care providers proactively in disaster preparedness.
5. Healthcare profession organizations and institutions caring for children should consider adding pediatric disaster preparedness curricula to their continuing education requirements.
6. Healthcare profession organizations caring for children should initiate discussions with their residency review committees, specialty boards and/or licensing bodies to include pediatric disaster preparedness in training program curricula to assure that trainees are prepared for their public health and advocacy role in pediatric disaster preparedness for their patients and families.
7. Healthcare profession organizations caring for children must work more directly and effectively with federal (eg, Department of Health and Human Services, HRSA, CDC) and state policy makers in the area of pediatric disaster readiness. Future HRSA and CDC disaster preparedness guidelines should have direct input from pediatric care experts as they are being written, not after the fact.

8. Federal and state policy makers should dedicate research funding for the development of redundant strategies for implementation in states to assure timely reunification of infants, toddlers, and children and with their correct parents and caregivers.

Source: Dolan, M. A., and Krug, S. E. 2006. Pediatric disaster preparedness in the wake of Katrina: Lessons to be learned. *Clinical Pediatric Emergency Medicine,* 7:59–66. © 2006 Elsevier. With permission. http://www.aap.org/disasters/pdf/PDP-in-the-Wake-of-Katrina.pdf.

Conclusion

A lot can be done to prepare children, caregivers, and the institutions and facilities that support them for a disaster. Involving all stakeholders in adapting your existing emergency operations plan to address the unique needs of children is critical. School officials and child care providers must develop emergency plans in advance of future disasters, and shelter operators must be aware of the needs of children and provide the appropriate resources to meet these needs. Programs in schools, summer camps, and child care facilities can help build confidence and resiliency in children as they prepare for the next disaster.

References

Agency for Healthcare Research and Quality. 2009. *School-based emergency preparedness: A national analysis and recommended protocol.* Pub. 09-0013. Rockville, MD: AHRQ. http://www.ahrq.gov/prep/schoolprep/schoolprep.pdf.

Dolan, M. A., and Krug, S. E. 2006. Pediatric disaster preparedness in the wake of Katrina: Lessons to be learned. *Clinical Pediatric Emergency Medicine,* 7: 59–66. http://www.aap.org/disasters/pdf/PDP-in-the-Wake-of-Katrina.pdf.

National Association of Child Care Resource and Referral Agencies (NACCRRA). 2006. *Is child care ready? A disaster planning guide for child care resource and referral agencies.* http://www.naccrra.org/disaster/.

National Commission on Children and Disasters. 2009. Interim report. October 14. http://www.childrenanddisasters.acf.hhs.gov/20091014_508IR_partII.pdf.

Save the Children. 2007. *The unique needs of children in emergencies: A guide for the inclusion of children in emergency operations plans.* September. http://www.savethechildren.org/publications/emergencies/Children-in-Emergencies-Planning-Guide.pdf.

Chapter 5

Response

Introduction

Recent disasters, starting with Hurricane Katrina, have brought the unique needs of children in disasters to the attention of emergency planners, medical officials, social service agencies, and voluntary groups involved in disaster response and recovery. The lessons learned and the knowledge gained from these recent events should inform the work to be done by emergency managers to better prepare for and respond to the needs of children in future disasters.

Learning Objectives

At the conclusion of this chapter, the participants will be able to:

- Evaluate case study information from real disasters
- Apply information to current response plans and operations

Developing a Functional Annex for Children to the Community Emergency Operations Plan

Emergency managers should consider adding a functional annex to their community's existing emergency operations plan (EOP). A functional annex is a plan that is organized around the performance of a broad task, issue, or concern. Each EOP functional annex focuses on one of the critical emergency functions that the jurisdiction will perform in response to, and often to recover from, an emergency. In certain instances, as is the case with this particular annex focusing on the needs of children, annexes will also address the preparedness and mitigation aspects of emergency management.

The number and type of functional annexes included in the EOP may vary from one jurisdiction to another, depending on needs, capabilities, and organization. Common functional annex topics include direction and control, communications, warning, emergency public information, mass care, evacuation, and others. Annex topics that are increasing in prevalence include pets in disasters, volunteer management, and vulnerable populations. Since functional annexes are oriented toward operations, their primary audience consists of those responsible for the tasks described. Annexes do not repeat general information contained in the community's basic EOP.

Some jurisdictions may choose to insert the children-specific information into the EOP as an emergency support function (ESF) rather than as an annex. An ESF is a functional area of response, recovery, mitigation, or preparedness activity established to facilitate the delivery of assistance required either before or after a disaster occurs, for the purpose of saving lives, protecting property and public health, and maintaining public safety. They are much like annexes, but are included in the base EOP, and their enactment is anticipated in a large percentage of, if not all, emergency situations. A community may choose not to include this information as a separate ESF only because of the additional effort involved with incorporating it into the base plan. Because the ESF and the functional annex operate in almost the same manner when enacted, the inclusion method selected should reflect the preferences of the emergency management agency itself.

In developing a children's annex to the community EOP, an emergency planner should consider the following areas of need for response and recovery operations.

Area 1: Child Safety and Security

Response and Recovery

- Enact badging, credentialing, and background check systems for anyone who will be working primarily with children
- Track all affected children, including those who are evacuated, sheltered at off-site locations, hospitalized, and sheltered in place, using tracking bracelets wherever and as soon as possible
- Warn all facilities in the care of children, as required
- Provide security to children in shelters
- Designate pediatric safe areas in shelters, hospitals, and other places where children are being sheltered or housed
- Conduct ongoing child safety and security inspections in shelters housing children
- Designate and reserve areas in shelters for families with children and pregnant mothers
- Ensure that sheltered children cannot gain access to dangerous medications (for other sheltered victims), and that areas where children are placed are generally childproof (away from stairs, dangerous equipment and materials, overhangs, kitchens, etc.)
- Make every effort to keep families together within the emergency medical system, within shelters, and during evacuations

Area 2: Nutrition

Response and Recovery

- Monitor the nutrition of children in emergency shelters
- Identify, track, and accommodate children and pregnant mothers with special dietary needs
- Assist unaccompanied children in all aspects of nutrition
- Distribute feeding and other nutritional supplies between shelters as needed

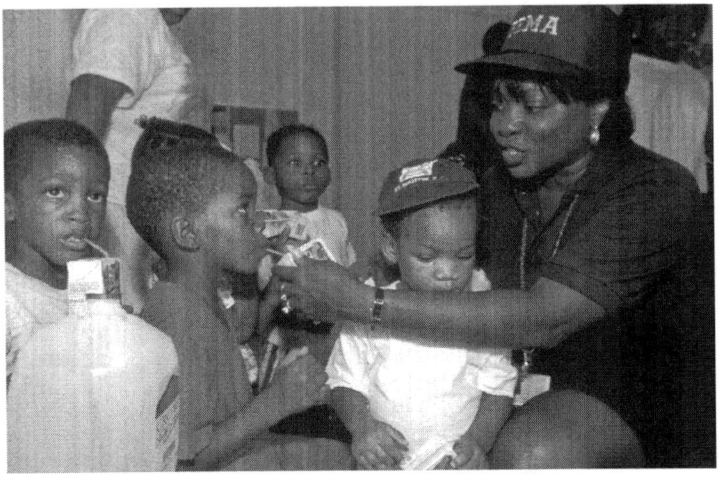

FIGURE 5.1 St. Thomas, Virgin Islands, September 16, 1995. FEMA worker cared for children after a hurricane in the Virgin Islands. (FEMA News Photo)

- Ensure adequate child nutritional supplies are available and ongoing, by means of multiple distributors (to reduce the risk of service interruptions)
- Provide equipment and materials necessary to prepare baby food and formula, and a designated area to do so (Figure 5.1)

Area 3: Clothing and Shelter

Response and Recovery

- Designate areas within shelters for families with children that allow for more privacy and that provide a sense of home to children, keeping in mind that crying and distressed babies and children can have a negative effect even on evacuees with no children of their own
- Ensure children, who require more sleep, have dark, quiet, secure places to rest during daytime (napping) hours as well as nighttime
- Allow private areas for nursing mothers
- Establish routines within the shelter for children
- Locate climate-appropriate clothing for small children and babies, as well as laundry facilities for soiled clothing and bedding

- Establish healthy environment areas in shelters where children are located, free from smoke, alcohol, drugs, weapons, and inappropriate or stress-inducing language and discussions (including discussions about response and recovery)
- Make arrangements for children with special health care needs, including providing for child patients on long-term medications
- Identify, track, and address the needs of sheltered special needs children
- Track all children who are sheltered in place, and assist the facility in providing for the needs of those children
- Provide children with a sense of normalcy as soon as possible after the critical phase of the emergency has ended

Area 4: Hygiene

Response and Recovery

- Monitor child health and hygiene in emergency shelters, and provide information and assistance to parents regarding good child hygiene practices
- Set up and maintain baby-changing facilities, stocked with supplies (diapers, wipes, individual packets of skin cream), and provide facilities for diaper disposal
- Provide families with materials and supplies necessary for cleaning babies and children (including infant baths and bathing stations, child-size toothbrushes, child-safe soaps and shampoos, and larger shower stalls)
- Assign individual sleeping mats and bed linens for each child, ensuring that mix-ups do not occur, and ensure that sleeping linens, towels, and other children's supplies are regularly cleaned

Area 5: Evacuation and Transportation

Response and Recovery

- Provide secure transportation within the shelter and the medical care and resources systems (including appropriate official supervision of and accountability for unattended children)

FIGURE 5.2 **New Orleans, Louisiana, September 4, 2005. Evacuees from New Orleans were taken by helicopter to the international airport, given food and water, and sent out on planes to shelters around the country. New Orleans was being evacuated as a result of flooding from Hurricane Katrina. (Liz Roll/FEMA)**

- Provide transportation for children to pediatric health and medical facilities
- Ensure that families remain together during evacuation
- Track all evacuated children, and provide a central repository of this information for concerned parents and family members
- Provide for the needs of special needs children during evacuations
- Provide psychological counseling and care to children during evacuation (Figure 5.2)

Area 6: Health and Hospital Care

Response and Recovery

- Assess emergency management damages and needs relevant to children's health
- Enact ongoing child health screening in shelters to ensure that problems are recognized as soon as possible

- Make medical information resources available to parents (computers, posters, phone referral lines, etc.) to aid in appropriate use of medical resources
- Provide standardized health care data collection for children at shelters and places where children may be congregated
- Address the pediatric medical needs of special needs children (dialysis, preexisting physical therapy, disability related)
- Provide on-site pediatric emergency and primary health care at emergency shelters
- Identify, track, and prevent the spread of illnesses more typical in children in shelters and among the affected population in general
- Ensure that children requiring medication for ongoing health problems (e.g., asthma) are able to replace lost subscriptions and refill them when necessary
- Isolate sick children within shelters to contain the spread of childhood illnesses
- Establish temporary pediatric clinics for the special needs of children (including well visits)
- Direct the care of pediatric patients (overflow) in general hospitals not accustomed to child patient issues

Area 7: Emergency Medical Care and Emergency Response

Response and Recovery

- Monitor the emergency response needs of children
- Provide family-centered emergency care to families with children
- Incorporate use of a pediatric-specific triage system by all first responders and hospital personnel (e.g., JumpSTART Pediatric Multiple Casualty Incident Triage)
- Conduct a child-focused damage and needs assessment
- Ensure that all emergency vehicles and teams are supplied and resupplied with child-appropriate equipment and materials

Area 8: Supervision, Day Care, and Educational Facilities

Response and Recovery

- Establish day care facilities at all community shelters
- Establish safe play areas in all shelters to foster natural childhood development
- Provide an outlet for community-based organizations to provide toys and bedside sitter support at shelters
- Establish routines for children in shelters to foster a safe, calm, nurturing, and normalizing environment
- Allow opportunities for children to play with and socialize with other children
- Treat or attend to the special needs of children in shelters
- Establish continuity of nurturing care for children (care by the same person for children between 0 and 18 months is considered very important)
- Provide communication assistance for children who require it (e.g., children who do not speak English, children with speech or sensory disabilities)
- Assist in the social integration of children, especially those who are separated from their families and friends or who are otherwise displaced
- Minimize parent-child separation
- Maintain strong communication with parents about the well-being of children both while in supervised care and while in the care of the parents, to track (and inform the parents/guardians of) any potential problems
- Document all care
- Staff vacated day care positions from both within and outside the community

Area 9: Education

Response and Recovery

- Establish safe spaces within the shelter for children to release creative energy
- Establish areas within shelters for educational development (including instruction, homework, and studies)

- Provide temporary replacements for educators who have been affected by the disaster
- Assist educators in returning to work, and replace any vacated teaching staff

Area 10: Psychological Care

Response and Recovery

- Mobilize the family information and support center
- Mobilize the assistance of pediatric psychiatric specialists to assist in the recognition and treatment of pediatric psychiatric trauma and illness
- Perform interventions to minimize pediatric psychological trauma, especially in shelter and school settings
- Incorporate childhood psychosocial recovery into ongoing in-school recovery programs and curricula
- Ensure that children with preexisting mental health conditions are not excluded from eligibility for mental health care after a disaster or crisis
- Mobilize outreach support teams to go into the community (e.g., schools, day care centers, churches) to provide stress debriefing, triage, and long-term monitoring
- Conduct community memorial and grieving services geared toward children
- Identify parents who are having difficulty in coping with the event, and refer them to appropriate support networks (children's recovery depends a great deal upon the status of their parents)
- Conduct early interventions with all children in the affected area, especially school-based interventions where children are most comfortable

Area 11: Emergency Management Education for Children, Parents, and Caregivers

Response and Recovery

- Provide postdisaster response and recovery information to parents about the disaster needs of children, and the facilities that are currently offering to meet those needs

- Advise parents and all other caregivers, as well as the media and public officials, about ways to help children cope during times of stress (anniversaries of the event, holidays, life changes, etc.) after a disaster
- Apply a family-centered approach after a disaster that includes, but is not limited to, assessment, early intervention, and treatment with primary caregivers and other family members

Area 12: Other Needs

Response and Recovery

- Ensure that transient children (children of tourists, nonresidents in community facilities, including camps and boarding schools) are identified, tracked, and cared for
- Communication (translation services)
- Family and parental support
- Pregnant and lactating mothers
- Transient children
- Illegal children or children of illegal alien parents

Notification

Emergency managers should develop and maintain a list of schools and child care providers in their community that should be notified of potential or pending disaster events.

The Agency for Healthcare Research and Quality, in its 2009 study entitled *School-Based Emergency Preparedness: A National Analysis and Recommended Protocol*, provided guidance to school officials for how to use notification information that would lead to an evacuation/relocation, shelter-in-place, or lockdown scenario. The recommended actions for an evacuation/relocation are presented in Sidebar 5.1.

SIDEBAR 5.1 NOTIFICATION ACTIONS

Evacuation/relocation recommendations.

The principal will:

- Make an announcement over the PA system while crisis team members deliver instructions to key staff.

The crisis team will:

- Initiate the response,
- Inspect the building and direct all students to exits and assembly areas,
- Carry walkie-talkies and cell phones,
- Communicate with town emergency response teams, and
- Communicate regularly with staff regarding the status of the emergency.

The secretarial staff will:

- Bring the attendance roster for students and staff to the alternate site, and take the crisis kit.

Teachers and other support staff will:

- Assist children with mobility difficulties,
- Take their classroom crisis kit,
- Lead students through evacuation using designated routes,
- Check lavatories and other areas of the building where students may be unsupervised in order to assure evacuation is complete,
- Take attendance and report any missing students to a crisis team member,
- Lead their students to the off-site location in the event of relocation following the designated route, and
- Stay with their students until further instructions are given.

The school nurse will:

- Bring the emergency medical kit and the first aid kit,
- Bring student emergency cards and medical information, and
- Monitor students with special medical needs and notify the administration of any urgent medical needs.

Custodians will:

- Maintain communication with the administration who may assign specific tasks,
- Inspect the building following an evacuation, and
- Assume responsibility for building safety and carry a school floor plan, which includes the location of utility shut-off valves.

The role of the PTO. Parent-teacher organizations have a poorly defined role in the construction of a school-based plan. On the one hand, the PTO can have a very valuable role in disseminating information and providing input on all aspects of the plan's creation and implementation. However, many families prefer not to have details of disaster preparedness plans, finding them anxiety provoking. A useful approach would be for the principal to present an overview of plans at a PTO meeting, giving the group the option of being involved in all aspects of planning (e.g., discussions about stockpiling of potassium iodide or details of lockdown or sheltering-in plans). For those PTOs that request full participation, reports and feedback can be incorporated into the plan.

Source: Agency for Healthcare Research and Quality. 2009. *School-based emergency preparedness: A national analysis and recommended protocol*. Pub. 09-0013. Rockville, MD: AHRQ. http://www.ahrq.gov/prep/schoolprep/schoolprep.pdf.

Evacuation

A sudden onset disaster event such as an earthquake may require that schools and child care facilities in a community evacuate and relocate students and children to a new location. Emergency managers must work with local school officials and child care providers to ensure plans are in place as to how such an evacuation would proceed, how parents will be notified about the evacuation, and to where the children will be evacuated.

Lessons Learned: Inadequate Strategies for the Evacuation of Children with Their Parents, Families, or Caretakers

During and after Hurricane Katrina, scores of children were found wandering alone in search of lost adults. Some children later described swimming past bloated human and animal corpses and lacerating their legs on unseen objects in the water below in efforts to find their parents. Some parents reported that during the evacuation, they placed their children on earlier buses in the mistaken belief that when the adults got seats on a later bus, the whole family would end up in the same place. In some cases, the children who were found were too young to give their names or too traumatized to speak, even if they were of age to talk. In other cases, investigators had no photographs of the children to circulate because the pictures were left behind in the floods. In the Houston Astrodome, a center was set up where volunteers worked to reunite children with their parents. Digital photographs were taken of each child. The photos and any information obtained were placed in the database of the National Center for Missing and Exploited Children. The volunteers also had a very long list of children who had been reported missing by a parent [Figure 5.3].

Source: Dolan, M. A., and Krug, S. E. 2006. Pediatric disaster preparedness in the wake of Katrina: Lessons to be learned. *Clinical Pediatric Emergency Medicine*, 7:59–66. © 2006 Elsevier. With permission. http://www.aap.org/disasters/pdf/PDP-in-the-Wake-of-Katrina.pdf.

FIGURE 5.3 **New Orleans, Louisiana, September 5, 2005. New Orleans was being evacuated and these evacuees were at the convention center. From the convention center they were flown by helicopter to the airport, where they were given food, water, and any medical attention they needed. They were then flown out of the area to one of the many shelters across the United States. (Liz Roll/FEMA)**

The National Association of Child Care Resource and Referral Agencies (NACCRRA) has developed a Sample Outline for a child care program evacuation plan and an evacuation kit for child care programs (see Sidebars 5.2 and 5.3).

SIDEBAR 5.2 SAMPLE OUTLINE FOR A CHILDCARE PROGRAM EVACUATION PLAN

I. Who Can Direct an Evacuation
- Local Official
- State Official
- Program Representative

II. How the Parents Will Be Notified
III. What the Children Will Be Told
IV. What Signal Will Be Given to Notify Everyone in the Facility?
- If Power Available
- If No Power Available
- Signal for Different Types of Disasters

V. How All Staff, Children, Volunteers and Others in Facility Will Be Accounted For
VI. How Children and Staff Will Be Transported
- Infants
- Toddlers
- Older Children
- Children or Staff with Special Needs

VII. Medications, Supplies, and Records Taken During Evacuation
VIII. Coordinating Actions with Community Public Safety and/or Emergency Management Officials
IX. Evacuation Site
- Near
- Within Area
- Outside Area

X. Person/s Responsible for Each Action
XI. Transportation Plan
- Program Vehicles
- Staff Vehicles

- Additional Vehicles from Volunteers and Neighbors
- Gas in Vehicles
- Keeping Vehicles in Workable Condition
- First-aid Kits in Vehicles

XII. Additional Information

- Location of Electricity Shut-off
- How to Shut Off Electricity
- Location of Gas Shut-off
- How to Shut Off Gas
- Location of Water Shut-off
- How to Shut Off Water
- Location of Air Vent Shut-off (if applicable)
- How to Shut Off Air Circulation System
- Location of Emergency Evacuation Kit
- Location of Additional Emergency Supplies
- Location of Cell Phone

Source: National Association of Child Care Resource and Referral Agencies (NACCRRA). 2006. *Is childcare ready? A disaster planning guide for childcare resource and referral agencies*. http://www.naccrra.org/disaster/.

SIDEBAR 5.3 EVACUATION KITS FOR CHILDCARE PROGRAMS

(One for each group or room, if possible. Avoid making so cumbersome they are difficult to handle or can cause back injury.)

- First-aid kits
- Critical medications for staff and children
- Emergency contact information children:
  - Parents' work phone
  - Parents' cell phone
  - Parents' home phone
  - Parents' home and work e-mail addresses
  - Two emergency contacts in area (preferably individuals who don't live or work with parents)
  - Two emergency contacts out of area
  - Phone number and e-mail of parents' supervisors
  - Critical medical information
  - Permission to transport and seek medical treatment

- Emergency contact information on staff
  - Spouse or family member's work phone
  - Staff member's cell phone
  - Spouse or family member's cell phone
  - Home phone
  - Staff member's home e-mail address
  - Spouse or family members' work e-mail address
  - Two emergency contacts in area
  - Two emergency contacts out of area
  - Critical medical information
- Dry or canned infant formula
- Gallons of water
- Disposable cups
- Baby food and plastic spoons
- Food bars in individual wrappers
- Games, books, and other materials to keep children occupied

Source: National Association of Child Care Resource and Referral Agencies (NACCRRA). 2006. *Is childcare ready? A disaster planning guide for childcare resource and referral agencies.* http://www.naccrra.org/disaster/.

Shelters

Historically, the American Red Cross has been responsible for standing up and managing emergency shelters in the immediate aftermath of a disaster event. The Red Cross has relied on other voluntary agencies such as the Church of the Brethren and the Southern Baptists Convention to provide child care services to families living in shelters. Post Hurricane Katrina, the Red Cross and Save the Children signed a memorandum of understanding (MOU) for Save the Children to establish safe spaces in Red Cross shelters.

Lessons Learned: Inadequate Preparations for Culturally and Developmentally Appropriate Critical Incident Mental Health Interventions for Children Affected by the Disaster

Thousands of children were among the 25,000 people crowded into the New Orleans Superdome and the New Orleans Convention Center for protection from Katrina and the subsequent flooding.

Refugees within these centers reported excessive heat, crowding, acts of violence, poor sanitation, inadequate fluids and food, and the overt presence of medically ill and dead persons. For many reasons, including interagency delays and confusion, relief personnel were unable to access these refugees with basic essentials, including mental health services. Evacuation of the refugees from these centers did not begin for 2 days after the hurricane was over. Mental health services, including play therapy and art therapy for the children, did not begin until well after the evacuations and certainly did not include all of the affected children or all shelters. In one instance, women residing in the neighborhood near one of these shelters were the ones to finally provide crayons and paper for the evacuated children so that these children could finally begin to express the experiences they had been through.

INADEQUATE RESOURCES FOR NON-ENGLISH-SPEAKING CHILDREN

In the aftermath of the hurricane, many families were disrupted as they moved from shelter to shelter and city to city. Six weeks after the hurricane, The Center for Missing and Exploited Children reported that there were still more than 2500 children who were separated from their families. Many of these children were from in flux family situations and/or from families with questionable immigration status, intimidated by public safety agencies, yet in great need of assistance. The Center reported that many of the displaced were adolescents younger than 21 and Spanish-speaking. Many shelters did not have sufficient translation support for Spanish-speaking victims.

Source: Dolan, M. A., and Krug, S. E. 2006. Pediatric disaster preparedness in the wake of Katrina: Lessons to be learned. *Clinical Pediatric Emergency Medicine*, 7:59–66. © 2006 Elsevier. With permission. http://www.aap.org/disasters/pdf/PDP-in-the-Wake-of-Katrina.pdf.

Voluntary Organizations Involved with Children in Disasters

There are several voluntary agencies that have been involved with children in disasters for many years, including Feed the Children, Brethren Children's Disaster Services, Southern Baptist Disaster Relief, and Save the Children (see Sidebar 5.4).

SIDEBAR 5.4 LIST OF VOLUNTARY AGENCIES

The following is a list of organizations that may provide for the needs of children in disasters. A complete listing of National Voluntary Organizations Active in Disasters is available from http://www.nvoad.org/.

This list is **not** intended to be all-inclusive. You should also check for local organizations that may exist in your area.

- American Red Cross

  http://www.redcross.org
- Brethren Children's Disaster Services

  http://www.brethren.org/site/PageServer?pagename=serve_childrens_disaster_services
- Church World Service Emergency Response Program

  http://www.disasterrecoveryhelp.org
- KaBOOM!

  http://kaboom.org/
- Habitat for Humanity

  http://www.habitat.org
- Mercy Corps

  http://www.mercycorps.org
- National Center for Missing and Exploited Children

  http://www.missingkids.com
- North American Mission Board: Southern Baptist Disaster Relief (see Sidebar 5.6)

  http://www.namb.net/site/c.9qKILUOzEpH/b.224451/k.A400/Disaster_Relief.htm
- The Salvation Army

  http://www.salvationarmyusa.org
- Save the Children

  www.savethechildren.org

Source: NVOAD. http://www.nvoad.org/.

Feed the Children's disaster website notes: "With our own fleet of semi-tractor trailers, Feed The Children is frequently one of the first relief agencies to reach disaster-affected communities. In response to the devastation caused by Hurricane Ike in September 2008, Feed The Children dispatched dozens of truckloads of relief supplies to the victims in Texas. Vital supplies included blankets, bottled water and snack foods" (Feed the Children, http://www.feedthechildren.org/site/PageServer?pagename=org_disaster_relief).

The Church of the Brethren website (http://www.brethren.org/site/PageServer?pagename=serve_childrens_disaster_services) notes (see Sidebar 5.5):

> Since 1980 Children's Disaster Services (CDS) has been meeting the needs of children by setting up childcare centers in shelters and disaster assistance centers across the nation. Specially trained to respond to traumatized children, volunteers provide a calm, safe and reassuring presence in the midst of the chaos created by tornados, floods, hurricanes, wildfires, or any natural or human caused disaster.
>
> Volunteers from across the country participate in specialized experiential training, undergo a rigorous screening process, learn to work with children after a disaster, are capable of mobilizing rapidly and responding both locally and nationally. Volunteers arrive to a disaster location with a "Kit of Comfort" containing carefully selected toys that promote imaginative play. Volunteers give children individualized attention and encourage them to express themselves, thereby starting the healing process. Although many volunteers are motivated by faith, CDS' training is open to anyone over 18 years old.
>
> CDS provides respite, education and individualized consultation for parents about their child's unique emotional needs after a disaster. Through consultation or workshops specifically tailored to each situation, CDS also works with parents, community agencies, schools or others to help them understand and meet the special needs of children during or after a disaster.

SIDEBAR 5.5 CHILDREN'S DISASTER SERVICES—A CHURCH OF THE BRETHREN DISASTER MINISTRY

Since 1980 Children's Disaster Services (CDS) has been meeting the needs of children by setting up child care centers in shelters and disaster assistance centers across the nation. Specially trained to respond to traumatized children, volunteers provide a calm, safe and reassuring presence in the midst of the chaos created by tornados, floods, hurricanes, wildfires — any natural or human caused disaster.

Volunteers from across the country participate in specialized experiential training, undergo a rigorous screening process, learn to work with children after a disaster, and are capable of mobilizing rapidly to respond both locally and nationally. Volunteers arrive after a disaster with a "Kit of Comfort" containing carefully selected toys that promote imaginative play. Volunteers give children individualized attention and encourage them to express themselves, thereby starting the healing process. Although many volunteers are motivated by faith, CDS workshops are open to anyone over 18 years old.

CDS also provides respite, education and individualized consultation for parents about their child's unique emotional needs after a disaster. Through consultation or workshops specifically tailored to each situation, CDS also works with groups of parents, community agencies, schools or others to help them understand and meet the special needs of children during or after a disaster.

Critical Response Childcare Team

The Critical Response Childcare (CRC) team is a group of experienced Children's Disaster Services volunteers who have received additional training that prepares them to work with children after an aviation incident or other mass casualty event. The presence of a compassionate caregiver, along with carefully selected play activities, has a significant impact on the recovery of a child who has experienced the trauma of such a loss.

A six-member team is on call each month, ready to travel within four hours of deployment by the American Red Cross. When the volunteers arrive, they work in a Family Assistance Center, where those impacted by the incident participate in briefings and receive support from the American Red Cross. This partnership between the American Red Cross and Children's Disaster Services ensures that children's needs are being met in an appropriate and compassionate manner.

Since 1997 the CRC team has responded to the terrorist attacks of September 11, 2001, and 8 aviation incidents.

CDS Volunteer Workshop

Participants in the 27-hour, Volunteer Workshop learn to provide comfort and encouragement to children by offering the healing young children need in traumatic situations. They learn to create a safe, friendly environment that gives children the chance to engage in therapeutic play activities designed to relieve stress and calm fears.

This workshop includes a simulated shelter experience (an overnight stay) and will be provided to any group of 15 or more adults interested in working with children after a disaster. Participants completing the course will have the opportunity to become certified Children's Disaster Services volunteers.

Because children can experience personal disasters (when a friend moves away, a pet dies, etc.) people who come in contact with a distressed child can benefit from this workshop. Many of the concepts taught in the Volunteer Workshop are appropriate to use at those times as well as after disasters.

Supporting Families and Communities

Supporting Families

Children's Disaster Services provides respite, education and individualized consultation for parents about their child's unique emotional needs after a disaster.

When picking up their children, parents often start to talk with CDS volunteers. Parents share concerns and worries with the volunteers who have cared for their children for the past few hours. The volunteers, who have been trained in what is typical behavior for children after a disaster, can reassure parents about the child's adjustment, give parents printed resources about helping a traumatized child, or refer parents to appropriate community resources.

Supporting Communities

Children's Disaster Services will provide workshops and/or consultation to communities (agencies, schools, etc.) about their unique needs relative to disaster, trauma and children.

CDS will provide consultation to schools, hospitals and other community agencies with concerns about childcare after a disaster. In addition to consultative phone calls and meetings, workshops or webinars can be presented to committees, groups of volunteers and others who want to know more about children and disasters.

CDS also presents at conferences, allowing even more people to learn about the needs of children after a disaster and the guiding principles behind our work.

Source: Church of the Brethren. http://www.brethren.org/site/PageServer?pagename=serve_childrens_disaster_services.

SIDEBAR 5.6 SOUTHERN BAPTIST DISASTER RELIEF

Fires, Tornadoes, Floods and Earthquakes

SBDR volunteers are ministering to neighbors whose lives have been turned upside down across the plains, in the southeast, and in L'Aquila, Italy as we celebrate the resurrection of our Lord Jesus this Easter Season.

2008 Disaster Relief Activity

	Volunteer Days	118,951
	Meals Prepared	7,914,391
	Chainsaw Jobs	9,289
	Gospel Presentations	3,487
	Professions of Faith	448

Complete 2008 Activity Report

Affiliation:	Southern Baptist Disaster Relief is a partnership ministry of the state Baptist conventions and the North American Mission Board, Southern Baptist Convention.
Resources:	Approximately 2,000 mobile units (feeding, chainsaw, mud-out, command, communication, childcare, shower, laundry, water purification, repair/rebuild, generators, and others).
	More than 88,000 trained volunteers, including trained disaster relief chaplains
Partnerships:	American Red Cross
	The Salvation Army

	Federal Emergency Management Agency (FEMA), Department of Homeland Security
	Convoy of Hope
	National Voluntary Organizations Active in Disasters (NVOAD)
	Mercy Medical Airlift
	Baptist Global Response
Organization:	Disaster relief units are owned and staffed by Southern Baptist churches, regional Baptist associations, and state Baptist conventions. Volunteer teams respond to disasters within their own state and work cooperatively with other states in larger emergencies. Teams also work overseas when Baptist Global Response requests help.
History:	The first Southern Baptist Disaster Relief response took place in 1967 when a small group of Texas volunteers helped victims of Hurricane Beulah by serving hot food cooked on small "buddy burners."
	Forty years later, in 2008, Southern Baptist volunteers prepared almost 8 million meals. All assistance is provided to individuals and communities free of charge.

2008 Activity Report

Volunteer Days	118,951
Meals Prepared	7,914,391
Mudout Jobs	2,647
Chainsaw Jobs	9,289
Repair Jobs	243
Roofing Jobs	295
Children Cared For	1176
Showers	90,497
Laundry Loads	33,775
Water (Gallons)	247,113

Source: Southern Baptist Disaster Relief. http://www.namb.net/site/c.9qKILUOzEpH/b.224451/k.A400/Disaster_Relief.htm.

CASE STUDY: Save the Children Safe Spaces

PARTNERING WITH THE AMERICAN RED CROSS AND NEW YORK CITY'S EMERGENCY MANAGEMENT AGENCY

Save the Children has a national partnership with the American Red Cross to create *Safe Spaces* in Red Cross evacuation shelters after disasters. We worked together to create *Safe Spaces* after wildfires forced thousands to evacuate their homes in Southern California in fall 2007. We also partnered in response to Hurricanes Gustav and Ike in 2008, floods in the Midwest, and smaller-scale emergencies in 2007. In addition, the agency works with federal, state and local emergency responders and advocates to improve U.S. emergency management systems.

In New York City, for example, Save the Children and the city's Office of Emergency Management (OEM) signed an agreement to incorporate Save the Children's *Safe Spaces* program into New York City's emergency sheltering plan. Under the initiative, Save the Children will provide 1,075 Safe Space Kits for use in emergency shelters in New York City. As part of the plan, more than 1,000 volunteers will be trained to lead activities for children in shelters. The kits will be stored in OEM's shelter stockpile, along with other supplies that can be quickly deployed to as many as 509 pre-identified shelter locations.

Source: Save the Children. http://www.savethechildren.org/programs/us-literacy-and-nutrition/safe-spaces-us.html. Safe Space slide show. http://www.savethechildren.org/programs/us-literacy-and-nutrition/safe-spaces.html. Safe Space video. http://multimedia.savethechildren.org/video/california-wildfires/video-box-california-wildfires.html.

CASE STUDY: Save the Children Responds to Wildfires in Southern California

As wildfires forced thousands from their homes in Southern California this October, Save the Children helped over 12,000 affected children and caregivers recover.

On October 23, 2007, just days after the fires began spreading across southern California, Save the Children dispatched an emergency response team to hardest-hit San Diego County. One of the first response teams from a national nonprofit to arrive in the area, Save the Children's emergency responders first focused on establishing Safe Spaces, safe play areas in evacuation shelters and local assistance centers.

Safe Spaces provide children with a designated area where they can play, socialize and get back to the business of being children through structured activities such as art, songs, games, drama and sports. Structured activities can be comforting to children, providing them with a sense of normalcy, strengthening their ability to bounce back and allow them to begin to process their experiences. Within a week, Save the Children had established 13 Safe Spaces serving over 1,500 children. The agency worked in partnership with the American Red Cross and Children's Disaster Services, Save the Children's national partners in an effort to provide Safe Spaces to children affected by emergencies.

As the fires were contained, Save the Children focused on the hardest-hit areas of San Diego County. The agency worked with local organizations to reach out to families and communities, while providing a program to help children build coping skills and prepare for future emergencies. Save the Children supported community organizations to provide essential items, including clothing, textbooks, car seats and cribs, and helped several schools, childcare centers and other child-focused organizations replace damaged materials or expand their services. Save the Children also helped recover four playgrounds.

Save the Children also provided R&R: Resilient and Ready, a program to help children build coping skills and feel a sense of safety and control while living in a fire-prone area. At the end of each R&R workshop, every child who participated received a backpack filled with evacuation supplies for future use. R&R was accompanied by a care-for-the-caregiver program, Journey of Hope, which Save the Children has used successfully in Hurricane Katrina-affected Louisiana and Mississippi.

Source: Save the Children. http://www.savethechildren.org/programs/us-literacy-and-nutrition/southern-california-wildfires.html.

Separation from Family

Thousands of children were separated from their families during the frantic evacuation caused by Hurricane Katrina (Sidebar 5.7). The federal government worked with the National Center for Missing and Exploited Children (NCMEC) to reunite these children with their families. The Children's Bureau of the American Bar Association (Sidebar 5.8) and the American Academy of Pediatrics have developed guidelines for how to reduce the chances that children will be separated from their families during a disaster event (Sidebar 5.9).

Lessons Learned: Inadequate Strategies for the Reunification of Children with Their Parents/Caretakers, Especially Infants and Preverbal Toddlers

This is a long-standing problem in disasters where children are involved. School-aged children can recognize their parents, making reliable reunification possible. This is not the case for infants and preverbal toddlers. After the 2004 tsunami, a highly publicized example of this occurred when an infant boy in Sri Lanka was claimed by 9 sets of desperate parents. His true identity and true parentage was eventually confirmed by DNA testing, and he was eventually reunited with his parents. In the high technology world of egg donors and artificial insemination for conception, or had that child been adopted, this outcome would not have been possible. As of January 2006, several hundred children separated from their families after Katrina have not been reunited.

After Hurricane Katrina, the Center for Missing and Exploited Children posted photos and names of missing children on its website as they were received from evacuation shelters. This is a good first step but does not completely resolve the problem of accurate reunification of infants and nonverbal toddlers with their caretakers in the event a child is claimed by more than one adult or if the correct parent is not a genetic parent.

Parents and family are the single most important source of security for children. These children who have already endured the trauma of a natural disaster now have the additional trauma of being without the support of their families and caregivers for extended periods.

Source: Dolan, M. A., and Krug, S. E. 2006. Pediatric disaster preparedness in the wake of Katrina: Lessons to be learned. *Clinical Pediatric Emergency Medicine*, 7:59–66. © 2006 Elsevier. With permission. http://www.aap.org/disasters/pdf/PDP-in-the-Wake-of-Katrina.pdf

CASE STUDY: National Center for Missing and Exploited Children

NATIONAL CENTER FOR MISSING & EXPLOITED CHILDREN REUNITES LAST MISSING CHILD SEPARATED BY HURRICANES KATRINA AND RITA

After Six Months, All Missing/Displaced Children Are Back Home With Their Families

Alexandria, VA—March 17, 2006—After working tirelessly for more than six months to track down the 5,192 children reported missing/displaced to the National Center for Missing & Exploited Children as a result of Hurricanes Katrina and Rita, the non-profit organization is thrilled to report it has reunited the final child who was separated from her family after Hurricane Katrina. On Thursday, March 16, 2006, four-year-old Cortez Stewart was reunited with her mother and siblings in Houston, Texas, bringing a close to NCMEC's unprecedented efforts to reunite children and families during one of the worst natural disasters in U.S. history.

"Our team has worked non-stop with searching parents, concerned family members, law enforcement agencies across the country, social service agencies, and other non-profit organizations to ensure that the thousands of children reported to us, like Cortez, found their way back home."

During the storm, 4-year-old Cortez was with her godmother, Felicia Williams, and they became separated from Cortez's mother, Lisa Stewart, and her five other children. As families were evacuated out of New Orleans, Cortez and Felicia landed in Atlanta and Lisa and her family found themselves in Houston. For months both Lisa and Felicia were trying to locate each other but to no avail. That was until the National Center for Missing & Exploited Children got involved. NCMEC tracked down information about Felicia through her previous employer and then used computer databases at NCMEC to locate Felicia's family members in Georgia. With the active assistance of the U.S. Postal Inspection Service, NCMEC secured the proper address and phone number for Felicia in Atlanta and successfully resolved the case.

"This is a remarkable recovery and we are overjoyed that it had a happy ending," added Allen. "We are thrilled the National Center could play such a vital role in bringing families together in the aftermath of such a devastating disaster."

Finding Cortez was just one more example of how NCMEC used investigative techniques and a staff of well qualified and dedicated, retired law enforcement officers and case managers to reunite fractured families across more than 40 states. From crosschecking sophisticated NCMEC databases to knocking on doors and working with local law enforcement, children were being located and reunited on a daily basis.

Since September 5, 2005 when NCMEC established the Katrina Missing Persons Hotline (1-888-544-5475) at the request of the U.S. Department of Justice, more than 34,112 phone calls have been logged related to separated families and missing persons. The number of reports to NCMEC of children separated from their families due to Hurricanes Katrina and Rita resulted in a total of 5,192 children.

In the months following Katrina, the agency received reports of 4,710 children missing or displaced in Louisiana,

339 in Mississippi and 39 in Alabama. Hurricanes Katrina and Rita resulted in a total of 5,192 children. After Rita, another 28 children were reported missing or displaced in Louisiana; 76 were reported in Texas.

Of the cases reported to NCMEC, the most serious were those children arriving at shelters separated from parents/guardians with no adult supervision. There were a total of 45 unaccompanied children "found" and reported to NCMEC. As of October 7, 2005, all 45 cases were resolved.

In addition to reports of missing/displaced children, approximately 12,342 missing adults were reported to NCMEC's Katrina/Rita Missing Persons Hotline and referred to the National Center for Missing Adults (NCMA) for case handling. Fifteen of NCMEC's Project ALERT volunteers assigned to NCMA have helped resolved more than four thousand adult cases.

The Katrina Missing Persons Hotline was operational from 8:00am ET to 12:00 midnight, ET, seven days per week, and staffed by 40 former law enforcement officers from NCMEC's Team Adam and Project ALERT.

Twenty Team Adam consultants were deployed in Louisiana, Mississippi, Alabama and Texas, for weeks. They visited shelters to photograph "found" children and take missing child reports. They worked collaboratively with local law enforcement, social services, and child protective services to help reunite children with their families.

Media interest, partnering agencies and concerned people from around the world drove traffic and viewers to the www.missingkids.com website in record numbers. At its peak, the site was receiving 10–20 million hits per day with site visitors from 220 countries. The site normally receives an average 1 million hits per day.

The relief efforts of NCMEC were strengthened by its partnerships with organizations across the country. In addition to the U.S. Department of Justice's Office of Juvenile Justice and Delinquency Prevention, NCMEC worked with the network of state missing child clearinghouses, the Federal Bureau of Investigation, other state and local law enforcement agencies, children's protective services bureaus, Project Angel Flight, the American Red Cross, media outlets and many other organizations.

Long-time NCMEC corporate partners are to be commended for providing valuable equipment and services that proved invaluable to recovery efforts. Digital cameras and scanners were supplied by Canon U.S.A. At the request of the parent or guardian, Lifetouch National School Studios provided school photographs of children, as possible, when no photograph was available of a missing child. Sprint Nextel Corporation equipped Team Adam and Project ALERT representatives with cellular technology. American Airlines helped reunite separated family members by donating flights. The National Association of Broadcasters generously donated portable, battery-operated television/radios to Team Adam consultants deployed to Louisiana, Alabama, Texas, and Mississippi.

"We are grateful for the support of our private sector partners and for the dedicated volunteers that answered the Katrina/Rita Missing Persons Hotline," added Allen. "This was a coordinated effort made possible by the dedication of many."

About the National Center for Missing & Exploited Children

NCMEC is a 501(c)(3) nonprofit organization that works in cooperation with the U.S. Department of Justice's Office of Juvenile Justice and Delinquency Prevention. NCMEC's congressionally mandated CyberTipline, a reporting mechanism for child sexual exploitation, has handled more than 340,000 leads. Since its establishment in 1984, NCMEC has assisted law enforcement with more than 116,000 missing child cases, resulting in the recovery of more than 94,000 children. For more information about NCMEC, call its toll-free, 24-hour hotline at 1-800-THE-LOST or visit www.missingkids.com.

Source: Missing Kids. http://www.missingkids.com/missingkids/servlet/NewsEventServlet?LanguageCountry=en_US&PageId=2317.

SIDEBAR 5.7 PROTOCOL TO RAPIDLY IDENTIFY AND PROTECT DISPLACED CHILDREN

- Survey all children in your hospital, medical clinic, or shelter to identify children who are not accompanied by an adult; these children have a high probability of being listed as missing by family members. Find out where they are sleeping/being held and the name and age of person(s) who is/are supervising them, if available.
- Place a hospital-style identification bracelet (or, ideally, a picture identification card) on the child and a matching one on the supervising adult(s), if such an adult is available. Check frequently to make sure that the wristband matches that of the adult(s) seen with the child in the hospital or shelter. If there is no supervising adult, the child should be taken to the hospital's pre-determined Pediatric Safe Area where he/she can be appropriately cared for until a safe disposition or reunification can be made.
- The names of all children identified through the survey as not being with their legal guardians or who are unaccompanied should be considered at high-risk and immediately reported to the hospital's emergency operations center. Additional reporting should also be made to the National Center for Missing and Exploited Children (NCMEC) at 1-888-544-5475. The NCMEC can then crosscheck them with the names of children who have been reported missing.
- After the "high risk" children have been reported, a complete list of all children names in the hospital, clinic or shelter should be sent to the office of emergency management or other agency responsible for tracking (if activated and the information is requested.)

- Unaccompanied children and those who are not with their legal guardians should undergo a social and health screening taking into consideration an assessment of the relationship between the child and accompanying adult, ideally performed by a physician with pediatric experience.

Source: Save the Children. 2007. *The unique needs of children in emergencies: A guide for the inclusion of children in emergency operations plans*. September. http://www.savethechildren.org/publications/emergencies/Children-in-Emergencies-Planning-Guide.pdf. Adapted from CDC Health Advisory. 2005. *Instructions for identifying and protecting displaced children*. September 28.

Case Study: Searching for Foster Kids after Katrina

Nearly, 2,000 foster children were displaced by Katrina. Over a month after Hurricane Katrina made landfall, officials with the Louisiana Department of Community Services were still searching for 51 foster children who had not been accounted for after the storm. Officials asked the National Center for Missing and Exploited Children for assistance in locating the missing foster children. The evacuation of nearly 600 case workers and inability of officials to publish pictures of the missing children because of state confidentiality laws were cited by officials as hindering the efforts to locate the missing foster children. Marketa Garner Gautrau, assistant secretary for the Department of Community Services, noted in a report by Reuters filed on October 10, 2005 that “calls are trickling in daily from foster families who have moved to other areas and have found jobs and schools for their children” (Reuters, 2005).

SIDEBAR 5.8 THE NATIONAL CHILD WELFARE RESOURCE CENTER ON LEGAL AND JUDICIAL ISSUES: A SERVICE OF THE CHILDREN'S BUREAU

Help in Child Welfare Legal and Judicial System Responses to Children and Families Affected by Disasters

The ABA Center on Children and the Law, working with our partners the National Council of Juvenile and Family Court Judges and the National Center for State Courts, continues to work on aiding legal and judicial system responses to the needs of children and families affected by future disasters (like Hurricanes Katrina and Rita of 2005).

This page will be updated with additional information related to child welfare legal/judicial interventions with children and families affected by disasters.

Our responses in 2005 and 2006 centered around three areas of assistance:

1. Determining and Helping Meet the More Immediate Needs of Dependency Courts and Child Welfare Legal Offices in the Hurricane-Affected Areas
2. Helping Serve the Legal Needs of Katrina-Affected Children and Families Through Provision of Pro Bono Child Welfare Law Experts
3. Studying Child Welfare Legal Issues Affecting Children and Families in Katrina-Like Disasters, Including Needed State and Federal Legislative Responses

Source: Excerpted from *Help in child welfare legal and judicial system responses to children and families affected by disasters*, published by the American Bar Association with The National Child Welfare Resource Center on Legal and Judicial Issues, a service of the Children's Bureau.

Lessons Learned: Increased Risk of Morbidity and Mortality for Children with Special Healthcare Needs during and after the Disaster

Children with special healthcare needs (CSHCN), particularly the subset of technology-dependent children, experienced increased morbidity and mortality because of inadequate planning to provide for backup electricity to run essential life-sustaining equipment, such as suction, ventilators, and nebulizers. Local emergency medical services (EMS) agencies were generally unaware of the technology-dependent children in their catchment areas who needed immediate evacuation to centers with electricity and medical personnel and were therefore unable to provide such assistance. The press contained accounts of CSHCN being evacuated in private vehicles on interstate highways with essential equipment, such as respirators, running out of battery power. Although the American Academy of Pediatrics (AAP) and American College of Emergency Physicians (ACEP) Emergency Information Form (EIF), which was designed to assist in the short-term care for CSHCN, is increasingly being used by primary care providers, subspecialists, and emergency departments (EDs), it has not been widely disseminated to EMS agencies.

Source: Dolan, M. A., and Krug, S. E. 2006. Pediatric disaster preparedness in the wake of Katrina: Lessons to be learned. *Clinical Pediatric Emergency Medicine*, 7:59–66. © 2006 Elsevier. With permission. http://www.aap.org/disasters/pdf/PDP-in-the-Wake-of-Katrina.pdf.

SIDEBAR 5.9 LEGAL CONSIDERATIONS

Legal Considerations for Working With Children in Disasters

The following are legal questions and issues that may arise during a disaster. Having policies and procedures in place prior to an event should be considered.

- For unaccompanied children during a disaster, consent is not needed to treat for a life or limb-threatening situation. Is parental consent needed to treat a child victim with minor injuries? With psychological injuries?
- Is parental consent required to decontaminate an unaccompanied child? What if child is asymptomatic? What if child is refusing?

- What medical or social information can be released and to whom during a disaster?
- Check HIPAA rules and your legal counsel concerning the unidentified patient locator protocols, such as posting Polaroid photographs of unidentified children.
- Who can children be released to and if not the parent or caregiver, what permission or information is needed? What is your protocol for releasing children if no legal guardian or parent can be found or if no permission document is provided?

Source: New York City Department of Health and Mental Hygiene (NYC Health). 2006. *Hospital guidelines for pediatrics in disasters*. Centers for Bioterrorism Preparedness Program Pediatric Task Force.

Conclusion

Responding to the unique needs of children in a disaster can be complicated and involve a wide variety of individuals (i.e., school officials, child care providers, social service workers, pediatricians, etc.) and organizations. The lessons learned and the actions prescribed by such groups as the American Academy of Pediatrics, the National Association of Child Care Resource and Referral Agencies, and others have outlined the steps that emergency managers need to take to ensure that the unique needs of children are addressed in all phases of the response to a disaster event.

References

Abanet. http://www.abanet.org/child/disasters.pdf.

Agency for Healthcare Research and Quality. 2009. *School-based emergency preparedness: A national analysis and recommended protocol.* Pub. 09-0013. Rockville, MD: AHRQ. http://www.ahrq.gov/prep/schoolprep/schoolprep.pdf.

Brethren Children's Disaster Services. http://www.brethren.org/site/PageServer?pagename=serve_childrens_disaster_services.

CDC Health Advisory. 2005. *Instructions for identifying and protecting displaced children.* September 28.

Church of the Brethren. http://www.brethren.org/site/PageServer?pagename=serve_brethren_disaster_ministries.

Dolan, M. A., and Krug, S. E. 2006. Pediatric disaster preparedness in the wake of Katrina: Lessons to be learned, *Clinical Pediatric Emergency Medicine*, 7: 54–66. http://www.aap.org/disasters/pdf/PDP-in-the-Wake-of-Katrina.pdf.

Feed the Children, http://www.feedthechildren.org/site/PageServer?pagename=org_disaster_relief.

Missing Kids. http://www.missingkids.com/missingkids/servlet/NewsEventServlet?LanguageCountry=en_US&PageId=2317.

National Association of Child Care Resource and Referral Agencies (NACCRRA). 2006. *Is child care ready? A disaster planning guide for child-care resource and referral agencies*. http://www.naccrra.org/disaster/.

New York City Department of Health and Mental Hygiene (NYC Health). 2006. *Hospital guidelines for pediatrics in disasters*. Centers for Bioterrorism Preparedness Program Pediatric Task Force.

NVOAD. http://www.nvoad.org.

Reuters. 2005. http://www.redorbit.com/news/general/266965/louisiana_still_searching_for_katrina_foster_kids/index.html.

Save the Children. Safe Space slide show. http://www.savethechildren.org/programs/us-literacy-and-nutrition/safe-spaces.html.

Save the Children. Safe Space video. http://multimedia.savethechildren.org/video/california-wildfires/video-box-california-wildfires.html.

Save the Children. http://www.savethechildren.org/programs/us-literacy-and-nutrition/southern-california-wildfires.html.

Save the Children. http://www.savethechildren.org/programs/us-literacy-and-nutrition/safe-spaces-us.html.

Southern Baptist Disaster Relief. http://www.namb.net/site/c.9qKILUOzEpH/b.224451/k.A400/Disaster_Relief.htm.

Chapter 6

Recovery

Introduction

The ability of a community to effectively recover from a major disaster event has a direct impact on the long-term health and development of the children of that community. While the unique disaster recovery needs of children have long been acknowledged by the various groups tasked with their care, this special needs group had received no significant attention from the federal, state, and local agencies responsible for recovery operations until Hurricane Katrina exposed the consequences of failing to adequately consider these needs.

Beginning in the early 1990s, psychologists began to recognize the critical importance that crisis counseling played in helping children to handle the traumatic images and impacts of major disasters they and their families had sustained. However, it was also found in subsequent events, as counseling was applied with greater regularity, that the counseling alone was insufficient to deal with the greater range of long-lasting physical and emotional effects that children had sustained (Figure 6.1).

Like with the frail elderly, the physiology of developing children makes them much more vulnerable to infection and illness in the

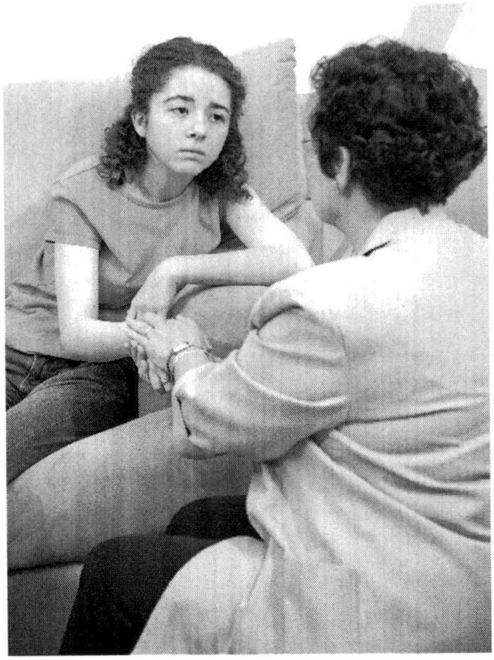

FIGURE 6.1 **Crisis counseling, while playing a critical role, is one of many considerations in helping children recover from traumatic experiences in disasters.**

aftermath of a disaster. Coupled with the significant psychological anxiety caused by the loss of home, separation from family members, witnessing the weakness or trauma of their primary caregivers, and interruption in their routines of care, this physical vulnerability puts children at unique risk in the interim period between the disaster event and a return to stability. Stress, confusion, and anxiety left unaddressed during this period of uncertainty will ultimately impact educational progress, physical development, self-confidence, and the ability of a child to enjoy the same opportunities of his or her peers.

The Recovery Needs of Children Are Recognized

The efforts of federal, state, local, and private sector stakeholders to repair or reconstruct community infrastructure have indirectly benefited children, but in the absence of a conscious effort to understand and address their unique needs, the efficiency and effectiveness of these efforts are limited. Thanks to the failures, struggles, and successes identified in the aftermath of an event as catastrophic as Hurricane Katrina was, we are beginning to witness a change in recovery approaches with regards to children's needs. The huge displacement of children throughout the Gulf Coast region, the death of hundreds of parents and caregivers upon which many children depended, and the destruction of homes and disruption to child care services have each helped to bring about much greater attention to this issue—and likewise have helped to identify best practices to better manage in the future.

Tangible recognition of the postdisaster recovery needs of children were initiated in earnest following the passage of the Post Katrina Emergency Management Reform Act of 2006 (PKEMRA), and the establishment of a National Commission on Children and Disasters. These two events began what has evolved into a rapidly growing awareness of the need to better support children during their recovery from major disaster events. Sidebar 6.1, which contains language from the provisions of the commission, illustrates the degree to which lawmakers responded.

SIDEBAR 6.1 INTERIM REPORT LANGUAGE ON RECOVERY

The Post Katrina Emergency Management Reform Act of 2006 (PKEMRA) requires the development of a National Disaster Recovery Strategy to coordinate long-term recovery resources following major disasters. Tangible progress is slow in the development of the Strategy. The Commission strongly urges that FEMA aggressively intensify efforts to develop the Strategy by the close of 2009, with the assistance of governmental and non-governmental stakeholders who provide health, educational, and social services to children.

A National Disaster Recovery Strategy that benefits children would ensure:

- The immediate availability and continuity of disaster case management services to families;
- Continuous access to a medical home;
- Federal disaster assistance through grants for all medical facilities damaged or destroyed by a disaster, such as primary medical, dental and mental health care practices and clinics;

- Access to appropriate crisis, bereavement and mental health services;
- Academic continuity and immediate educational access by enrolling and placing disaster-affected children in educational and related services in compliance with the McKinney-Vento Homeless Education Assistance Improvements Act;
- Priority for families with school-aged children, especially for those families with children having special health, mental health or educational needs, for disaster housing assistance and permanent housing; and
- The provision of developmental and age-appropriate play and recreation options, particularly quality day care and after-school services.

The overarching principle for recovery from disasters must be to create self-sufficient families and a "new and improved normalcy" for all children, especially children who are socially and economically disadvantaged. The development of a National Disaster Recovery Strategy would specify guiding principles for services that must be provided to children affected by disasters: safe, stable living environments; health care, mental health and oral health; academic continuity and supervised after school activities; childcare; and disaster case management. The guiding principles would govern the request for and provision of federal disaster and recovery funding for these services, to ensure the economic recovery of communities as a whole. Strategies, roles, and responsibilities for recovery must be established and emphasized as critical components of federal, state and local disaster plans, and should include the roles and contributions of systems responsible for the education, care and welfare of children.

Source: National Commission on Children and Disasters. 2009. Interim report. October 14. http://www.childrenanddisasters.acf.hhs.gov/20091014_508IR_partII.pdf.

As the commission requested in its 2009 interim report, the awareness of these recovery phase needs must be supported by prioritized actions that ensure plans and efforts adequately meet these postdisaster recovery requirements determined to be unique to children. Experts agree that the areas of priority for children in the long-term recovery phase should include:

1. Restoring the infrastructure that supports children in a community, including providing and restoring temporary housing, schools, and child care facilities
2. Providing mental health support and services

Both of these priorities will be detailed throughout this chapter, illustrated with case studies typical of the innovative programs that have been adopted to address these needs. Sidebar 6.2, which is drawn from the recovery plan of the New Mexico Children, Youth, and Families Department, highlights one example of a recognized set of child-focused actions a government agency has identified as key to addressing in the recovery phase of a major disaster.

SIDEBAR 6.2 RECOVERY FUNCTIONS IDENTIFIED IN A STATE EMERGENCY RESPONSE PLAN

When the immediate emergency situation is over, New Mexico Children, Youth, and Families Department (CYFD) staff will continue to work with local and state emergency operations personnel to assist in recovery activities. These activities will include, but are not limited to:

- Returning to normal business operations;
- Reuniting children separated from their families;
- Informing biological parents and other caregivers of the location and status of their children who are in CYFD protective custody;
- Providing or securing psychosocial support (crisis response, short and long term counseling, etc.) for survivors, victims, and responders, including CYFD PS personnel;
- Assisting foster care providers in obtaining other support needed in the aftermath of an emergency, including housing, food, clothing, medical care, etc.;
- Documenting any expenses incurred during the emergency for possible reimbursement from FEMA or other agencies;
- Debriefing the agency's efforts during the emergency to identify lessons learned and revise emergency response plans as necessary.

Source: New Mexico Children, Youth. and Families, Department of Protective Services. *All-hazard emergency response plan.*

Providing and Restoring the Infrastructure That Supports Children in a Community, Including Temporary Housing, Schools, and Child Care Facilities

The traditional disaster recovery process has always prioritized the rebuilding of the community's damaged physical infrastructure. Of highest priority is the repair or reconstruction of roads and bridges essential for the access of public health, safety, and emergency response vehicles. Any other infrastructure that supports the rapid restoration of critical governmental services and the economy followed closely behind. Infrastructure that is of critical importance to children, however, is of secondary and further tiered priority. This includes, for instance, the rebuilding of schools, clinics, child care centers, and other social and community service providers.

Starting in the 1990s, as communities began to recognize the strong link between the ability of the labor market to return to their jobs and the ability of the economy to quickly recover, the low rankings of children's and other social needs began to reverse. For example, transit systems needed to be brought back quickly so people could travel to their offices or job sites. Parents were unable to return to work if their children were staying home due to ongoing school closures. Parents of very young children who were suddenly without child care—a purely private sector market and therefore outside any scope of government purview—could find themselves bound to their households indefinitely.

However, such efforts have not been standardized through national- or even state-level guidance, and as such these positive trends follow only the direct impact and experience of disaster. Therefore, it is a patchwork of progress that has resulted across the nation's communities, and the process continues to evolve as more and more disasters highlight needs to those exposed. Clearly, a very determined and conscious national-level effort, such as what was seen in the aftermath of September 11 with regards to planning standards, is what is needed to educate emergency managers and local recovery planners such that every community proactively adopts the necessary approach (Figure 6.2).

FIGURE 6.2 **Marianna, Florida, May 12, 2009. FEMA Human Services Group Supervisor Judith Thomas hands out information about FEMA services to the Jackson County School Board. This FEMA outreach effort is to get information to families through school children about services available for those affected by a recent storm/flood. (George Armstrong/FEMA)**

The criticality of infrastructure supportive of children, and thus the community as a whole, is not necessarily self-evident to those planning in the absence of experience. These components include:

- Schools
- Child care centers and facilities
- Social services organizations
- Facilities that support after-school programs
- Pediatric health and medical services

The Robert T. Stafford Act provides the legal authority and funding to support recovery programs, including support for essential facilities that are nongovernmental, private nonprofit entities. Included in this definition are power (energy), water, sewer, communications, and emergency medical. Currently, child care is not included in the definition of critical services. This means that the vast majority of child care facilities are not eligible to receive federal funds to rebuild after a disaster.

As such, in order to rebuild or repair any damages to child care facilities, the owners of these facilities must apply for a Small

Business Administration (SBA) loan or a loan from the private sector. Obtaining such financing can be a very long process, especially through the SBA, and many child care facility owners do not have the financial resources to sustain such delays. The result is that many of these facilities end up closing their doors for good—resulting in a net loss of child care services in the community. In Katrina alone, the number of licensed child care facilities that ceased providing services due to impact from the events (direct or indirect) in Louisiana alone stands at 356 (Save the Children, www.savethechildren.com). This can have devastating effects on all sectors of society, as workers in government, nongovernmental organizations, critical infrastructure, transportation, and more are the parents of these children who are suddenly faced with no alternative.

There has been considerable research that has documented that child care facilities are essential to restoring the economic health and vitality of a community after a disaster strikes. And in the longer term, quality child care, early learning, and education are key to building a future workforce. Therefore, it is in the best economic interest of the nation to apply federal dollars for the rebuilding of child care facilities in communities impacted by disasters. Organizations such as Save the Children, as well as the National Commission on Children in Disasters, will continue to argue for changes to the Stafford Act that will add child care facilities to the definition of critical facilities under that legislation (see Sidebar 6.3).

SIDEBAR 6.3 FACT SHEET: PROTECTING CHILDREN DURING U.S. EMERGENCIES: HOW SAFE ARE OUR SCHOOLS AND DAY CARE CENTERS WHEN DISASTER STRIKES?

Some 67 million children are enrolled in U.S. kindergartens, schools and child-care centers. Many parents assume these facilities are fully equipped to safeguard their children. However, for millions of parents this confidence may be misplaced.

New research commissioned by Save the Children has found that most states have not taken the necessary steps to ensure that thousands of child-care facilities are prepared to respond to the needs of children in the event of emergencies such as tornados, earthquakes or industrial accidents, which can strike during school hours. The research—the result of an April 2008 review of state child-care licensing regulations and quality standards conducted by Mississippi State University Early Childhood Institute—also examined state standards for K–12 schools and found that 18 states do not require K–12 schools to have written procedures for general disaster planning.

More American children than ever before are in out-of-home care each day. Over 11 million children in the United States under the age of 5 are in some type of child-care arrangement while their parents work. Meanwhile more than 90 percent of the nation's children up to 18 years of age, and over 88 percent of low-income children, live in counties at high risk of hurricanes, earthquakes or tornadoes.

Upon evaluation of emergency preparedness regulations and requirements for licensed child-care facilities and K–12 schools in all 50 states and the District of Columbia, the survey found that many states are falling short when it comes to protecting children in times of disaster.

In fact:

- Only nine states require licensed child-care facilities to have a designated relocation site and evacuation route in the event of a disaster. When a child-care facility does not have a relocation site or evacuation route, neither staff nor children evacuating a building know where to go or the most direct route to safety. This absence of planning and practice may create confusion and panic during times of crisis. In the event of an unexpected disaster like a tornado, fire or chemical spill, minutes lost due to panic and confusion can have a profound impact on the safety of children and staff.
- Only 15 states require licensed child-care facilities to have a reunification plan for children and families in the event they become separated during an emergency. Children often spend a great deal of time in day-care facilities, and parents trust that if they need to reach their children, they know exactly where they are. If an emergency makes it impossible for a parent or caregiver to reach the day-care center, reunification plans ensure that parents can safely reunite with their young children and babies.
- Only 14 states require licensed child-care facilities to make provisions for children with special needs in case

of a disaster. During emergencies all children are vulnerable; in the case of children with special needs, these vulnerabilities can be even more striking. If a child is confined to a wheelchair or has a sight or hearing impairment, a plan must be put into place to make sure they are cared for and not put in harm's way during an emergency.

- The review also found that 18 states do not require K–12 schools to have written procedures for general disaster planning. Without written procedures for disaster preparedness, any emergency response effort can falter due to variables such as staff changes, communication failures or misunderstandings about staff roles and responsibilities. Child safety requires that school disaster plans are written, easily available, practiced often and consistently improved.

Source: Save the Children. 2008. http://www.savethechildren.org/publications/reports/Disaster-Preps-Issue-Brief-Final-1.pdf.

In the aftermath of Katrina, the recovery of child care became a critical bottleneck in the ability of many of the nation's key energy sector businesses—a main driver behind the economy of the Gulf Coast. Many of these businesses turned to creative answers to address the need for their employees, many of them parents, to find safe, affordable, quality child care for their children. Without such action these businesses, which constitute a major tax base of the region's local and state governments, could not operate to capacity or at all. In one instance, detailed in the following case study, a business worked closely with a university to address the recovery of child care when government action fell short of what was ultimately needed.

CASE STUDY: Rebuilding Childcare in Mississippi

In 2005, Chevron's Pascagoula Refinery in Mississippi prepared to help refinery employees and the surrounding communities recover from the unprecedented destruction caused by Hurricane Katrina. The leadership team overseeing the recovery saw that many of the childcare centers serving local communities and Chevron employees had been damaged by the storm, and many Chevron employees could not return to work until safe, secure childcare services were restored.

"After the hurricane, it was obvious how interconnected things were," said Steve Renfroe, a member of the Chevron leadership team overseeing local recovery efforts. "A disaster of the magnitude of Katrina has the power to stop the economy, but how do you restart it? Think of the portable electric generators that provided the initial energy to restart the refinery. Childcare is like that generator. It enables parents to go back to work. But childcare was not on the federal government's list of critical services so it was not immediately eligible for federal funds."

Chevron partnered with the Early Childhood Institute (ECI) at Mississippi State University to map the level of destruction to the childcare infrastructure in the three Mississippi coastal counties—Jackson, Harrison and Hancock—devastated by Hurricane Katrina. Results "reported on October 6 [2005] found that from 62 percent to 94 percent of licensed slots in the three coastal counties were lost or potentially lost" (Mississippi State University Early Childhood Institute, 2006).

Chevron contributed $500,000 and provided work crews to repair and rebuild 40 childcare centers in Jackson County. In Harrison County, Chevron partnered with Save the Children, which made a $795,000 donation, Help and Hope Foundation, the Mississippi Low Income Child Care Initiative and U.S. Fund for UNICEF to repair and rebuild 42 childcare centers. In November 2006, Chevron made a $2 million donation to Save the Children to construct two new childcare centers in the communities of Bay St. Louis and Bay Waveland. In addition, childcare center owners invested over $1.6 million in insurance payouts, their savings and countless hours of sweat equity to repair and rebuild their centers.

Immediately after Hurricane Katrina struck, ECI had joined in the formation of Embrace Mississippi's Children and collected tons of supplies and gifts and about $128,000 in cash contributions from around the country to resupply the centers with books, toys and furniture. ECI received grants or contracts totaling $1.55 million from the W.K. Kellogg Foundation, the Community Foundation of Northwest Mississippi and individual donors (Mississippi State University Early Childhood Institute, 2006). At the same time, ECI provided training and technical assistance to upgrade childcare center staff capabilities in the three counties.

All told, ECI estimates that in Jackson County, 3,412 childcare slots (a childcare slot is a space for one child in a childcare center or family childcare home) received teaching and material kits and 2,805 childcare slots received furnishings and/or reconstruction aid. In Harrison County, 2,678 childcare slots received material kits, 1,036 childcare slots received furnishings and 2,235 childcare slots received reconstruction aid.

"Realizing its importance, we began rebuilding this infrastructure. Others decided to help and in the end, the partnership included university, philanthropic, state government and private sector support," said Renfroe.

Source: Save the Children. 2007. *Child care: An essential service of disaster recovery*. Issue brief. June. http://www.savethechildren.org/publications/issue-briefs/issuebrief3_07.pdf.

For parents who have lost their homes, finding suitable child care services for their children becomes minor in comparison to their quest to locate and secure safe and appropriate shelter for their families—and ultimately a permanent housing solution to meet longer-term needs. In the interim period, the provision of temporary housing is critical to stabilizing the family's situation, and likewise ensuring the physical and psychological safety and security of children. Current federal policy was created in the absence of any consideration of how the resulting approaches might impact the lives or development of children who become recipients of such aid. While temporary housing, be it in travel trailers, converted facilities, rental or hotel units, or "FEMA-ville" congregate camps, might be appropriate as designed to a generic target population, there are factors unique to each of these solutions that have profound effects of the children who occupy them. For example, most housing recovery solutions look at the requirements of a healthy adult. These facilities allow for sleeping, eating, access to utility services, and access to employment. However, children have developmental needs that go far beyond these basic requirements of an adult. Children need to play for social development. Children need protection from predators to reduce their likelihood of victimization. Children have greater susceptibility to many of the chemicals and other environmental impacts associated with temporary housing. The list goes on and on. Without incorporating the needs of children into such policies at the national level, programs will continue to fail children. Again, Hurricane Katrina was highly illustrative of the effects that result from recovery policies developed without due consideration of the unique needs of children. Housing relocations separated children from their extended families and friends, which are of much greater psychological and developmental importance than in adults who can manage such separations. Children were exposed to chemicals that caused asthma, skin infections, and other health problems. Children fell victim to child predators when placed within close contact of a hotel, trailer park, or other congregate situation. And children were exposed to situations where their lack of supervision, and difficulty of receiving an adequate education, caused them to fall behind their peers nationwide.

CASE STUDY: The Purgatory of Temporary Housing

Ask child advocates what families need most and they respond: housing, housing, housing. More than 70 percent of New Orleans flooded. By now, much of the painful, nasty work of cleaning up, gutting and throwing away a lifetime of now-ruined possessions has been done. But many residential neighborhoods still remain empty except for an occasional trailer in a driveway. Of New Orleans' pre-Katrina population of 484,000, only about 200,000 live there today—though not necessarily in the same location.

An informal survey of the 41 children in the Children's Defense Fund's Freedom Schools® program in

New Orleans one afternoon found that just 16 live in the same house or apartment as they did before. Many children and families yearn to return to New Orleans but cannot. As of mid-January 2007, 258 Louisiana homeowners (out of 101,657 applicants) had received their share of the billions in federal dollars intended to help them repair or replace their homes. Families who rented pre-Katrina are not in line for any of these funds, and many are priced out of returning because the scarcity of livable units has driven monthly rents from $676 to $978 for a two-bedroom unit and from $868 to $1,256 for three bedrooms.

While some displaced families have settled comfortably, though perhaps a little sadly, into other cities, many remain in the purgatory of temporary housing—or what one social worker calls "long-term temporary housing." Of the nine displaced children profiled in a CDF "Katrina's Children" report last April, only one family had been able to return to New Orleans by November 2006. Two other families are fairly well situated with jobs, housing and schools in Houston and in Simmesport, Louisiana. Five families continue to wait, in trailers, mobile homes and family members' houses, to go home or at least obtain more permanent housing and a sense of stability in their upturned lives. The ninth family could not be located.

A surprisingly large number of evacuees still live in FEMA-provided travel trailers—8 by 30 foot boxes that were not designed for extended stays, large families or high winds. From a high of 107,623 travel trailers in Louisiana, Mississippi and Alabama in July 2006, 92,409 remained in place in January 2007.

FEMA does not keep track of the number of children in trailers but visits to FEMA trailer parks suggest that many trailers house children, often more than one. Valerie, who until recently lived in a FEMA trailer park near Baton Rouge, said that her trailer housed seven family members, three adults and four children.

"We slept in shifts," she said. During this time her seven-year-old grandson, Hakeem, who was abandoned by his mother right after the storm, kept saying, "Looks like I'm going to have to go to a foster home."

Families living in FEMA trailers that are parked in the driveways of their damaged houses in New Orleans worry about their children's exposure to mold, dust and even rats, which are said to live in houses untouched since the storm. Parents worry, too, about their children living in largely abandoned neighborhoods [Figure 6.3].

The one profiled family that has returned to New Orleans, Cheryl and her daughters Montrelle, 14, and Maliyah, 4, live in a four-plex in the upper Ninth ward, which their former landlord repaired and rented to

FIGURE 6.3 **Columbia, Mississippi, December 15, 2005. Tony "Chappy" Hodge stands on the steps of his FEMA mobile home. Hodge, a member of the Mississippi Air National Guard, was deployed to the Gulf Coast prior to Hurricane Katrina's landfall and assisted hurricane victims. His wife and children lost their home at the same time due to tornadoes spawned by Hurricane Katrina. (Patsy Lynch/FEMA)**

them at a reasonable price. But theirs is one of only three inhabited houses in the entire block, and public bus service, which Montrelle takes to get to her Catholic high school, is infrequent. Only 17 percent of the pre-Katrina New Orleans buses were running in January 2007. "I'm concerned about who's out there—workers from out of state, homeless people living under houses," Cheryl said.

Montrelle is happy to be back at St. Mary's, a rigorous all girls' school she much prefers to the large public high school that she attended in Houston last year. But once she gets home, she said, "I don't go out."

Source: Children's Defense Fund. 2007. *Katrina's children: Still waiting.* http://www.childrensdefense.org/child-research-data-publications/data/katrinas-children-still-waiting-hurricane-2007.pdf.

The following case study illustrates how the unmet special needs of children, most notably those of temporary housing, can quickly and profoundly affect other groups associated with them—most notably their primary caregivers (Figure 6.4).

FIGURE 6.4 San Diego, California, October 24, 2007. Bashi Yusuf's children enjoy a movie with their father at Qualcomm Stadium where they camped out with thousands of other people driven from their homes by wildfires. (Michael Raphael/FEMA)

CASE STUDY: Women's Media Center Katrina Campaign: New Study Explores the Aftermath for Women

Peggy Simpson
July 10, 2007

Some women displaced by Hurricane Katrina have had to choose between finding basic shelter and guarding their personal safety.

Of the estimated 142,000 New Orleans apartments or houses destroyed by the storm, nearly four-fifths were affordable to low-income families. People rendered homeless and unable to rebuild took refuge with extended family and friends. That gave them a place to call home but also left women and children vulnerable to sexual assault and domestic violence, says a new report by the Institute for Women's Policy Research.

The "overcrowding has led to abuse specifically linked to the Katrina experience," said Avis A. Jones-DeWeever of the IWPR.

Much has been written about the race and class fault lines exposed by the disaster nearly two years ago when Katrina ravaged an area the size of Great Britain. The IWPR study, with excerpts released at a congressional briefing June 22, examines the disproportionate impact on women. In addition to overcrowding and an increased threat of domestic violence, women face problems involving health needs, childcare and jobs, among other issues.

In some ways, women faced plights after Katrina similar to those confronting victims of other international catastrophes, including the tsunami. Because of their dual roles—as paid workers but also caregivers to children, the elderly and the disabled—women have limited mobility. And those at the bottom of the economic rung before the storms found intensified peril in their wake.

"Women and children are fourteen times more likely to die than men are during a disaster," said Leigh Wintz, executive director of Soroptimist, which funded the

IWPR study on women after Katrina. "Following the Asian tsunami, for instance, Oxfam found that women made up more than seventy percent of the casualties."

Jones-DeWeever's study found that women's part of the Gulf Coast workforce has declined since Katrina. Ironically, wages have gone up due to the competition for workers—but costs for shelter, food and health care have shot up. A two-bedroom home that used to rent for $601 is $978 today, she said. And women competing for the higher paid jobs in the building trades face job discrimination, said Joan Kuriansky of Wider Opportunities for Women. A flyer she displayed illustrated the problem. It sought "healthy and hardy men" to help rebuild the Gulf Coast.

The scarcity of childcare is another formidable obstacle, post-Katrina. More than 3,000 licensed Gulf Coast childcare facilities were damaged or destroyed, and most remain out of service today. Only 10 in Louisiana and one in Mississippi got federal assistance to reopen. A Mississippi Delta congressman whose district was hard hit by Katrina, Rep. Bennie Thompson, is sponsoring legislation that would add emergency childcare to the "critical service" category for federal disaster relief funds, along with such others as shelter, food and medical care.

Partnerships forged between business, nonprofit groups, foundations and Mississippi State University got results in reopening childcare centers even without federal funds. More than $600,000 was raised to rebuild centers in Harrison and Hancock Counties in Mississippi, as a result of efforts by the Mississippi Low Income Child Care Initiative with foundations and relief agencies. Chevron, which has a refinery in Pascagoula, worked with the university to map the destruction to the childcare infrastructure in three counties, provided funds and work crews to rebuild 40 childcare centers and partnered with Save the Children to reconstruct others.

Source: Ms. Foundation for Women. http://www.ms.foundation.org/wmspage.cfm?parm1=475.

FIGURE 6.5 **Baker, Louisiana, October 27, 2006. Entertainer Rosie O'Donnell appears at the grand opening of the Children's Plaza at FEMA's Renaissance Village trailer park. O'Donnell's charitable foundation was the leading force in establishing the center for residents of the park, victims of Hurricane Katrina. The plaza includes facilities for Early Head Start, elementary after-school programs, adult education, and social services. (Keith Riggs/FEMA)**

However, despite that current federal programs supporting temporary disaster housing are inadequate, and lack innovation to support the needs of children, it is still possible for change to be effected at the state and local levels. Through proper planning and intervention at these levels, emergency management officials responsible for providing and managing the temporary housing efforts can instill a flexibility and atmosphere of adaptation that better provides for these critical postdisaster needs of children. The experience in Pass Christian, Mississippi, after Hurricane Katrina is but one example where local innovation was applied to better meet these needs (Figure 6.5).

CASE STUDY: Emergency Childcare Established to Support Housing Recovery Efforts

When Hurricane Katrina struck Pass Christian, Mississippi, virtually all of the homes, buildings, and businesses were damaged or destroyed. Five months later, nearly all of Pass Christian's 7,000 residents still lived in temporary travel trailers on what was left of their property. Another 200 people lived in a FEMA tent camp called "The Village."

For the community to begin recovery, people needed to return to work—which meant that quality childcare was a critical need. Unfortunately, the childcare centers had all been destroyed.

To help parents return to work, a tented childcare center was established in The Village—the first of its kind to be constructed in an emergency setting in the U.S. The childcare center was the result of Save the Children's partnership with the city of Pass Christian, the Mississippi Department of Health's childcare licensure office, and Ginger Holmes, the owner of the Pass Christian Child Development Center. In addition, educational materials, an outdoor play structure, and childcare supplies were donated from the *Bright Horizons Foundation* and *Bridging the Gulf*. The site, located in four tents in the center of the town, served more than 40 children daily—from infancy through pre-school age.

The emergency childcare tents in Pass Christian provided an innovative solution that could be used as a model to be replicated in other crisis situations throughout the United States.

Source: Save the Children. *Emergency Childcare in Mississippi Gets Parents Back to Work*. http://www.savethechildren.org/emergencies/us/us-gulf-coast-hurricanes/emergency-child-care-in-mississippi-gets-parents-back-to-work.html.

CASE STUDY: Project Rebuild Plaquemines

Project Rebuild Plaquemines is a non-profit organization started in September of 2005, shortly after Hurricane Katrina, for the purpose of aiding in the community recovery effort. It's board consists of representatives from major sponsors and members of the Plaquemines Parish community.

The organization's work began with a "Welcome Home" fair that was free and open to all parish residents in celebration of its residents returning home. The organization also co-sponsored health fairs in the largest FEMA community parks in partnership with United Way, Hands of Hope and many local, state and federal agencies.

Project Rebuild Plaquemines addressed a number of recovery sectors, and children were one key focus. The organization built their first playground in the community of Diamond in cooperation with KaBOOM!, Save the Children and Plaquemines Parish Government. This effort was supported by a number of volunteers, from organizations that included the Red Cross, AmeriCorps, the Belle Chasse Naval Air Station, ConocoPhillips, South Plaquemines High School students, the Plaquemines Parish Orange Queen 2007 (Ashley Johnson), Leon Duplessis and Sons and many others.

Their largest undertaking, in fact, was focused on something that helped bring about the long-term recovery of children—play and recreation. The Plaquemines Parks Project was a partnership with the Plaquemines Parish Government to rebuild and improve five parks at parish sites that restored and improved recreation access in the parish. Each park is designed to benefit each of the families' members, which in turn encourages not only children but also their caregivers to get outside and take a break from the stress of the lengthy recovery process.

Source: Project Rebuild Plaquemines. http://www.projectrebuildplaquemines.org/.

Providing Mental Health Support and Services

Children, and the caregivers of children, have been found to require more substantial psychosocial support than is typically needed by members of the general population. These two groups face much more complex problems. The caregivers are suddenly struggling to meet their own survival needs, which are quickly compounded by the dependence of the children whose needs become additive to their own. For the children, who suffer the impacts of exposure to trauma and disruption of security and routines, there exists an intrinsic deficiency of resources and experience from which to address these problems. The result is that both of these groups require not only more support, but also specialized kinds of support that is designed to deal with the emotional, psychological, and social needs that arise in the aftermath of a major disaster event. For children and caregivers, quality mental health services will be a necessity during the whole recovery process and often long after community recovery in other sectors has ceased (Figure 6.6).

Psychosocial services are specialized, especially those that manage the posttraumatic stress of a disaster. While it is often the case that organizations and agencies from outside the community come in to assist with their provision, it is possible for the community

FIGURE 6.6 **New Orleans, Louisiana, May 8, 2006. A Katrina Child Watch roundtable program for parents, sponsored by the Children's Defense Fund, is held at the St. Roch FEMA Trailer Park in New Orleans to address health and educational issues of the children. The Children's Defense Fund delegation is made up of national celebrities visiting the area and the St. Roch FEMA Trailer Park to address the mental health, health, and education issues of children traumatized by Hurricane Katrina. (Marvin Nauman/FEMA)**

to develop these resources from within their own ranks. With a level of training that matches the background and experience of the individual, it is possible for school psychologists, teachers, pediatricians, child care providers, and even parents, among many others, to become adequately equipped to independently meet these needs. The following points address the different ways in which communities can prepare for or respond to the postdisaster psychosocial needs of disaster-impacted children:

- Community programs and services focused on or tasked with the care of children can research existing psychosocial programs and train staff in the skills needed to offer such services.
- Local mental health programs can explore different critical incident stress methodologies that better meet the needs of children to add to their list of options, including such things as puppet/playhouse games and play as therapy (see Sidebar 6.4).
- Schools can ensure that all counselors and teachers are able to address the needs of all children, or that they can augment their internal capacity by identifying and partnering with outside resources prior to a disaster onset.
- Social services staff can plan for the systems required to meet a sudden increase in their caseload as families find themselves unable to adequately cope with the stress brought on by a disaster.
- Nongovernmental and faith-based organizations can be encouraged to, and supported in their efforts to, create a capacity to meet the psychosocial needs of their youngest members or service recipients, recognizing that these groups are already held in a high level of trust and confidence not only by the children themselves, but also their parents, who may otherwise be reluctant to put their children in the care of a stranger (see Sidebar 6.5).

In the aftermath of Hurricane Katrina in 2005, Save the Children developed a psychosocial program called the Journey of Hope, which was designed to help children in the Gulf Coast region to cope with the emotional impacts of the storm. The program was administered by school officials trained by Save the Children. It became evident very quickly that school administrators, counselors, and teachers were having problems coping with the impacts of the storm. To meet these unexpected needs, Save the Children developed a special Journey of Hope program that was focused on these caregiver needs (see Sidebar 6.6 and Figure 6.7).

SIDEBAR 6.4 HOW FAMILIES CAN HELP CHILDREN COPE WITH FEAR AND ANXIETY

Whether tragic events touch your family personally or are brought into your home via newspapers and television, you can help children cope with the anxiety that violence, death, and disasters can cause.

Listening and talking to children about their concerns can reassure them that they will be safe. Start by encouraging them to discuss how they have been affected by what is happening around them. Even young children may have specific questions about tragedies. Children react to stress at their own developmental level.

The *Caring for Every Child's Mental Health Campaign* offers these pointers for parents and other caregivers:

- **Encourage children to ask questions.** Listen to what they say. Provide comfort and assurance that address their specific fears. It's okay to admit you can't answer all of their questions.
- **Talk on their level.** Communicate with your children in a way they can understand. Don't get too technical or complicated.
- **Find out what frightens them.** Encourage your children to talk about fears they may have. They may worry that someone will harm them at school or that someone will try to hurt **you**.
- **Focus on the positive.** Reinforce the fact that most people are kind and caring. Remind your child of the heroic actions taken by ordinary people to help victims of tragedy.
- **Pay attention.** Your children's play and drawings may give you a glimpse into their questions or concerns. Ask them to tell you what is going on in the game or the picture. It's an opportunity to clarify any misconceptions, answer questions, and give reassurance.

- **Develop a plan.** Establish a family emergency plan for the future, such as a meeting place where everyone should gather if something unexpected happens in your family or neighborhood. It can help you and your children feel safer.

If you are concerned about your child's reaction to stress or trauma, call your physician or a community mental health center.

The **Caring for Every Child's Mental Health Campaign** is part of The Comprehensive Community Mental Health Services Program for Children and Their Families of the Federal Center for Mental Health Services. Parents and caregivers who wish to learn more about mental well-being in children should call 1-800-789-2647 (toll-free) or visit mentalhealth.samhsa.gov/child/ to download a free publications catalog (Order No. CA-0000). The Federal Center for Mental Health Services is an agency of the Substance Abuse and Mental Health Services Administration, U.S. Department of Health and Human Services.

Source: U.S. Department of Health and Human Services, Substance Abuse and Mental Health Services Association (SAMHSA), National Mental Health Information Center. *How Families Can Help Children Cope with Fear and Anxiety*. http://mentalhealth.samhsa.gov/publications/allpubs/Ca-0022/.

FIGURE 6.7 **Houston, Texas, September 3, 2005. Counselors and volunteers help stressed and grief-stricken evacuees deal with the trauma of Hurricane Katrina in the Astrodome. Many volunteers provided child care to give mothers a break during the day. (Andrea Booher/FEMA)**

SIDEBAR 6.5 SAVE THE CHILDREN: HURRICANE KATRINA RECOVERY FACT SHEET 2007

Classroom and Community Based Intervention: A school and community-based emotional support program addressing children's need for safety and trust remains a focal point of our response. We train teachers, school counselors and other caregivers to facilitate a series of structured sessions that use art, drama, music and movement to guide children through their thoughts and feelings about the disaster. The program focuses on building community, enhancing self-esteem and helping participants identify their inherent coping skills. From the start of program activities in fall 2005 through December 2006, 1,100 adults had been trained and over 11,600 children had completed the program.

Journey of Hope: In response to the needs of teachers and other adult caregivers who experienced devastating losses, Save the Children conducts a "Journey of Hope" care-for-caregivers workshop. As of December 2006, the program had assisted some 700 adults as they recovered from their own stresses and helped them to better understand the needs and reactions of children in their care. In addition, we had also successfully reached out to 80 teens in the region through Journey of Hope.

Protection Activities: Temporary arrangements for housing displaced families can be dangerous and unhealthy places for children, as Save the Children recognizes from decades of international relief work and an assessment of temporary housing sites in the Gulf Coast. Poorly planned facilities invariably lead to deterioration in social conditions, putting already vulnerable children further at risk.

Safe and Protective Communities Project: During summer 2006, Save the Children and the U.S. Department of Homeland Security, Federal Emergency Management Agency (FEMA) announced a new pilot program to improve services for children and families living in temporary housing group sites in the Gulf Coast. The Safe and Protective Communities Project seeks to foster a protective environment for children by helping to build a sense of community among residents. Save the Children establishes community spaces, works with residents to identify issues of concern, and helps them take action. As part of the project, we help connect local service organizations and officials with residents of the sites. As of January 2007, we are working in the 400-trailer Diamond group housing site and the 100-trailer Davant site, both in Plaquemines Parish, Louisiana. We plan to expand to 10 sites total during 2007.

Child Care Recovery: Save the Children plays a leadership role in a child care recovery coalition that is repairing and re-supplying 39 child care centers in seven Mississippi counties. The importance of this work cannot be understated—working parents need quality child care so that they can return to jobs and help contribute to the region's economic recovery. The project will create over 2,300 child care slots, and as of December 2006, work was complete at 29 of the sites. During 2007, the rebuilding coalition will also build two new child care centers in Harrison County, Mississippi, to be located on site with elementary schools. Save the Children has offered technical, material and financial support to child care centers in Louisiana and Mississippi to help them stay in business or extend their services to more children. Currently, we are working with Community Playthings, a manufacturer of children's furniture, to supply three New Orleans child care centers with furniture that will help them open their doors.

Playgrounds: One important aspect of our programs is to provide communities with places where their children can play and recover. Working with local partners and donors, Save the Children has created three state-of-the-art playgrounds in Mississippi. By building universally accessible playgrounds, we strive to create places where all children can play together and that symbolize hope for communities. Plans are in the works for a fourth playground at the Diamond FEMA transitional housing site in Louisiana.

Source: Save the Children. *Hurricane recovery fact sheet*. http://www.savethechildren.org/emergencies/us/us-gulf-coast-hurricanes/.

SIDEBAR 6.6 JOURNEY OF HOPE: HELP FOR CAREGIVERS

The *Journey of Hope* is a one-day workshop (available in 2hr, 4hr, & 6hr versions) designed to support teachers, administrators, parents and childcare providers in efforts to process recent events, cope with current challenges, and realize healthier futures.

Background

While Save the Children typically focuses on programs for children, support for the caregivers of children (teachers, administrators and parents) has emerged as an urgent unmet need on the Gulf Coast. School staff members have reported feeling overwhelmed by new curriculum standards, resource needs in the face of budget shortfalls, uncertainty about the future, and a workload that leaves little time and space to process grief, loss and anxiety. Unaddressed, the ongoing stress can potentially lead to burnout, interpersonal conflicts, and anger and frustration in the classroom. Facing the challenges of daily living in new environments without familiar communities and usual supports, teachers and parents are likely experiencing similar struggles as they try to meet the needs of their children and families. Addressing their own needs for self-care and strengthening community cohesion increases the capacity of caregivers to be fully present and attentive to the needs of children.

Project Description

Journey of Hope provides the opportunity for teachers and parents to understand the journey of their own lives through and beyond the recent disaster. The model draws on the ideas and experiences of teachers, school social workers, administrators and others working for children's well-being. *Journey of Hope* gathers participants around a circle in order to build trust and a sense of community. Activities utilize creative methods including silent storytelling, music and cooperative games adapted for adults, as well as practical knowledge and skills for self-care. The workshop facilitates the creation of a safe space for teachers and other caregivers in:

- Building trust and community
- Understanding reactions to stress and enhancing skills for coping

- Collective processing of grief and loss
- Identifying and amplifying community strengths and assets
- Collaborative planning for future community-led action and support.

The aim is to provide space for individual and group reflection of their journey, and to develop a sustainable plan for strengthening the school and living community.

Source: Save the Children. http://www.savethechildren.org/emergencies/us/us-gulf-coast-hurricanes/feature-AJOH.html.

SIDEBAR 6.7 "JOURNEY OF HOPE" HELPING GULF COAST CHILDREN COPE WITH POST-HURRICANE STRESS

When hurricanes slam into communities, the physical damage can be measured. What can't be measured is the toll such disasters take on children's sense of security and safety.

Years after Hurricane Katrina, children and teen-agers in New Orleans still face tremendous challenges—from attending schools in temporary locations to social pressures stemming from frequent moves, substandard housing and high crime and poverty rates.

Katrina was the catalyst for Save the Children to partner with the New Orleans Recovery School District to create school-based support programs for children in grades K–12. The result—the "Journey of Hope"—helps children cope with uncertainties, build their resiliency and strengthen their network of social support.

To date, over 48,000 children affected by Katrina and every major Gulf Cost hurricane since have completed grade-specific "Journey of Hope" programs.

Through site visits and interviews with children, teachers and school administrators, an independent evaluation of "Journey of Hope" in 2009 documented its significant success in helping children express their emotions, regain self-esteem and respect others.

"We had a lot of discipline behavior problems," said one high school principal. "Children experienced things they should not experience. They needed some sort of outlet.... Save the Children was able to really get at the kids' concerns in a way we could not reach them...."

Children notice the difference "Journey of Hope" has made in their lives as they deal with daily challenges in and out of school.

"I learned about helping each other," an 8-year-old girl said. "To take time out. To calm down. To let it go."

Source: Save the Children. http://www.savethechildren.org/emergencies/stories/journey-of-hope.html.

The following case study provides an illustration of a Journey of Hope project in its implementation.

CASE STUDY: New Orleans Students on a Journey of Hope

Since Hurricane Katrina struck the Gulf Coast, Save the Children has been responding to the needs of children and their caregivers in impacted communities. In 2008, we focused our Katrina recovery efforts on disaster recovery and resilience-building programs, which offered structured play activities designed to restore a sense of normalcy and strengthen children's coping skills, trust and self esteem.

Many of those affected by Katrina were uprooted by the storm. Children were forced to change schools, lost loved ones and experienced other disturbing or stressful events. Compounding their problems, many New Orleans children attending city schools experienced a rise in violence in their communities as well as drugs and fights at school since Katrina.

In the fall of 2006, a fight erupted in a New Orleans public elementary school affecting many students, staff and security guards. Save the Children partnered with the New Orleans Recovery School District to implement a structured play and resilience-building program addressing the challenges children were facing at the school. Seeing the positive effect of the program with these students, Save the Children created Adolescent

Journey of Hope (AJOH), and offered the program at other New Orleans schools.

Preet and Tara, two Save the Children staff members, were working in the school when they learned that two groups of boys participating in AJOH were threatening to hold a fight using weapons. Preet, Tara and the school counselor held an emergency session to help the boys talk through their disagreement. The successful session demonstrates how structured play programs like AJOH—which experts refer to as psychosocial programs—can empower children to confront and resolve the problems they face. Preet and Tara tell the story below:

The boys had divided into two groups, the "Blood Hounds" and the "Black Mafia." They said their fight would take place after an upcoming statewide test, and that it would involve guns and knives. We had started working with students at the school because of problems with fighting, and the last thing the school needed was another fight.

When we brought the boys together, we asked them to sit in a circle and discussed respect for one and other. We told them they all had the capacity to succeed, but were at a point in life when they could go either way and that we wanted them to meet their potential. We asked the boys why they were fighting.

The leader of the "Blood Hounds" began by telling his side of the story: he had heard the leader of the other group was saying he wanted to fight him, and that he felt he had to defend himself. There were also smaller disagreements between individuals: two boys from opposing sides were fighting over a girl; another two fought because the brother of the leader was trying to defend his sibling.

Before Hurricane Katrina, the boys said, they had all gotten along, but they had formed opposing groups after the storm, when their school was moved to the other side of town. As the conversation continued, they began to say it was "stupid" that were fighting, and to reminisce about how much fun they used to have when they were friends.

We asked the boys what they could do about the situation, and whether they thought miscommunication had led to their fights. One of the leaders eagerly chimed in that they should talk to each other directly before starting fights—rather than listening to rumors about what other boys had said about them. "That way we will know exactly what the other person said!" he added.

The other group members agreed. As the session closed, the leader of the "Blood Hounds" spoke up.

"Hey, why don't we sit together at lunch and see what everyone else in the school says?" he suggested. "They won't believe it! They will have no idea what's going on."

As we left, we thought about the transformation between the boys. The emergency session had helped them confront their differences head-on in a safe environment and empowered them to solve their problems without violence. We hoped that through the program, they would build trust in each other, strengthen their sense of safety and community, learn how to handle their anger and aggression, and raise their self-esteem.

Source: Save the Children. http://www.savethechildren.org/emergencies/us/us-gulf-coast-hurricanes/feature-AJOH.html.

Sometimes, meeting the psychosocial needs of affected children is as simple as returning their opportunities for play. Several NGOs in the aftermath of Katrina focused their efforts entirely on the recovery of parks and playgrounds, knowing that children have few other outlets to escape the reality of disasters that are frightening to them and expose their vulnerability (and that of their parents) in a way that is especially traumatic to the young. Playgrounds are, unfortunately, rarely seen as a priority of government, and therefore may stay in a state of disrepair or even in hazardous conditions, until long after other sectors have been addressed. However, as the Katrina experience has shown, the existence of outlets like parks and playgrounds can be the key to preventing or minimizing much greater impacts later on. The following case study illustrates a partnership that was developed between the NGO Save the Children and a local fire department to rebuild a playground that served especially hard-hit children in Mississippi.

CASE STUDY: New Playground for Children Displaced by Hurricane Katrina Opens In Mississippi

Long Beach, MS. (April 29, 2006)—Eight long months after Hurricane Katrina destroyed their hometown and school, the students of North Bay Elementary School in Bay Saint Louis, Miss., finally have a place to play.

Save the Children, working in partnership with the New Jersey Firefighters Mutual Benevolent Association (NJFMA), Mercy Corps and the school, have completed building one of the first fully accessible playgrounds in the state. Some 20 New Jersey firefighters traveled to Mississippi last week to undertake the construction project.

The playground project is the culmination of a long relationship between the New Jersey firefighters and North Bay Elementary. Following the tragic events of 9/11, the children and teachers at the school reached out to support the fire crews who played a major role in the response that day. The children sent notes of encouragement and thanks—as well as a handmade mailbox, which adorns the entrance of a firehouse in Elizabeth, NJ, today.

When Hurricane Katrina struck, the firefighters immediately moved to help children on the Gulf Coast, including the students at North Bay Elementary. They successfully raised more than $300,000 in support of Save the Children's Katrina after-school, child care and structured-activity programs that help children work through their traumatic experience.

"New Jersey's firefighters have been instrumental in helping children recover from Katrina. This playground will give the North Bay students a sense of normalcy," said Charles F. MacCormack, President and CEO of Save the Children. "Their school is a cluster of portable trailers located on a muddy field. When they go home—often to other trailers—at the end of the day, it is to streets and communities still full of debris. They have no safe place to play and to just be kids."

A recent visit by NJFMBA members to see Save the Children's Mississippi programs inspired the firefighters to give the children a chance to have some fun.

"We were blown away that people were still living in tents and children were going to school in trailers," said Bill Lavin, NJFMBA president. "But when we asked the children what they really needed, they all said a playground."

Bay Saint Louis was one of the communities hit hardest by Hurricane Katrina, and the elementary school was completely destroyed. Temporary trailers, set up on the grounds of the facility, serve as classrooms.

The NJFMBA is raising an additional $25,000 for this project, with Save the Children and Mercy Corps matching those funds.

Source: Save the Children. http://www.savethechildren.org/newsroom/2006/new-playground-for-children-in-mississippi.html.

National Disaster Recovery Framework

In 2010, FEMA began a process to establish a National Disaster Recovery Framework (NDRF) that would complement the National Response Framework (see Sidebar 6.8). FEMA's ongoing efforts are part of a White House Long Term Disaster Recovery Working Group established by the Obama administration to examine how the federal government should approach disaster recovery. This effort is being co-chaired by FEMA and the Department of Housing and Urban Development (HUD). It is anticipated that HUD will be requested to take on a more prominent role in recovery, especially because of continuing problems with the temporary housing program and with HUD's expertise in housing (see Sidebar 6.9). What is important about this framework is that it will ultimately form the structure within which all recovery, including that of children, is guided by all stakeholders—governmental, nongovernmental, business sector, individual, and otherwise.

SIDEBAR 6.8 NATIONAL DISASTER RECOVERY FRAMEWORK INITIATIVE

On August 27, 2009, FEMA Administrator Craig Fugate announced the establishment of a National Disaster Recovery Framework Working Group. Elizabeth Zimmerman, Assistant Administrator for Disaster Assistance, was appointed to lead the effort. The goal is to engage recovery stakeholders to create a comprehensive coordinating structure that will enhance our ability to work together and effectively deliver recovery assistance.

On September 29, 2009, President Obama announced an effort to examine lessons learned during previous catastrophic disaster recovery efforts, areas for improved collaboration between federal agencies and between the federal government and state and local governments and stakeholders. At the President's request, the Secretaries of Homeland Security and Housing and Urban Development are co-chairing a Long-Term Disaster Recovery Working Group composed of the Secretaries and Administrators of more than 20 departments, agencies and offices. This high-level, strategic initiative will provide operational guidance for recovery organizations as well as make suggestions for future improvement. An intensive stakeholder outreach effort during October and November, 2009, involving State, local, and tribal government representatives, as well as a wide array of private organizations and private non-profit organizations, will inform these efforts.

The National Disaster Recovery Framework Working Group is now co-chaired with HUD and comes under the umbrella of the White House's Long-Term Disaster Recovery Working Group effort. It will provide one of the two main outcomes of the effort. The other outcome is a Report to the President that will summarize the findings of the Working Group.

The National Disaster Recovery Framework will:

- Define the Federal, State, local, Tribal, private non-profit, private sector roles and individual citizen's roles in disaster recovery.
- Design and establish an effective coordinating structure for disaster recovery programs.
- Identify gaps, as well as, duplications, in recovery programs and funding.
- Establish performance standards for the Federal support of State and local recovery.

Desired Outcome:

Recovery programs and capabilities at all levels of government and in all sectors that function together harmoniously, supported by:

- A coordinating structure with defined roles and responsibilities.
- Clearly defined measures of success.
- A communications strategy designed to keep all stakeholders informed about the recovery arena.

Outcomes are subject to further refinement.

Approach:

- Merging efforts with the Long-Term Recovery Working Group, the team will engage Federal agency partners and State, Tribal, local governments, and nongovernmental organizations in a comprehensive collaborative review and shaping of the national approach to managing disaster recovery.
- Develop the Framework based on the stakeholders' perceptions of how recovery should be organized and managed.
- Include all stakeholders, particularly those representing traditionally underserved communities, such as children and adults with disabilities, low income, multi-cultural and rural communities.

Timeline:

- Phase I—Stakeholder Engagement and Concept Design by December 31, 2009.
- Phase II—Coordination and Publication by June 1, 2010.

Source: FEMA. *National Disaster Recovery Framework Initiative*. http://www.fema.gov/recoveryframework/.

SIDEBAR 6.9 DISASTER RECOVERY WORKING GROUP: STRENGTHENING DISASTER RECOVERY FOR THE NATION

Purpose Statement

Background

It is widely agreed that a greater focus is needed on disaster recovery issues—especially over the longer-term, after the response efforts are completed. Communities devastated by a disaster face complex challenges as they work to restore quality of life, rebuild infrastructure and public services, revitalize social services and networks, and reestablish economic viability, environmental sustainability and resilience against future hazards.

Statement of Intent

At the President's request, the Secretaries of Homeland Security (DHS) and Housing and Urban Development (HUD) are co-chairing a *White House Long-Term Disaster Recovery Working Group* composed of the Secretaries and Administrators of more than 20 departments, agencies and offices. This high-level, strategic initiative will provide operational guidance for recovery organizations as well as make suggestions for future improvement. An intensive stakeholder outreach effort during October and November, 2009, involving State, local, and Tribal government representatives, as well as a wide array of private organizations and private non-profit organizations, will inform these efforts.

Areas of Focus

Our goal is to ensure a more resilient Nation—one in which individuals, communities, and our economy can adapt to changing conditions as well as withstand and rapidly recover from disasters. In order to develop a better national strategy for an effective approach to long-term disaster recovery, the Working Group on Long-Term Disaster Recovery will:

- Provide operational guidance for Federal, State, Tribal and local authorities to provide for unified, and effective disaster recovery. This includes defining roles and responsibilities, detailing recovery management and operational coordination, articulating communications strategies and establishing measurements for success;
- Review disaster recovery programs and the framework of disaster recovery, and identify gaps as well as overlapping and/or conflicting sources of authority for disaster recovery efforts;
- Examine areas for improved interagency planning and collaboration among Federal agencies;
- Examine methods to build capacity within State, local and Tribal governments as well as within the nonprofit,

faith-based, and private sectors; both in recovery operations and in pre-disaster recovery planning; and
- Examine successful practices and Lessons Learned during previous disaster recovery efforts, with particular attention to catastrophic disasters such as Hurricanes Katrina and Rita.

The Secretaries will provide the President with recommendations to improve long-term catastrophic disaster recovery and will help develop a *National Disaster Recovery Framework* that provides more detailed operational guidance to recovery organizations under existing authorities.

Participation

The Working Group is taking a bottom's up approach to implementing this important national initiative and there are multiple opportunities for stakeholder participation.

An intensive stakeholder outreach effort is now underway to solicit input from a broad range of recovery stakeholders. To ensure broad representation, input is solicited from Federal, State, Tribal and community leadership; policy- and decision-makers; public and private recovery partners and practitioners; nonprofits; disaster recovery stakeholders and citizens. Participants are asked to identify their existing perceptions of disaster recovery; articulate what they think recovery assistance should look like going forward; identify best practice examples; raise challenges and obstacles to success; and share their thoughts, experiences and Lessons Learned.

A series of Ten (10) Regional Video Teleconferences hosted by HUD and FEMA Regional Offices have just completed. Five (5) Stakeholder Forums sponsored in partnership with select States and local communities are now being organized across the nation. Both series of events provide an opportunity for participants to discuss disaster recovery management issues and opportunities—a discussion that will help shape two important products:

- The *White House Working Group Report to the President*, which will identify opportunities for improving the delivery of recovery assistance in the future and,
- The *National Disaster Recovery Framework*, which will provide guidance for the delivery of recovery assistance using current resources and authorities.

To facilitate further stakeholder input, DHS/FEMA and HUD have also developed the www.DisasterRecoveryWorkingGroup.gov Web site. Recovery stakeholders are invited to submit written input and see updates and information regarding this important national initiative.

Schedule

The *Report to the President* is scheduled for delivery the first of April 2010. A DRAFT of the *National Disaster Recovery Framework* is anticipated for comment first quarter of 2010 with a final publication date scheduled for June 1, 2010.

Source: Disaster Recovery Working Group. http://disasterrecoveryworking-group.gov/purpose-statement.cfm.

Conclusion

The word *crisis* takes its root from the Latin term signifying a turning point. It is during the recovery period where the crisis shifts most profoundly from the general population to those groups that are most vulnerable. While some groups may come out of the emergency phase relatively unscathed, children have physical and emotional weaknesses that require a concerted, long-term effort to address. Therefore, the recovery phase becomes a critical period in the affected child's life wherein his or her needs must be immediately and adequately addressed. However, elected officials and career officials in state and local government, and in the emergency management community, are (as a group) not yet taking a uniform, concerted effort to address the disaster-related needs of children either prior to or in the aftermath of a disaster. Despite that organizations such as the American National Commission on Children and Disasters have each taken great strides to assess and highlight the problems with the existing legislation, rules, and regulations, little has been done to formalize their proposed changes. Each and every one of these obstacles can be overcome with the introduction of simple policy changes at the federal level that mandate consideration of the unique and critical disaster recovery needs of the very vulnerable children population. At a minimum, the authors recommend that such changes be adopted by the federal government, state government, and local communities as they consider their disaster recovery planning. There are five actions that could be taken that would dramatically improve recovery for our community's children:

- Designate child care facilities as an eligible essential function under the Robert T. Stafford Act
- Establish flexible rules and programs for the provision of temporary disaster housing that would promote families staying together and within their own communities
- Make restoration of community infrastructure that supports children a top priority, including rebuilding of schools, public transit systems, etc.
- Provide enhanced mental health services to children and caregivers in communities impacted by a disaster
- Support research on children's disaster issues

References

Children's Defense Fund. 2007. *Katrina's children: Still waiting.* http://www.childrensdefense.org/child-research-data-publications/data/katrinas-children-still-waiting-hurricane-2007.pdf.

Disaster Recovery Working Group. http://disasterrecoveryworkinggroup.gov/purpose-statement.cfm.

FEMA. *National Disaster Recovery Framework Initiative.* http://www.fema.gov/recoveryframework/.

Mississippi State University Early Childhood Institute. 2006a. *After Katrina: Rebuilding Mississippi's early childhood infrastructure; the first six months.* Mississippi State University Early Childhood Report 1. Mississippi State University.

Mississippi State University Early Childhood Institute. 2006b. *The first year: Child care restoration in Mississippi's Katrina region.* Mississippi State University Early Childhood Report 3. Mississippi State University.

Ms. Foundation for Women. http://www.ms.foundation.org/wmspage.cfm?parm1=475.

National Commission on Children and Disasters. 2009. Interim report. October 14. http://www.childrenanddisasters.acf.hhs.gov/20091014_508IR_partII.pdf.

New Mexico Children, Youth, and Families, Department of Protective Services. *All-hazard emergency response plan.*

Project Rebuild Plaquemines. http://www.projectrebuildplaquemines.org/.

Save the Children. 2007. *Child care: An essential service of disaster recovery.* Issue brief. June. http://www.savethechildren.org/publications/issue-briefs/issue brief3_07.pdf.

Save the Children. 2008. *Protecting children in US emergencies.* August. http://www.savethechildren.org/publications/reports/Disaster-Preps-Issue-Brief-Final-1.pdf.

Save the Children. *Emergency childcare in Mississippi gets parents back to work.* http://www.savethechildren.org/emergencies/us/us-gulf-coast-hurricanes/emergency-child-care-in-mississippi-gets-parents-back-to-work.html.

Save the Children. *Hurricane recovery fact sheet.* http://www.savethechildren.org/emergencies/us/us-gulf-coast-hurricanes/.

Save the Children. http://www.savethechildren.org/emergencies/us/us-gulf-coast-hurricanes/feature-AJOH.html.

Save the Children. http://www.savethechildren.org/emergencies/stories/journey-of-hope.html.

Save the Children. http://www.savethechildren.org/newsroom/2006/new-playground-for-children-in-mississippi.html.

Save the Children. http://www.savethechildren.org/publications/reports/Disaster-Preps-Issue-Brief-Final-1.pdf.

U.S. Department of Health and Human Services, Substance Abuse and Mental Health Services Association (SAMHSA), National Mental Health Information Center. *How families can help children cope with fear and anxiety.* http://mentalhealth.samhsa.gov/publications/allpubs/Ca-0022/.

Chapter 7

Emergency Management Resources Focused on Children's Needs

The emergency manager, planner, administrator, parent, or other individual charged with planning for or responding to the unique needs of children can benefit greatly from the existing material that has been developed to guide their efforts. Owing to the diversity of both the stakeholders involved in meeting children's needs and the target audience of these publications, there is a wide range of fact sheets, guides, primers, courses, training materials, reports, and more. In most cases, there is no need to reinvent the wheel, as so much time and effort has already been dedicated to meeting these unique needs on the scale of a university, a community, a hospital, or a particular disaster response, for example. As such, this chapter is provided to present an exhaustive list of academic, professional, case study, and other resources that may be used in the planning for and meeting the unique needs of children in disasters.

This chapter is organized into the following sections:

- Emergency planning
- Sample plans
- Psychosocial recovery

- Training and education courses and materials
- Technical assistance
- Reports
- Organizations
- Web links

Emergency Planning

Emergency planning resources are those that can be used to guide the actual emergency planning process. These resources have a range of target audiences, including government emergency planners, pediatricians, hospitals, child care providers, educators, and parents.

- Agency for Healthcare Research and Quality. 2006. *Pediatric Terrorism and Disaster Preparedness: A Resource for Pediatricians*. http://www.ahrq.gov/research/pedprep/.

  Practical resources that pediatricians can consult in planning for and responding to natural disasters and bioterrorist events.

- American Academy of Pediatrics. 2010. *Disaster Preparedness and Pediatric Preparedness: An Online Tool*. http://practice.aap.org/disasterpreptool.aspx.

  An interactive Web-based tool developed by the AAP Disaster Preparedness Advisory Council that provides an easy way for members to review resources and take steps to develop a written disaster preparedness plan for their office practices.

- American Red Cross. n.d. *Your Evacuation Plan: Evacuation Planning for Persons with Disabilities and Caregivers*. http://www.redcross.org/preparedness/cdc_english/evac_dis-3.html.

  Online fact sheet to guide the evacuation planning process.

- The Center for Effective Collaboration and Practice. 1998. *Safe Schools Guide*. http://www.naccrra.org/for_parents/traumatic-events/docs/safe_schools_guide.pdf.

This guide presents a brief summary of the research on violence prevention and intervention and crisis response in schools. It tells communities what to look for and what to do.

- Columbia University Mailman School of Public Health. 2010. *Pediatric Preparedness.* http://www.ncdp.mailman.columbia.edu/program_pediatric.htm.

  Website providing a range of preparedness information focused on children, including model wording for state emergency plans.

- Department of Education. 2007. *Practical Information on Crisis Planning: A Guide for Schools and Communities.* http://www2.ed.gov/admins/lead/safety/emergencyplan/crisisplanning.pdf.

  The guide is intended to give schools, districts, and communities the critical concepts and components of good crisis planning, stimulate thinking about the crisis preparedness process, and provide examples of promising practices.

- Federal Emergency Management Agency. 2009. *Developing and Maintaining State, Territorial, Tribal, and Local Government Emergency Plans (CPG101).* http://www.fema.gov/pdf/about/divisions/npd/cpg_101_layout.pdf.

  FEMA's official guidance on the development of emergency operations plans. This document only makes one reference to children, but its influence on the planning process is unparalleled.

- FEMA. n.d. *Are You Ready? An In-Depth Guide to Citizen Preparedness.* http://www.fema.gov/areyouready/.

  FEMA's public preparedness guidebook.

- FEMA. n.d. *How Schools Can Become More Disaster Resistant.* http://www.fema.gov/kids/schdizr.htm.

  Website that explains the hazard risk management process to school administrators.

- HHS. 2009. *School-Based Emergency Preparedness: A National Analysis and Recommended Protocol.* http://www.ahrq.gov/prep/schoolprep/schoolprep.pdf.

  This report is an analysis of emergency response plans from school districts in Massachusetts, Florida, Wisconsin, Colorado, and California. Using the findings in conjunction with existing recommendations on the development of school-based preparedness programs, the authors developed a template that provides an overview, including best practices for school districts to use in their development of a comprehensive emergency response plan.

- NACCRRA. 2006. *Is Child Care Ready? A Disaster Planning Guide for Child Care Resource and Referral Agencies.* http://www.naccrra.org/disaster/docs/Disaster_Guide_MECH.pdf.

  A guide designed specifically for use by child care resource and referral agencies in training child care providers both in center-based and family child care. The guide is designed to ensure that child care programs are prepared to respond to disasters and to continue to serve the children and families that need child care.

- NACCRRA. Emergency Planning Forms. http://www.naccrra.org/disaster/docs/Disaster_Forms.doc.

  User-friendly forms that offer templates for child care providers and others to use to fully prepare for disasters.

- NCTSN. n.d. *The 3 Rs of School Crises and Disasters: Readiness, Response, and Recovery.* http://www.nctsnet.org/nccts/nav.do?pid=ctr_aud_schl_3rs_desc.

- Needle, Scott. n.d. *A Disaster Preparedness Plan for Pediatricians.* http://www.aap.org/disasters/pdf/DisasterPrepPlanforPeds.pdf.

  A technical guide that facilitates the disaster planning process for pediatric professionals.

- Save the Children. 2007. *The Unique Needs of Children in Emergencies: A Guide for the Inclusion of Children in Emergency Operations Plans.* http://www.savethechildren.org/publications/emergencies/Children-in-Emergencies-Planning-Guide.pdf.

  Guide to assist emergency management agencies in including the needs of children in their standard emergency operations plans.

- Source Forge. n.d. *Special Population Planner.* http://sourceforge.net/projects/spc-pop-planner/.

  A free downloadable GIS-based emergency planning tool for all-hazards analysis. It is tailored for planning for the needs of persons with special needs, but can be easily adapted to other uses. It runs within ESRI ArcGIS 9.x software.

- UCLA Center for Public Health and Disasters. n.d. *Head Start Disaster Preparedness Workbook.* http://www.cphd.ucla.edu/headstartwb.html.

  An eight-part workbook with information, tools, and activities to assist programs in disaster planning and preparedness.

- U.S. Department of Education. 2006. *Helpful Hints for School Emergency Management.* http://www.ed.gov/about/offices/list/osdfs/gokits.pdf.

  Checklist to help schools create an emergency "go kit."

Sample Plans

The following resource is provided to illustrate how a community has successfully incorporated the unique needs of children into its preparedness, mitigation, response, and recovery operations:

- County of Tulsa. n.d. *Tulsa County Emergency Operations Plan: Annex G—Children's Emergency Response Plan.* http://www.ccrctulsa.org/pdfs/childrenresponse.pdf.

Psychosocial Recovery

One of the greatest needs of children that fall victim to disasters is protection of their psychosocial health. Their underdeveloped ability to comprehend what is happening, coupled with their sense of dependence, makes even smaller disasters terribly traumatic. There has long been a focus on planning for and addressing the psychosocial needs of children, but this issue continues to evolve in practice. The following resources address psychosocial protection of children from a number of vantage points.

- American Academy of Pediatrics. 1994. *Psychological Issues for Children and Families in Disasters: A Guide for the Primary Care Physicians.* http://mentalhealth.samhsa.gov/publications/allpubs/SMA95-3022/default.asp.

  The focus of this manual is on how the child health care provider may better prepare, assess, and treat youngsters and their families in the event of a disaster. As a recognized leader in a community, the physician also may be called upon to address community needs in case of such events. This manual also will aid the physician in assuming this role.

- American Association of Pediatrics. 2009. *Guidelines for Care of Children in the Emergency Department.* http://www.aap.org/visit/Checklist_ED_Prep-022210.pdf.

  Checklist that ascribes different recommended disaster-related tasks to different individuals, which can be used to assess preparedness of the emergency room to handle the needs of children in major emergencies and disasters.

- American Association of Pediatrics. n.d. *Infant Nutrition during a Disaster: Breastfeeding and Other Options.* http://www.aap.org/breastfeeding/files/pdf/InfantNutritionDisaster.pdf.

  Fact sheet with basic information, action steps, and decision analysis to support families with infants during a disaster.

- CDC. 2007. *Maintain a Healthy State of Mind.* http://emergency.cdc.gov/preparedness/mind/.

Online fact sheet providing information about helping children deal with the psychosocial impacts of disasters, including terrorism. Provides common reactions exhibited by different groups, including children of different ages. Developed in partnership with the American Red Cross.

- CDC. 2008. *Coping with Depression and Thoughts of Suicide after a Disaster.* http://emergency.cdc.gov/disasters/psa/suicide.asp.

  Series of PSAs geared at preventing postdisaster depression among various groups, including children.

- CDC. 2009. *Coping with Traumatic Events.* http://www2c.cdc.gov/podcasts/player.asp?f=303306.

  Podcast on managing reactions to disaster-related stress.

- CDC. 2009. *Preventing Violence after a Natural Disaster.* http://emergency.cdc.gov/disasters/violence.asp.

  Website providing information on the prevention of post-disaster child abuse and other violence children face due to the increased stress of a disaster.

- CDC. n.d. *Helping Parents Cope with Disaster.* http://emergency.cdc.gov/mentalhealth/pdf/Helping-Parents-Cope-with-Disaster.pdf.

  Provides information for parents dealing with the stress of raising a family in the midst of disaster response and recovery.

- CDC. n.d. *Helping Parents Prepare for Disaster.* http://emergency.cdc.gov/mentalhealth/pdf/Helping-Parents-Prepare-for-Disasters-Final.pdf.

  Fact sheet describing the steps involved in making a family disaster plan and making a disaster kit.

- Centers for Disease Control and Prevention. 2009. *Coping with a Traumatic Event.* http://emergency.cdc.gov/masscasualties/copingpub.asp.

Public information resource that gives basic details about posttraumatic stress disorder.

- The Child Trauma Academy. 2002. *Helping Traumatized Children: A Brief Overview for Caregivers.* http://www.naccrra.org/docs/emergency/Helping_Traumatized_Children-Brief_Overview.pdf.

  This booklet addresses some of the key issues related to the child's complex set of reactions that often follow traumatic events. While focused on caregivers, this information may be helpful to caseworkers, teachers, other family, and other adults working and living with traumatized children. This simple guide is intended to inform and provide general principles.

- Cincinnati Children's Hospital. n.d. *Listen, Protect, and Connect: Psychological First Aid for Children, Parents, and Other Caregivers after Natural Disasters.* http://www.cincinnatichildrens.org/svc/alpha/s/school-crisis/psych-aid.htm.

  Psychological first aid brochure.

- County of Ventura. 2010. *Special Needs Children and Disasters.* http://portal.countyofventura.org/portal/page/portal/HCA/PUBLICHEALTH/DISEASECONTROL/EMERGENCYPREPAREDNESS/Special%20Needs%20Children%20and%20Disasters.

  Website with key planning tasks in bullet form.

- Ehrenreich, J. H. 2001. *Coping with Disasters: A Guidebook to Psychosocial Intervention.* http://www.mhwwb.org/CopingWithDisaster.pdf.

  Provides practical knowledge about managing disaster psychosocial needs for a number of vulnerable groups, including children.

- FEMA. 2004. *Helping Children Cope with Disasters.* Publication FEMA 478. http://www.fema.gov/pdf/library/children.pdf.

This booklet offers parents, caregivers, and other adults suggestions on how to help children cope with the effects of disaster, as well as how to be prepared before a disaster strikes.

- Florida EMSC. 2004. *Hospital Pediatric Equipment Inventories for Disaster Response.* http://www.childrensnational.org/files/PDF/DepartmentsandPrograms/CHAI/EMSC/products/Hospital_Pediatric_Equipment_Inventories_for_Disaster_Respon.pdf.

  Describes the different equipment and supplies that would be needed to manage the medical needs of children affected by disasters.

- Goodman, R. n.d. *Talking to Kids about Terrorism and Acts of War.* NYU Child Study Center. http://www.aboutourkids.org/articles/talking_kids_about_terrorism_or_acts_war.

  Fact sheet providing information to anyone charged with the care of a child exposed to terrorism, either directly or indirectly.

- Gurian, A. n.d. *Talking to Kids about Disasters.* NYU Child Study Center. http://www.aboutourkids.org/articles/talking_kids_about_disasters.

  Fact sheet provided for caregivers of children affected by disaster.

- Gurian, A. n.d. *Talking to Kids about World Natural Disasters.* NYU Child Study Center. http://www.aboutourkids.org/articles/talking_kids_about_world_natural_disasters.

  Fact sheet provided for caregivers of children affected by disaster.

- Gurian, A., et al. n.d. *Helping Children and Teens Cope with Traumatic Events and Death: The Role of School Health Professionals.* NYU Child Study Center. http://www.aboutourkids.org/articles/helping_children_teens_cope_traumatic_events_death_role_school_health_professionals.

Psychosocial fact sheet provided for school health professionals who may interact with disaster-affected children.

- Gurian, A., et al. n.d. *Helping Children with Developmental Disabilities Cope with Traumatic Events and Death: The Role of School Health Professionals.* NYU Child Study Center. http://www.aboutourkids.org/articles/helping_children_developmental_disabilities_cope_traumatic_events.

  Fact sheet provided for teachers of children with developmental difficulties affected by disaster.

- HHS. 2002. *How Families Can Cope with Fear and Anxiety.* http://mentalhealth.samhsa.gov/publications/allpubs/Ca-0022/.

  Information to help families talk about, and deal with, the psychosocial impacts of disasters on children.

- HHS. 2005. *Helping Families Deal with the Stress of Relocation after a Disaster.* http://www.atsdr.cdc.gov/publications/100233-RelocationStress.pdf.

  This handout gives information and tips that explain basic information about stress, signs of and ways to help family members deal with relocation stress, signs of stress in young people of different age groups (preschool to high school age), ways to help young people deal with stress (preschool to high school age), how to help the elderly deal with relocation stress, and where to find further information on these topics.

- HHS. 2005. *Tips for Talking to Children in Trauma: Interventions at Home for Preschoolers to Adolescents.* http://mentalhealth.samhsa.gov/publications/allpubs/tips/intervention.pdf.

  Fact sheet providing parents of young children with information they need to help their children deal with the psychosocial impacts of disasters.

- HHS. n.d. *Helping Children and Adolescents Cope with Violence and Disasters: What Parents Can Do.* http://www.aap.org/disasters/pdf/helping-children-and-adolescents.pdf.

Checklists for parents on coping with trauma and information on helping their children.

- HHS. n.d. *Helping Children and Adolescents Cope with Violence and Disasters: What Rescue Workers Can Do.* http://www.nimh.nih.gov/health/publications/helping-children-and-adolescents-cope-with-violence-and-disasters-rescue-workers/helping-children-and-adolescents-cope-with-violence-and-disasters-what-rescue-workers-can-do.pdf.

  Provides information to help first responders respond to the needs of children in an emergency.

- HHS. n.d. *Marking Disaster Anniversaries in the Classroom.* http://mentalhealth.samhsa.gov/cmhs/EmergencyServices/oneyear.asp.

  Fact sheet prepared as a resource to help children deal with normal recovery issues that may be triggered by the anniversary of a disaster. The activities suggested help teachers anticipate and address issues that may emerge. It can be adapted for use with any disaster and can be used any time from the first day following the disaster to one or more years later.

- HHS. n.d. *Questions to Help Children Talk about a Disaster.* http://mentalhealth.samhsa.gov/cmhs/EmergencyServices/questions.asp.

  Short fact sheet to help educators manage the psychosocial reactions of children exposed to disasters.

- HHS. n.d. *What's Going on in the Mind of a Child Who's Lived through a Hurricane.* http://download.ncadi.samhsa.gov/ken/Disasterrelief/ZGRY6848.wmv.

  One component of a PSA campaign designed to help children who have been impacted by hurricanes and are in need of mental health services.

- HHS. n.d. *When Talking Doesn't Help: Other Ways to Help Children Express Their Feelings Following a Disaster.* http://mentalhealth.samhsa.gov/cmhs/EmergencyServices/other ways.asp.

Website that provides alternatives to traditional discussion-based psychosocial therapy.

- Mercy Corps. 2005. *What Happened to My World.* http://www.mercycorps.org/publications/11846.

  Intended to help parents, and all those who work with families and children, during times of natural disaster to cope with the stresses and other psychosocial problems that occur.

- NACCRRA. 2005. *Nurturing Children after Natural Disasters: A Book for Child Care Providers.* http://www.naccrra.org/docs/pubs/Disasters_10131.pdf.

  Provides basic disaster preparation information, as well as specific guidance on helping children cope with the aftermath of natural disasters.

- NACCRRA. n.d. *Helping Children Cope with Fear and Anxiety.* http://www.naccrra.org/for_parents/traumatic-events/ docs/FearandAnxiety5-02.pdf.

  One-page fact sheet with simple tips for caregivers.

- National Association of School Psychologists. 2003. *Helping Children after a Natural Disaster: Information for Parents and Teachers.* http://www.nasponline.org/resources/crisis_safety/naturaldisaster_ho.pdf.

  A short informational guide for parents and teachers to explain the need for, and steps required in, conducting postdisaster child counseling.

- The National Child Traumatic Stress Network. 2005. *After a Disaster: Helping Young Children Heal.* http://main.zerotothree.org/site/DocServer/NCTSN_Disaster_Guidelines.pdf?docID=2162&AddInterest=1142.

  One-page fact sheet with a checklist of suggested actions.

- The National Child Traumatic Stress Network. n.d. *Building Community Resilience for Communities and Nature.* http://www.nctsnet.org/nctsn_assets/pdfs/edu_materials/BuildingCommunity_FINAL_02-12-07.pdf.

This guidebook provides information about building community resilience, helping communities improve their capacity to respond effectively to natural or man-made disasters or acts of terrorism. To be most effective, community plans must address the emotional well-being of residents, including children. Putting strategies in place before an incident occurs enhances the community's ability to improve its outcomes after an event.

- National Mental Health America. 2010. *Helping Children Handle Disaster Related Anxiety.* http://www.nmha.org/index.cfm?objectid=e2a880ae-1372-4d20-c886e4e4aa69eea1.

  Fact sheet for parents on postdisaster stress in children.

- NYU Child Study Center. n.d. *Posttraumatic Stress Disorder.* http://www.aboutourkids.org/families/disorders_treatments/az_disorder_guide/posttraumatic_stress_disorder.

  Online course to provide information about the psychosocial impacts of disasters on children.

Training and Education Courses and Materials

The following resources link to or provide information to educate various audiences (either caregivers or the children themselves) about disasters, their impacts, and the things that can be done to prepare for and respond to them.

- American Academy of Pediatrics. *Calendar of Disaster Preparedness Events.* http://www.aap.org/disasters/events.cfm.

  List of conferences and training courses and events that focus on children in disasters.

- American Association of Pediatricians. n.d. *Caring for Your Family.* http://www.aap.org/family/frk/aapfrk1.pdf.

  Handout that includes a general overview of how families can prepare for disasters.

- American Bar Association. 2007. *Help in Child Welfare: Legal and Judicial System Responses to Children and Families Affected by Disasters.* http://www.abanet.org/child/disasters.pdf.

  Describes the ABA responses in 2005 and 2006 centered around three areas of assistance: (1) determining and helping meet the more immediate needs of dependency courts and child welfare legal offices in the hurricane-affected areas, (2) helping serve the legal needs of Katrina-affected children and families through provision of pro bono child welfare law experts, and (3) studying child welfare legal issues affecting children and families in Katrina-like disasters, including needed state and federal legislative responses.

- American Medical Association. 2010. *Basic Disaster Life Support Course.* http://www.ama-assn.org/ama/no-index/physician-resources/12618.shtml.

  Direct delivery course that addresses the health care professional's role in public health and incident management systems, community mental health, and special needs of vulnerable populations (including children).

- American Red Cross. 2010. *Masters of Disaster.* http://www.redcross.org/disaster/masters/.

  The American Red Cross *Masters of Disaster*® curriculum is centered on a series of ready-to-go lesson plans that help organizations educate youth about important disaster safety and preparedness information. *Masters of Disaster* contains lessons, activities, and demonstrations on disaster-related topics that organizations can incorporate into daily or thematic programming. The curriculum is nonsequential, allowing organizers to choose the lesson plans that best fit into their programming. The *Masters of Disaster* curriculum materials meet national educational standards and are specifically tailored for lower elementary (K–2), upper elementary (3–5), and middle school (6–8) classes.

- American Red Cross. 2010. *Preparing and Getting Trained: Children.* http://www.redcross.org/portal/site/en/menuitem.d8aaecf214c576bf971e4cfe43181aa0/?vgnextoid=e4a20c45f663b110VgnVCM10000089f0870aRCRD&vgnextfmt=def.

  Short website explaining the training and informational needs of children.

- American Red Cross. *Disaster Preparation Training.*http://www.redcross.org/services/prepare/0,1082,0_239_, 00.html.

- California Office of Emergency Services. *Be Smart, Be Prepared, Be Responsible! Coloring Book.* http://www.oes.ca.gov/Operational/OESHome.nsf/PDF/Be%20Smart%20Coloring%20Book/$file/ColorBk.pdf.

  Coloring book that provides children with basic disaster preparedness information.

- Children's Hospital Los Angeles Pediatric Disorder Resource and Training Center. n.d. http://www.chladisastercenter.org/site/c.ntJYJ6MLIsE/b.3569237/k.DEF0/Education__Training.htm.

  Website that provides training, resources, and new models of virtual linkages with health care centers throughout Los Angeles County.

- Children's National Medical Center. n.d. *Pediatric Disaster Web Based Training Program.* http://uat.dcchildrens.com/chexwizarding/pediatricdisasterwbtprogram_b/index.html.

  Online course that provides information to prepare for and respond to incidents or disasters involving children. This program offers continuing education credits upon completion of the course and posttest.

- Cincinnati Children's Hospital Medical Center. n.d. *Emergency, Safety, and Disaster Planning.* http://www.cincinnatichildrens.org/svc/alpha/c/special-needs/resources/emergencies.htm.

Includes a series of informational sheets on the following topics: emergency information forms, emergency plan, supply kit, child alarms and locators, and child identification products.

- Department of Homeland Security. n.d. *Ready Kids*. http://www.ready.gov/.

  Disaster planning website aimed at children.

- FEMA. 2009. *Student Tools for Emergency Preparedness (STEP).* http://www.nedrix.com/presentation/0309/STEP%20One%20Page.pdf.

  A fact sheet describing a preparedness education project supported by New England state emergency management. In this program, students at the fourth grade level are taught strategies for dealing with various types of emergencies and to act as “agents” to share this awareness with family members.

- FEMA. n.d. *Disaster Coloring Book*. http://www.fema.gov/kids/games/colorbk/original_color.htm.

  One of the first disaster preparedness coloring books for children, available for download.

- FEMA. n.d. FEMA for Kids website. http://www.fema.gov/kids/.

  Website aimed at training children in disaster preparedness basics.

- FEMA. n.d. Freebies for Disaster Action Kids. http://www.fema.gov/kids/freebie.htm.

  Website with information on ordering free educational resources on disasters for children.

- FEMA Emergency Management Institute. 2009. *EMI School Program*. http://training.fema.gov/emiweb/emischool/.

  Offers school officials courses supporting the implementation of NIMS as well as general courses aimed at building school emergency management capacity.

- FEMA Emergency Management Institute. n.d. *Interactive Web-Based Course: IS-362 Multi-Hazard Emergency Planning for Schools.* http://www.training.fema.gov/EMIWeb/IS/is3 62.asp.

  Independent study course that provides information on making a school emergency plan.

- FloridaDisaster.Org. n.d. Kids Get a Plan website. http://www.kidsgetaplan.com/.

  Interactive website that helps children learn about disaster planning.

- HHS. n.d. *Decontamination of Children.* http://www.ahrq.gov/research/decontam.htm.

  A twenty-seven-minute video that demonstrates for emergency responders and hospital emergency department staff how to safely decontaminate children who have been exposed to hazardous chemicals, including those from a bioterrorist attack.

- NACCRRA. n.d. *Disaster Preparation: A Training for Child Care Centers.* http://www.naccrra.org/disaster/docs/disaster_prep_ccc.pdf.

  A guide designed to help those responsible for training child care centers on disaster preparedness. It includes specific activities for training individuals who direct and work in child care centers.

- NACCRRA. n.d. *Disaster Preparation: A Training for Family Child Care Providers.* http://www.naccrra.org/disaster/docs/naccrra_fc_081506.pdf.

  A guide intended to assist those training family child care providers on disaster preparedness. It includes activities for training individuals who care for children in their homes.

- NACCRRA. n.d. *What's the Plan? Ask Your Child Care Provider before a Disaster.* http://www.naccrra.org/disaster/docs/ParentBroch.pdf.

One of the most important questions for all parents to consider and ask their child care program is: "What kind of emergency preparedness plan do you have in place?" To help parents ensure the safety and well-being of their children, this colorful brochure walks them through ten questions they should ask about the what, when, where, and how of their provider's disaster plan.

- Plan UK. 2007. *Indonesian Children's View on Disaster Risk Reduction*. http://www.childreninachangingclimate.org/docs/PLAN%20Booklet_Eng.pdf.

  Research on the relationship between risks, gender, and religion in child-centered disaster risk reduction.

- University of Illinois Extension. n.d. *Children, Stress, and Natural Disasters: A Guide for Teachers*. http://web.extension.uiuc.edu/disaster/teacher2/guide.html.

  A guide to inform teachers on how natural disasters can affect children's behavior and performance in the classroom, and what teachers can do to help children cope.

- U.S. Department of Education. n.d. *Readiness and Emergency Management for Schools*. http://rems.ed.gov/index.php?page=trainings.

  The U.S. Department of Education's Office of Safe and Drug-Free Schools (OSDFS) Readiness and Emergency Management for Schools (REMS) Technical Assistance (TA) Center conducts two trainings annually for grantees. The initial training introduces the National Incident Management System (NIMS) and focuses on the four phases of emergency management.

Technical Assistance

This section includes resources that are more programmatic in nature, or that provide more detailed or comprehensive technical assistance to those charged with meeting the unique needs of children affected by disasters.

- American Academy of Pediatrics. 2005. *Clinician Recommendations Regarding the Return of Children to Areas Impacted by Flooding and/or Hurricanes.* http://www.aap.org/disasters/pdf/Hurricanes-ReturnofChildren.pdf.

  Checklist that helps those charged with the care of children determine whether it is appropriate to return children to their former homes in the aftermath of the disaster.

- American Academy of Pediatrics. 2007. *Prehospital Preparedness for Pediatric Mass-Casualty Events.* http://pediatrics.aappublications.org/cgi/content/full/120/4/e756.

  Documents the preparedness of prehospital emergency medical services agencies in the United States for the care of children who are involved in mass-casualty events.

- American Academy of Pediatrics. n.d. *Pediatric First Aid for Caregivers and Teachers—The Book.* http://www.pedfactsonline.com/Thebook.cfm.

  Information on what teachers and caregivers need to do when a child is injured or ill.

- American Academy of Pediatrics. *Children and Disasters.* http://www.aap.org/disasters/schools.cfm.

  Provides links to a number of resources that help parents and other caregivers plan and prepare for the needs of children in disasters.

- American Red Cross. 2006. *Talking about Disasters: A Guide for Standard Messaging.* http://www.redcross.org/disaster/disasterguide/.

  Created to assist those who provide disaster safety information to the general public, including children.

- American Red Cross. Disaster preparedness materials. https://americanredcross.com/pubs/dspubs/genprep.html.

- Bhawan, V. 2009. *Child Protection in Emergency. Save the Children.* http://nidm.gov.in/idmc2/PDF/Presentations/Children_ Disasters/Pres1.pdf.

Series of presentation slides describing the role of Save the Children in international disaster response, notably their role regarding the protection of disaster-impacted children. This presentation provides guidance to emergency planners.

- California Department of Education. n.d. *Crisis Response Box: A Guide to Help Every School Assemble the Tools and Resources Needed for a Critical Incident Response.* http://www.cde.ca.gov/ls/ss/cp/documents/crisisrespbox.pdf.

  A guide to assist schools in crisis prevention planning.

- Church World Service Emergency Response Program. Disaster Recovery Help. http://www.disasterrecoveryhelp.org.

- Discovery Education. n.d. Ready Classroom. http://readyclassroom.discoveryeducation.com/.

  Emergency preparedness resources that can be used by teachers and families to help children adequately prepare for disasters.

- Federal Emergency Management Agency. 2003. *Mitigation Planning How-To Guide.* http://www.fema.gov/library/viewRecord.do?id=1867.

  This is a series of guides that discuss the activities and issues involved in performing community- and state-based mitigation planning. This is a practical guide that gives detailed step-by-step instructions.

- Federal Emergency Management Agency. n.d. Resources for parents and teachers. http://www.fema.gov/kids/teacher.htm and http://www.fema.gov/kids/tch_diz.htm.

  Offers a number of printable and downloadable disaster education materials for teachers and parents. The second site offers links to other organizations' resource pages.

- FEMA. 2009. *Planning for the Needs of Children in Disasters.* FEMA L 366.

Sample emergency operations plans.

- HHS. n.d. *Child Care Resources for Disasters and Emergencies.* http://nccic.acf.hhs.gov/emergency/index.cfm.

  List of key links that bring together information and key resources for emergency preparedness, disaster response, and recovery that relate specifically to child care.

- HHS. n.d. *Disaster Alternate Care Facilities: Report and Interactive Tools.* http://www.ahrq.gov/prep/acfselection/dacfrep.htm.

  Report and related interactive computer tools that help institutions and communities select alternate care facilities and determine which patients to send to them.

- India Disaster Management Congress. 2009. Children and disasters theme. http://nidm.gov.in/idmc2/pres_children.asp.

  Various slide shows presented at the Second India Disaster Management Congress.

- Kumar, M. B. 2009. *Child Care and Protection in Disasters.* National Institute of Public Cooperation and Child Development. http://nidm.gov.in/idmc2/PDF/Presentations/Children_Disasters/Pres2.pdf.

  Series of presentation slides on the protection of children in disaster situations.

- Mehta, N. 2009. *Child Centeredness in Disaster Response.* PLAN. http://nidm.gov.in/idmc2/PDF/Presentations/Children_Disasters/Pres6.pdf.

  Series of presentation slides detailing the child-focused disaster efforts of PLAN, most notably those of psychosocial protection.

- National Association of School Nurses. 2006. *Disaster Preparedness: School Nurse Role.* http://www.nasn.org/Default.aspx?tabid=221.

Explains the role school nurses can play in disaster preparedness.

- National Association of School Psychologists. n.d. School safety and crisis resources. http://www.nasponline.org/resources/crisis_safety/index.aspx.

  Website showing links to a number of fact sheets and other resources focusing primarily on psychosocial needs of children affected by disasters.

- National Center for Missing and Exploited Children. 2005. *Know the Rules: Safety Tips for Children Displaced in Natural Disasters and Their Caregivers.* http://www.missingkids.com/missingkids/servlet/ResourceServlet?LanguageCountry=en_US&PageId=2118.

  Fact sheet designed to help child victims of natural disasters acclimate to a new environment and to help caregivers provide the best assistance possible.

- Save the Children. 2009. *Child Centered and Community Based Disaster Risk Reduction.* http://nidm.gov.in/idmc2/PDF/Presentations/Children_Disasters/Pres3.pdf.

  Series of presentation slides detailing the inclusion of children in community disaster risk reduction efforts.

- Seltzer, J. M., et al. 2007. *Environmental Hazards for Children in the Aftermath of Wildfires.* http://www.aap.org/disasters/pdf/Wildfires-RecoveryPhase.pdf.

  Provides information that allows individuals and families to assess the safety of returning back to a community or home in the aftermath of a wildfire event, in terms of the risks to children.

- Seltzer, J. M., et al. 2007. *Health Risks of Wildfires for Children—Acute Phase.* http://www.aap.org/disasters/pdf/Wildfires-AcutePhase.pdf.

  Technical report geared toward preparing families for the hazards children will face during the acute phase of a wildfire.

- Trust for America's Health and the American Academy of Pediatrics. 2006. *Pandemic Influenza: Warning, Children at Risk*. http://aap.org/new/KidsPandemicFlufnl.pdf.

  Document with strategies for containing the spread of a pandemic influenza in children and adolescents.

- U.S. Department of Education. n.d. *Readiness and Emergency Management for Schools Technical Assistance Center*. http://rems.ed.gov/index.cfm?event=resources.

Reports

This section includes references to academic and professional reports that address a specific component of emergency management.

- Columbia University Mailman School of Public Health. 2007. *Pediatric Preparedness for Disasters and Terrorism*. http://www.ncdp.mailman.columbia.edu/files/peds2.pdf.

  Report detailing advances in knowledge and practice aimed at protecting young people and children from the affects of terrorism.

- Council on Accreditation. 2005. *Former Child Welfare Leader Offers Insights on Lessons Learned from Hurricane Katrina at COA's Public Agency Roundtable*. http://www.coanet.org/Files/RoundtableLuncheon.pdf.

  Luncheon address from the 2005 Council on Accreditation Public Agency Roundtable presentation.

- Foltin, G. 2009. *The Future of Pediatric Disaster Preparedness*. Elsevier. http://www.ncdp.mailman.columbia.edu/files/foltin_redlener.pdf.

  This article is part of a collaborative effort by experts in the field of emergency preparedness to form an overview of the current challenges and future directions in pediatric disaster readiness.

- Goodman, R. 2001. *Kids and Terrorism: Supporting Our Children in Times of Crisis.* NYU Child Study Center. http://www.aboutourkids.org/articles/kids_terrorism_supporting_our_children_in_times_crisis.

  Compilation of written and verbal testimony of Robin Goodman, PhD, Director, Public Education Programs and AboutOurKids.org, New York University Child Study Center, New York, New York, on behalf of the New York University Child Study Center.

- Government Accountability Office. 2006. *Gulf Coast Hurricanes: Lessons Learned for Protecting and Educating Children.* http://www.gao.gov/new.items/d06680r.pdf.

  A report generated to determine or learn more about: (1) the number of missing children and the challenges and lessons learned in locating them; (2) the number of foster and other children receiving child welfare services in Louisiana, in particular, who were affected by the storm, and the challenges and lessons learned in locating and serving them; and (3) the number of schoolchildren displaced by the storm, the damage to their schools, and the challenges and lessons learned for educating displaced school-aged children.

- National Center for Disaster Preparedness. 2007. *The Legacy of Katrina's Children: Estimating the Number of Hurricane Related At-Risk Children in the Gulf Coast States of Louisiana and Mississippi.* NCDP Research Brief 2007_12. http://www.ncdp.mailman.columbia.edu/files/legacy_katrina_children.pdf.

  Details the population of children exposed to posthurricane displacement and infrastructure loss, and considers how many are at elevated risk of a poor future outcome. This research brief sought to answer four questions: (1) How many children were displaced as a result of Hurricanes Katrina and Rita? (2) Among those who were displaced, how many children have since returned to their home state or home communities? (3) Among those who were displaced, how many children are still living in temporary or transient FEMA-subsidized group housing? (4) Regardless as to whether they have returned or are still living in temporary housing, how many of these displaced children are at risk for poor outcomes?

- National Commission on Children and Disasters. 2009. *Report of the National Commission on Children and Disasters.* http://www.childrenanddisasters.acf.hhs.gov/20091014_508IR_partII.pdf.
- NYU Child Study Center. n.d. *Children's Response to Hurricane Katrina. Tips for Schools and Teachers.* http://www.aboutourkids.org/articles/children039s_responses_hurricane_katrina_tips_schools_teachers.

  Fact sheet providing individualized disaster coping mechanisms for teachers and administrators.
- PriceWaterhouseCoopers Health Research Institute. *Closing the Seams: Developing an Integrated Approach to Health System Disaster Preparedness.* http://www.pwc.com/us/en/healthcare/publications/closing-the-seams.jhtml.

  A comprehensive report that examines the preparedness of the U.S. health care system, identifies gaps, and highlights emerging solutions and innovative best practices that can be leveraged to help providers and communities deliver health care in the face of the unknown.
- Senate Committee on Homeland Security and Governmental Affairs. 2009. *Focusing on Children in Disasters: Evacuation Planning and Mental Health Recovery.* http://hsgac.senate.gov/public/index.cfm?FuseAction=Hearings.Hearing&Hearing_ID=aa8241f6-6f0e-41a5-87c3-07c9 a58ecbfa.

  Testimony from a number of experts on government planning for children in disasters.
- The Urban Institute. 2006. *Federalism after Hurricane Katrina: How Can Social Programs Respond to a Major Disaster?* http://www.urban.org/UploadedPDF/311344_after_katrina.pdf.

Report describing how social programs fared under the extreme conditions of Hurricane Katrina and the aftermath.

- Yale University Medical Center. n.d. *Small Victims, Big Challenges: Pediatric Triage, Treatment, and Recovery in Disasters*. http://www.aap.org/disasters/pdf/YNH-fact-sheet.pdf.

  Fact sheet about disaster preparedness training courses for pediatric medical units and others affiliated with the treatment of postdisaster pediatric medical needs.

Organizations

The following is a list of organizations that often provide for the needs of children affected by disasters, or facilitate the reduction of disaster vulnerability among children. A more comprehensive list of organizations active in disasters, irrespective of their focus, may be found by accessing the website of the National Voluntary Agencies Active in Disasters, or http://www.nvoad.org/. This list is not intended to be all-inclusive.

- American Association of Pediatricians

  http://www.aap.org

- American Red Cross

  http://www.redcross.org

- Brethren Children's Disaster Services

  http://www.brethren.org

- Children's Health Fund

  http://www.childrenshealthfund.org/children-in-crisis

- Christian Children's Fund

  http://www.childfund.org

- Church World Service Emergency Response Program

  http://www.disasterrecoveryhelp.org, http://cwserp.org

- Cincinnati Children's National Center for School Crisis and Bereavement

  http://www.cincinnatichildrens.org/svc/alpha/s/school-crisis/default.htm

- Federal Emergency Management Agency

  http://www.fema.gov

- Habitat for Humanity

  http://www.habitat.org

- KaBOOM!

  http://kaboom.org/

- Mercy Corps

  http://www.mercycorps.org

- National Association of Child Care Resource and Referral Agencies (NACCRRA)

  http://www.naccrra.org/disaster/

- National Center for Missing and Exploited Children

  http://www.missingkids.com

- National Commission on Children and Disasters

  http://www.childrenanddisasters.acf.hhs.gov/

- North American Mission Board: Southern Baptist Disaster Relief

  http://www.namb.net/site/c.9qKILUOzEpH/b.224451/k.A400/Disaster_Relief.htm

- Salvation Army

  http://www.salvationarmyusa.org

- Save the Children

  www.savethechildren.org

- U.S. Department of Education

  http://www.education.gov
- U.S. Department of Health and Human Services

  http://www.hhs.gov

Web Links

The following Web links provide access to websites that contain other interesting information about planning for children in disasters.

- American Academy of Pediatrics: Children and Disasters (child care)

  http://www.aap.org/disasters/child-care.cfm
- American Academy of Pediatrics: Children and Disasters (families)

  http://www.aap.org/disasters/families.cfm
- American Academy of Pediatrics: Children and Disasters (pediatricians)

  http://www.aap.org/disasters/pediatricians.cfm
- American Red Cross Disaster Preparation Training

  http://www.redcross.org/services/prepare/0,1082,0_239_,00.html
- American Red Cross Masters of Disaster® Family Kit

  http://www.redcross.org/preparedness/familymodule/fam-cd-front-page-1.html
- Children's Health Fund

  http://www.childrenshealthfund.org
- Child Welfare Information Gateway: Disaster Preparedness

  http://www.childwelfare.gov/highlights/disaster/prepare.cfm

- Church World Service Emergency Response Program, Disaster Recovery Help

  http://www.disasterrecoveryhelp.org

- Council of State Archivists: Intergovernmental Preparedness for Essential Records Project

  http://www.statearchivists.org/iper/index.htm

- Dougy Center for Grieving Children and Families

  http://www.dougy.org/

- Emergency Medical Services for Children

  http://bolivia.hrsa.gov/emsc/

- Emergency Preparedness for Teachers, Students, and Families

  http://readyclassroom.discoveryeducation.com/

- EMSC National Resource Center

  http://www.childrensnational.org/EMSC/

- Helping Children after a Natural Disaster: Information for Parents and Teachers

  http://www.nasponline.org/resources/crisis_safety/naturaldisaster_ho.aspx

- Independent Study Course: IS-7 A Citizen's Guide to Disaster Assistance

  http://www.training.fema.gov/EMIWeb/IS/is22.asp

- Independent Study Course: IS-22 Are You Ready? An In-Depth Guide to Citizen Preparedness

  http://training.fema.gov/EMIWeb/IS/is7.asp

- Independent Study Course: IS-394.a Protecting Your Home or Small Business from Disaster

  http://training.fema.gov/EMIWeb/IS/IS394A.asp

- Institute for Business and Home Safety

  http://www.disastersafety.org/

- Lessons Learned Information Sharing: Children and Disasters (resource page)

  http://www.lls.dhs.gov/index.do

- Model for Child Care Readiness: Tulsa Partners

  http://tulsapartners.org

- National Association for the Education of Young Children

  http://www.naeyc.org/families/disaster.asp

- National Association of Child Care Resource and Referral Agencies, Children and Disasters

  http://www.naccrra.org/disaster/

- National Emergency Medical Services for Children Data Analysis Resource Center

  http://www.nedarc.org/nedarc/index.html

- Preparing for Disaster: The Parent View

  http://www.naccrra.org/for_parents/coping/disaster.php

- Ready Business

  http://www.ready.gov/business

- Ready Business (Spanish)

  http://www.listo.gov/negocios

- Resources for Parents and Teachers

  http://www.fema.gov/kids/teacher.htm

- Save the Children Journey of Hope

  http://savethechildren.org

- Save the Children Recovery and Resilience-Building Programs

  http://www.savethechildren.org/programs/us-literacy-and-nutrition/recovery-resilience.html

- Sesame Street Let's Get Ready!

  http://www.sesamestreet.org/ready

- Tips for Talking about Disasters

  http://mentalhealth.samhsa.gov/cmhs/EmergencyServices/after.asp

Appendix A
National Commission on Children and Disasters 2010 Report to the President and Congress August 23, 2010 Report Publication Date: October 2010

Executive Summary

The President and Congress charged the National Commission on Children and Disasters with carrying out the first-ever comprehensive review of Federal disaster-related laws, regulations, programs, and policies to assess their responsiveness to the needs of children and make recommendations to close critical gaps.

In this Executive Summary, the Commission assembles all the recommendations in this report. As is customary of a Federal advisory body such as the Commission, the recommendations are primarily directed toward the President, Federal agencies, and Congress. However, in order to achieve a coordinated national strategy on children and disasters at all levels of government—including Federal, State, tribal, territorial, and local—the Commission urges non-Federal executive and legislative branches of government to consider and apply the recommendations, as appropriate.

To assist Congress, Federal agencies, and non-Federal partners in quickly identifying recommendations most relevant to them, the Commission provides an index organized by the agency, group, or individual charged with implementing the recommendation.

Recommendation 1.1: Distinguish and comprehensively integrate the needs of children across all inter- and intra-governmental disaster management activities and operations.

- *The President should develop a National Strategy for Children and Disasters.*
- *The Executive Branch, Congress, and non-Federal partners should prioritize children separately from "at risk" population categories.*
- *The Executive Branch at all levels of government should establish and maintain permanent focal points of coordination for children and disasters, supported by sufficient authority, funding, and policy expertise. FEMA should establish Children's Integration Specialists at the regional level.*
- *The Executive Branch and non-Federal partners should incorporate children as a distinct priority in base disaster planning documents and relevant grant programs.*
- *The Executive Branch and non-Federal partners should incorporate education, child care, juvenile justice, and child welfare systems into disaster planning, training, and exercises.*
- *The Executive Branch and non-Federal partners should incorporate children as a distinct priority in relevant target capabilities, preparedness training, and exercises, with specific target outcomes and performance measures.*
- *The Executive Branch and Congress should institute accountability and progress monitoring measures to track implementation of Commission recommendations and capability improvements.*

Recommendation 1.2: The President should accelerate the development and implementation of the National Disaster Recovery Framework with an explicit emphasis on addressing the immediate and long-term physical and mental health, educational, housing, and human services recovery needs of children.

Recommendation 1.3: DHS/FEMA should ensure that information required for timely and effective delivery of recovery services to children and families is collected and shared with appropriate entities.

- *Government agencies and non-governmental organizations should collect information on children and families necessary to identify and support their immediate and long-term recovery needs.*
- *DHS/FEMA should expand information sharing with appropriate government agencies and non-governmental organizations to enable the delivery of recovery services.*
- *DHS/FEMA should pre-identify and credential additional local and out-of-State voluntary and non-governmental organizations and networks that provide disaster assistance to children and families.*

Recommendation 1.4: DHS/FEMA should establish interagency agreements to provide disaster preparedness funding, technical assistance, training, and other resources to State and local child serving systems and child congregate care facilities.

Recommendation 2.1: HHS should lead efforts to integrate mental and behavioral health for children into public health, medical, and other relevant disaster management activities.

- *Congress should direct HHS to lead the development of a disaster mental and behavioral health Concept of Operations (CONOPS) to formalize disaster mental and behavioral health as a core component of disaster preparedness, response, and recovery efforts.*

Recommendation 2.2: HHS should enhance the research agenda for children's disaster mental and behavioral health, including psychological first aid, cognitive-behavioral interventions, social support interventions, bereavement counseling and support, and programs intended to enhance children's resilience in the aftermath of a disaster.

- *HHS should convene a working group of children's disaster mental health and pediatric experts to review the research portfolios of relevant agencies, identify gaps in knowledge, and recommend a national research agenda across the full spectrum of disaster mental health for children and families.*

Recommendation 2.3: Federal agencies and non-Federal partners should enhance pre-disaster preparedness and just-in-time training in pediatric disaster mental and behavioral health, including psychological first aid, bereavement support, and brief supportive interventions, for mental health professionals and individuals, such as teachers, who work with children.

Recommendation 2.4: DHS/FEMA and SAMHSA should strengthen the Crisis Counseling Assistance and Training Program (CCP) to better meet the mental health needs of children and families.

- *Simplify the Immediate Services Program (ISP) grant application to minimize the burden on communities affected by a disaster and facilitate the rapid allocation of funding and initiation of services.*
- *Establish the position of Children's Disaster Mental Health Coordinator within State-level CCPs.*
- *Formally modify the CCP model to indicate and promote "enhanced services" where the mental health impact is unlikely to be adequately addressed by "typical" CCP services.*
- *Include bereavement support and education within services typically provided under the CCP.*

Recommendation 2.5: Congress should establish a single, flexible grant funding mechanism to specifically support the delivery of mental health treatment services that address the full spectrum of behavioral health needs of children including treatment of disaster-related adjustment difficulties, psychiatric disorders, and substance abuse.

Recommendation 3.1: Congress and HHS should ensure availability and access to pediatric medical countermeasures (MCM) at the Federal, State, and local levels for chemical, biological, radiological, nuclear, and explosive threats.

- *Provide funding and grant guidance for the development, acquisition, and stockpiling of MCM specifically for children for inclusion in the Strategic National Stockpile (SNS) and all other federally funded caches, including those funded by DHS/FEMA.*
- *Amend the Emergency Use Authorization to allow the FDA, at the direction of the HHS Secretary, to authorize pediatric indications of MCM for emergency use before an emergency is known or imminent.*
- *Form a standing advisory body of Federal partners and external experts to advise the HHS Secretary and provide expert consensus on issues pertaining specifically to pediatric emergency MCM.*
- *Within the HHS Biomedical Advanced Research and Development Authority, designate a pediatric leader and establish a pediatric and obstetric working group to conduct gap analyses and make research recommendations.*
- *Include pediatric expertise on the HHS Enterprise Governance Board or its successor and all relevant committees and working groups addressing issues pertaining to MCM.*
- *Establish a partnership between the proposed MCM Development Leader and key pediatric stakeholders both within and outside government.*

Recommendation 3.2: HHS and DoD should enhance the pediatric capabilities of their disaster medical response teams through the integration of pediatric-specific training, guidance, exercises, supplies, and personnel.

- *HHS should develop pediatric capabilities within each National Disaster Medical System (NDMS) region.*
- *HHS should establish a "reserve pool" of pediatric health care workers to assist in NDMS disaster response.*

- *HHS and DoD should establish a Pediatric Health Care Coordinator on each disaster medical response team and develop strategies to recruit and retain team members with pediatric medical expertise.*

Recommendation 3.3: HHS should ensure that health professionals who may treat children during a disaster have adequate pediatric disaster clinical training.

- *The President should direct the Federal Education and Training Interagency Group for Public Health and Medical Disaster Preparedness and Response (FETIG) to prioritize the development of pediatric core competencies, core curricula, training, and research.*
- *The FETIG should support the formation of a Pediatric Disaster Clinical Education and Training Working Group to establish core clinical competencies and a standard, modular pediatric disaster health care education and training curriculum.*

Recommendation 3.4: The Executive Branch and Congress should provide resources for a formal regionalized pediatric system of care to support pediatric surge capacity during and after disasters.

- *HHS should include pediatric surge capacity as a "Required Funding Capability" in the Hospital Preparedness Program.*
- *States and hospital accrediting bodies should ensure all hospital emergency departments stand ready to care for ill or injured children through the adoption of emergency preparedness guidelines jointly developed by the American Academy of Pediatrics, the American College of Emergency Physicians, and the Emergency Nurses Association.*

Recommendation 3.5: Prioritize the recovery of pediatric health and mental health care delivery systems in disaster-affected areas.

- *Congress should establish sufficient funding mechanisms to support restoration and continuity of for-profit and non-profit health and mental health services to children.*
- *The Executive Branch should recognize and support pediatric health and mental health care delivery systems as a planning imperative in the development and implementation of National Health Security Strategy and National Disaster Recovery Framework.*
- *HHS should create Medicaid and Children's Health Insurance Program incentive payments for providers in disaster areas.*
- *The American Medical Association should adopt a new code or code modifier to the Current Procedural Terminology to reflect disaster medical care in order to facilitate tracking of these services and as a means for enhanced reimbursement from public and private payers.*
- *Recommendation 3.6: EPA should engage State and local health officials and non-governmental experts to develop and promote national guidance and best practices on re-occupancy of homes, schools, child care, and other child congregate care facilities in disaster-impacted areas.*
- *EPA and HHS should expand research on pediatric environmental health risks associated with disasters.*

Recommendation 4.1: The President and Congress should clearly designate and appropriately resource a lead Federal agency for emergency medical services (EMS) with primary responsibility for the coordination of grant programs, research, policy, and standards development and implementation.

- *Establish a dedicated Federal grant program under a designated lead Federal agency for pre-hospital EMS disaster preparedness, including pediatric equipment and training.*

Recommendation 4.2: Improve the capability of emergency medical services (EMS) to transport pediatric patients and provide comprehensive pre-hospital pediatric care during daily operations and disasters.

- *Congress should provide full funding to the Emergency Medical Services for Children (EMSC) program to ensure all States and territories meet targets and achieve progress in the EMSC performance measures for grantees, and to support development of a research portfolio.*
- *As an eligibility guideline for Centers for Medicare & Medicaid Services reimbursement, require first response and emergency medical response vehicles to acquire and maintain pediatric equipment and supplies in accordance with the national guidelines for equipment for Basic Life Support and Advanced Life Support vehicles.*
- *HHS and DHS should establish stronger pediatric EMS performance measures within relevant Federal emergency preparedness grant programs.*
- *HHS should address the findings of the EMSC 2009 Gap Analysis of EMS Related Research.*

Recommendation 4.3: HHS should develop a national strategy to improve Federal pediatric emergency transport and patient care capabilities for disasters.

- *Conduct a national review of existing capabilities among relevant government agencies and the private sector for emergency medical transport of children.*

Recommendation 5.1: Disaster case management programs should be appropriately resourced and should provide consistent holistic services that achieve tangible, positive outcomes for children and families affected by the disaster.

- *The Executive Branch and Congress should provide sufficient funds to build, support, and deploy a disaster case management system with nationwide capacity.*
- *DHS/FEMA should clarify the transition from Federal to State-led disaster case management programs.*
- *Government agencies and non-governmental organizations should develop voluntary consensus standards on the essential elements and methods of disaster case*

management, including pre-credentialing of case managers and training that includes focused attention to the needs of children and families.

Recommendation 6.1: Congress and HHS should improve disaster preparedness capabilities for child care.

- *Congress should provide HHS the authority to require States to include disaster planning, training, and exercise requirements within the scope of their minimum health and safety standards for child care licensure or registration.*
- *Congress and HHS should require States to develop statewide child care disaster plans in coordination with State and local emergency managers, public health, State child care administrators and regulatory agencies, and child care resource and referral agencies.*

Recommendation 6.2: Congress and Federal agencies should improve capacity to provide child care services in the immediate aftermath of and recovery from a disaster.

- *FEMA should revise its Public Assistance regulations to codify child care as an essential service.*
- *Congress should codify child care as an "essential service of a governmental nature" in the Stafford Act.*
- *Federal agencies should incorporate child care as an essential service in the National Response Framework, the National Disaster Recovery Framework, the National Disaster Housing Concept of Operations, and Disaster Housing Practitioners' Guide.*
- *Congress should authorize a grant funding mechanism, such as an emergency contingency fund, to repair or rebuild private, for-profit child care facilities, support the establishment of temporary child care, and reimburse States for subsidizing child care services to disaster-affected families.*

Recommendation 6.3: HHS should require disaster preparedness capabilities for Head Start Centers and basic disaster mental health training for staff.

Recommendation 7.1: Congress and Federal agencies should improve the preparedness of schools and school districts by providing additional support to States.

- *Congress and ED should award disaster preparedness grants to State education agencies to oversee, coordinate, and improve disaster planning, training, and exercises statewide and ensure that all districts within the State meet certain baseline criteria.*
- *DHS/FEMA should partner with ED to provide funding and other resources to support disaster preparedness efforts of State and local education agencies, including collaborative planning, training, and exercises with emergency management officials.*

Recommendation 7.2: Congress and ED should enhance the ability of school personnel to support children who are traumatized, grieving, or otherwise recovering from a disaster.

- *Congress and ED should award funds to States to implement and evaluate training and professional development programs in basic skills in providing support to grieving students and students in crisis and establish statewide requirements related to teacher certification and recertification.*

Recommendation 7.3: Ensure that school systems recovering from disasters are provided immediate resources to reopen and restore the learning environment in a timely manner and provide support for displaced students and their host schools.

- *Congress should create a permanent funding mechanism to support recovery for schools and students.*
- *Congress should establish an emergency contingency fund within the Education for Homeless Children and Youth program and expeditiously provide grants to school districts serving an influx of displaced children.*

- *Congress and ED should support the immediate provision of expert technical assistance and consultation regarding services and interventions to address disaster mental health needs of students and school personnel.*
- *DHS/FEMA and other Federal agencies should clarify, consolidate, and publicize information related to the recovery programs, assistance, and services (i.e. transportation to schools) currently available to school systems through the Stafford Act and other Federal sources.*

Recommendation 8.1: Ensure that State and local child welfare agencies adequately prepare for disasters.

- *Congress should request a national assessment of child welfare disaster planning to determine if significant advances have been made since passage of the Child and Family Services Improvement Act of 2006 (CFSIA).*
- *HHS should develop detailed disaster planning criteria by regulation or other formal policy guidance to supplement the basic procedures mandated in CFSIA.*
- *Within each ACF regional office, child welfare staff and the region's emergency management specialist should collaboratively review and evaluate the State child welfare disaster plans required by CFSIA and assist States in developing comprehensive plans and meeting their statutory obligations.*
- *DHS/FEMA and HHS should provide funding, guidance, and technical assistance to child welfare agencies and encourage collaboration with emergency management, courts, and other key stakeholders.*

Recommendation 8.2: Ensure State and local juvenile justice agencies and all residential treatment, correctional, and detention facilities that house children adequately prepare for disasters.

- *Congress should require State and local juvenile justice agencies and all residential treatment, correctional, and detention facilities that house children to have comprehensive disaster plans in place.*

- *DHS/FEMA and DOJ should support disaster planning for State and local juvenile justice agencies and residential treatment, correctional, and detention facilities that house children by providing funding, technical assistance, and training.*

Recommendation 8.3: HHS and DOJ should ensure juvenile, dependency, and other courts hearing matters involving children adequately prepare for disasters.

- *HHS should include disaster preparedness as a component of the Court Improvement Program for dependency courts.*
- *DOJ should include disaster preparedness as a component of the proposed National Juvenile Delinquency Court Improvement Program.*
- *DOJ and the National Council of Juvenile and Family Court Judges should incorporate disaster preparedness into the Model Courts program.*

Recommendation 9.1: Government agencies and nongovernmental organizations should provide a safe and secure mass care shelter environment for children, including access to essential services and supplies.

- *Implement national standards and indicators for mass care shelters that are specific and responsive to children.*
- *Integrate essential age-appropriate shelter supplies for infants and children into shelter planning and fund the addition of child-specific supplies to caches for immediate deployment to support shelter operations.*
- *Implement common standards and training, including standards for criminal background checks, to mitigate risks unique to children in shelters such as child abduction and sex offenders.*

Recommendation 10.1: Prioritize the needs of families with children, especially families with children who have disabilities or chronic health, mental health, or educational needs, within disaster housing assistance programs.

- *Government agencies and non-governmental organizations should ensure that families with children in disaster housing, especially community sites, have access to needed services and are provided safe and healthy living environments.*
- *Congress should authorize DHS/FEMA to reimburse State and local governments for providing wrap-around services to children and families in community sites.*
- *DHS/FEMA should develop clear written guidance around emergency transportation planning and reimbursement for State and local governments that addresses the recovery needs of children and families.*
- *Government agencies and non-governmental organizations should identify and promote innovative programs to expedite the transition into permanent housing for families with children.*

Recommendation 11.1: Federal agencies and Congress should provide sufficient funding to develop and deploy a national information sharing capability to quickly and effectively reunite displaced children with their families, guardians, and caregivers when separated by a disaster.

- *DHS should lead the development of a nationwide information technology capability to collect, share, and search data from any patient and evacuee tracking or family reunification system.*
- *DHS should support the development of voluntary consensus-driven standards for data collection and data sharing through a joint Federal, non-Federal, and private sector process.*
- *Government agencies should ensure the collection of appropriate data on evacuated children, particularly unaccompanied minors.*

Recommendation 11.2: Disaster plans at all levels of government must specifically address the evacuation and transportation needs of children with disabilities and chronic health needs, in coordination with child congregate care facilities such as schools, child care, and healthcare facilities.

Appendix B

Standards and Indicators for Disaster Shelter Care for Children

The National Commission on Children and Disasters facilitated the development and dissemination of a draft document, *Standards and Indicators for Disaster Shelter Care for Children.* The document was being piloted in the field by the American Red Cross (ARC) and selected state and local emergency agencies during the 2009 hurricane season.

Purpose

To provide guidance to shelter managers and staff that ensures children have a safe, secure environment during and after a disaster—including appropriate support and access to essential resources.

Standards and Indicators for All Shelters

- Under most circumstances a parent, guardian or caregiver is expected to be the primary resource for their children, age 18 and younger.
- In cases where parents or guardians are not with their children, local law enforcement personnel and local child protective/child welfare services must be contacted to assist with reunification.
- Children are sheltered together with their families or caregivers.
- Every effort is made to designate an area for families away from the general shelter population.
- Family areas should have direct access to bathrooms.
- Parents, guardians and caregivers are notified that they are expected to accompany their children when they use the bathrooms.
- Every effort is made to set aside space for family interaction:
  - This space is free from outside news sources thereby reducing a child's repeated exposure to coverage of the disaster.
  - If age-appropriate toys are available they will be in this space, with play supervised by parents, guardians or caregivers.
- Shared environmental surfaces in shelters that are frequently touched by children's hands or other body parts should be cleaned and disinfected on a regular basis. High contact areas may include diaper changing surfaces, communal toys, sinks, toilets, doorknobs and floors. These surfaces should be cleaned daily with a 1:10 bleach solution or a commercial equivalent disinfectant based on the manufacturer's cleaning instructions. Local health department authorities may be consulted for further infection control guidance.
- When children exhibit signs of illness, staff will refer children to on-site or local health services personnel for evaluation and will obtain consent from a parent, guardian or caretaker whenever possible.

- When children exhibit signs of emotional stress, staff will refer children to on-site or local disaster mental health personnel and will obtain consent from a parent, guardian or caretaker whenever possible.
- Children in the shelters come in all ages and with unique needs. Age appropriate and nutritious food (including baby formula and baby food) and snacks are available, as soon as possible after needs are identified.
- Diapers are available for infants and children as soon as possible after needs are identified. General guidelines suggest that infants and toddlers need up to 12 diapers a day.
- Blankets, for all appropriate ages, are also available.
- A safe space for breastfeeding women is provided so they may have privacy and a sense of security and support (this can include a curtained off area or providing blankets for privacy).
- Basins and supplies for bathing infants are provided as soon as possible after needs are identified.

Standards and Indicators for Temporary Respite Care for Children

Temporary Respite Care for Children provides temporary relief for children, parents, guardians or caregivers. It is a secure, supervised and supportive play experience for children in a Disaster Recovery Center, assistance center, shelter or other service delivery site. When placing their child or children in this area, parents, guardians or caregivers are required to stay on-site in the disaster recovery center, assistance center or shelter or designate a person to be responsible for their child or children, who shall also be required to stay on-site.

In cases where temporary respite care for children is provided in a Disaster Recovery Center, assistance center, shelter and other service delivery site, the following Standards and Indicators shall apply:

- Temporary respite care for children is provided in a safe, secure environment following a disaster.

- Temporary respite care for children is responsive and equitable. Location, hours of operation and other information about temporary respite care for children is provided and easy for parents, guardians and caregivers to understand.
- All local, state and federal laws, regulations and codes that relate to temporary respite care for children are followed.
- The temporary respite care for children area is free from significant physical hazards and/or architectural barriers and remains fully accessible to all children.
- The temporary respite care for children area has enclosures or dividers to protect children and ensure that children are supervised in a secure environment.
- The temporary respite care for children area is placed close to restrooms and a drinking water source; hand washing and or hand sanitizer stations are available in the temporary respite care for children area.
- Procedures are in place to sign children in and out of the temporary respite care for children area and to ensure children are only released to the parent(s), guardian(s), caregiver(s) or designee(s) listed on the registration form.
- All documents—such as attendance records and registration forms (which include identifying information, parent, guardian or caregiver names and contact information), information about allergies and other special needs, injury and/or incident report forms—are provided, maintained, and available to staff at all times.
- Toys and materials in the temporary respite area are safe and age appropriate.
- Prior to working in the temporary respite care for children area, all shelter staff members must receive training and orientation. In addition, such staff must successfully complete a criminal and sexual offender background check. Spontaneous volunteers are not permitted. When inside the temporary respite area, staff shall visibly display proper credentials above the waist at all times.

- When children are present, at least two adults are to be present at all times. No child should be left alone with one adult who is not their parent, guardian or caregiver.
- All staff members must be 18 years or older. Supervision of the temporary respite care for children area is provided by a staff person at least 21 years of age.
- An evacuation plan will be developed with a designated meeting place outside the center. The evacuation plan will be posted and communicated to parent(s), caregiver(s), and guardian(s) when registering their child.
- The child to staff ratio is appropriate to the space available and to the ages and needs of the children in the temporary respite care for children area at any time.

Appendix C

Child ID Survey

Name:______________________________Hospital #_____________

Age:______Months/Years DOB__________________________

Gender: Male________Female________

Is the child currently accompanied by a supervising adult?
Yes No

Name of the currently supervising adult?_______________ Age___

Is this person a Parent? Yes No

A Grandparent? Yes No

Is this parent the usual guardian? Yes No

Was the child living with this person before the disaster?
Yes No

Does the supervising adult have any proof of legal guardianship or relationship to child? Yes No

If Yes, please describe or attach a copy:

____

If the adult(s) is not a Parent or Grandparent, what is the relationship to this child?

Aunt/Uncle__________________________________Age___

Sibling_____________________________________Age___

Friend______________________________________Age___

Other (next-of-kin, teacher)____________________Age___

Was the child treated for illness or have an injury? Yes No

If yes, please describe:__________________________________

Was the child admitted to the hospital? Yes No

If Yes, give room or location:____________________________

If No, give location or address where child is currently (lobby, Pediatric Safe Area, sent to shelter, etc.)________________________

Does this child have a history of medical problems? Yes No

If yes, please list:______________________________________

Does this child or family members have special needs? Yes No

If yes, please list:______________________________________

Sources: CDC. 2005. *Instructions for identifying and protecting displaced children.* CDC Health Advisory. September 28; Save the Children. 2007. *The unique needs of children in emergencies: A guide for the inclusion of children in emergency operations plans.* September. http://www.savethechildren.org/publications/emergencies/Children-in-Emergencies-Planning-Guide.pdf.

Appendix D

The Family Information and Support Center

Family Information and Support Center Main Objectives

1. Provide the necessary reliable information via a systematic organizational framework and assistance in the identification process.
2. Assist relatives coping with uncertainty, stress and stages of adaptation.
3. Enable the medical staff to concentrate freely on their treatment of the casualties, especially in the acute stage of the proceedings, while providing a formal support system for the bewildered and anxious relatives and friends.

Family Information and Support Center Main Functions

1. Provide accurate information.
2. Provide psychological first aid to distraught families.
3. Provide crisis counseling or refer for immediate mental health services.
4. Provide escort and "comfort" services to families.
5. Provide temporary childcare for well children of the injured or family members who need to assist the injured.
6. Assist with patient location and reunification of family within the hospital.
7. Assist in contacting family members to arrange care of children present at hospital.
8. Assist in making in-place shelter arrangements or community placement of children, i.e., (ACS) who do not have a safe place to be or a family member who can care for them.
9. Provide communications needs for families (phones, e-mail)
10. Protect families from intrusion by media or curious bystanders

Structure of the Family Information and Support Center

The FISC structure is divided into two main areas: The Main Unit that is the physical location of the FISC and the Hospital Peripheral Units that are the hospital units that staff will need to be in constant communication with during the immediate phase of a disaster.

The Main Unit

Recommendation: Identify physical space for the FISC, wired with telephone and computer/internet connections.

This unit should be able to have contact with the general public, via phone or in person. It deals with the widest range of activities and has the largest number of professional personnel allocated to it. The structure of the main unit is as follows:

Reception Area:

At any given time there may be hundreds of families and friends in contact with the FISC at varying stages of the disaster. The simultaneous presence of all these people, especially in the earlier stages, requires expertise in crowd management. Here, social workers or (assigned staff) may be allocated to the families and friends as they arrive. This social worker or assigned staff take in information from arriving family members and assigns them a social worker. Coordination among staff members prevents unnecessary doubling up and allows optimal use of manpower. A central waiting area should be large enough to accommodate family members seeking information. This area should be away from the Emergency Department area but ideally in close proximity or easily accessible to facilitate communication. There should be conveniently located bathroom facilities.

Suggestions: Consider utilizing the chapel; auditorium/conference room; clinic waiting room; cafeteria/dining room for the reception area. A nearby community center, school or church can be considered.

Information Desk:

This information provided by the social workers or assigned staff, operating the information desk in person and via telephone, is based on constantly updated data retrieved from the computer, social workers in the field and the Incident Command Center.

Suggestions: Consider a message center/area for families to communicate with each other; computer with e-mail availability, bulletin board or log book.

Photograph/Identification Room:

This room is utilized for those people without confirmatory information on a missing relative but when there is a high degree of probability that the person is among the casualties. At this stage of the proceedings, the need for support is at its greatest and requires sensitive and careful intervention. Only the closest relatives are brought to this room. This room will also service as the center for family reunification through photograph identification.

Consultation Areas:

Side rooms are used for those members of the public that express extreme stressful reactions (i.e., shock or pain). When the social worker or assigned staff, identifies a family reacting in an extremely volatile and agitated manner, and feels that they would benefit from personal, supportive attention in a quiet atmosphere, they are encouraged to withdraw to a side room provided for this purpose. This area separates the family from the rest of the public in order to prevent a panic chain reaction. These areas will at least minimally be furnished with chairs, desk or table, tissues, trashcan and a telephone.

Pediatric Safe Area:

As discussed in *Section 1, "Security Issues"*, the Pediatric Safe Area may be the located within the FISC. The Pediatric Safe Area is a designated place for unaccompanied children who have been discharged from the emergency department or had been separated from their caregivers. These children are awaiting reunification with appropriate family members or others. If the Pediatric Safe Area is located within the FISC, set aside a portion of the large room to accommodate child size furniture with a selection of toys, games, art materials and books. This area should have a regularly assigned adult, the Pediatric Safe Area Coordinator and appropriate security staff, (either staff or volunteer) to attend the children. If your organization has a Child Life Program, they are the most experienced to setup and monitor the Pediatric Safe Area.

Sources: New York City Department of Health and Mental Hygiene (NYC Health). 2006. *Hospital guidelines for pediatrics in disasters.* Centers for Bioterrorism Preparedness Program Pediatric Task Force; Save the Children. 2007. *The unique needs of children in emergencies: A guide for the inclusion of children in emergency operations plans.* September. http://www.savethechildren.org/publications/emergencies/Children-in-Emergencies-Planning-Guide.pdf.

Appendix E

Draft the Annex

The most effective format for an EOP annex is one that follows a standard format established for the basic plan and any other functional or hazard-specific annexes. While there are likely to be several subtle differences between each community's EOP format, most plans contain variations of essentially the same components—often appearing in the same order due to the logical nature of a plan's layout.

The following format, as suggested by FEMA, is based on an easily understood, commonsense approach: definition of objective, characterization of the situation, general plan of action, delegation of responsibilities, and information on resources and administrative support necessary for accomplishing the tasks. FEMA recommends a format consisting of: purpose, agencies involved, situation and assumptions, concept of operations, assignment of responsibilities, administration and logistics, plan development and maintenance, and authorities and references. Each of these components is described in greater detail below.

Annexes are added to plans in order to provide emergency response officials with more specific information and direction regarding unique or important issues. Annexes generally do not focus on general emergency operations; rather, they emphasize responsibilities, tasks, and operational actions that pertain to the function being covered. Annexes cover the activities to be performed by anyone with a responsibility under the function—in this case, meeting the needs of children in emergencies. The annex identifies actions that not only ensure effective response and recovery, but also that aid in preparing for and mitigating emergencies and disasters.

The Children in Emergencies annex is an example of a "generic" annex, a term assigned to functional annexes that are generally applicable to all hazards. The generic annexes are critically important to the effectiveness of the plan, since they enable the jurisdiction to cope with issues that are likely to arise with any unforeseen emergency. The annex should clearly define and describe the policies, processes, roles, and responsibilities inherent to the fulfillment of the associated tasks required before, during, and after any emergency period. To ensure adequate planning for all appropriate contingencies, the planning team may need to spend time projecting the consequences of various emergencies, ensuring that they do not restrict their efforts to those hazards found to be most threatening by the hazard analysis.

In general, the organization of the annexes parallels that of the basic plan. Specific sections can be developed to expand upon—but not to repeat—information contained in the basic plan. Each section is named and described below.

1. **Annex introduction**—The annex introduction introduces the document and explains its need. It includes the purpose, situation, and assumptions.
   a. **Purpose**—The purpose explains exactly what the annex is, why it was created, and what it does. It can be as simple or detailed as the planners wish to make it, from succinctly stating everything in one sentence to providing a brief explanation of each component of the annex to follow.

b. **Situation**—The situation defines the scope of the annex; it allows users to understand exactly for what it is needed. Components of the section may include: geographical limit of the jurisdiction affected by the annex; important, relevant information about the area (such as schools, daycare facilities, recreational centers, and shelters); a listing of hazards that could affect children; information on children in the community and their location at certain times (such as when they are in school, and the numbers); cultural and linguistic factors; maps; and other information as required. Like other components of the annex, it should not repeat information contained in the basic plan if possible.
c. **Assumptions**—The assumption describes those details the annex template users must assume to be true, or that which they believe would be true during the annex's activation. They show the annex's limitations, allowing users to understand the ways in which they may need to improvise or modify the information included when reality clashes with what was assumed during the planning phase. Some of the assumptions may appear obvious, but if their inclusion helps to limit misunderstanding when the plan is enacted, they should not be left out.

2. **Concept of operations**—The concept of operations section explains how the actions prescribed in the annex will play out, most notably that of emergency response. Topics covered could include what situations will initiate activation of the annex, when and how the emergency operations center will be staffed by appropriate child-focused officials, what other general actions will be taken (when and by whom), and additional logical, planned sequences actions to take place. Predisaster issues are covered in this section as well, including warning and evacuation.
3. **Organization and assignment of responsibilities**—This section describes and illustrates the actual organizational structure of the disaster management actions prescribed by the plan as they relate to the four phases of emergency management (mitigation, preparedness, response, and recovery).

Organizational charts and other illustrative tools may be used. This section includes a detailed list of the actual organizational titles (roles are used in lieu of names to ensure that the annex outlasts changes in position, and to allow for substitutes in case individuals are unable to fulfill their responsibilities) that will be involved in the response to a disaster. For each of the listed roles, the actual responsibilities assigned to the person filling the role are listed, complete with information dictating how and when those responsibilities are carried out, if such information is relevant. In cases where responsibilities require the involvement of several individuals, primary and supportive designations to each action may be required. The method by which planners organize the appearance of responsibilities in this section should be the same used throughout the other components of the plan that already exist. Common methods include:

a. Organize by role (e.g., fire chief or mass care coordinator)
b. Organize by action area (e.g., security and safety)
c. Organize by emergency management functional area (e.g., preparedness or response)
d. Organize by government organizational level (e.g., local, state, or federal)

4. **Authorities/references**—This section provides a list of the statutory authorities upon which the actions contained in the annex are based, and provides references to sources used in the creation of the annex.
5. **Appendices**—Appendices allow for the inclusion of more detailed information that supports actions or other items contained in the annex.

Review and Comments

Once a draft of the annex is complete, it is important to present it to a wider audience representative of the community's stakeholders. In doing so, the planning team increases the likelihood that the actions prescribed in the plan will be accepted by all stakeholders involved, and minimizes the chance that mistakes or omissions were made. One of the most important stakeholders to include in the review and comment period is the general public, who are ultimately the recipients of most of the assistance listed in the annex. This process helps to ensure that their concerns are adequately met, and that the direction taken by the planning team matches the expectations of the emergency operations plan's "customers."

There are several methods by which annex review and comments may be achieved, including:

- Review by the local planning and development commission
- Review by all agencies, organizations, and individuals included in the annex
- Town hall meeting
- Invited comments from all local elected officials
- Public hearing
- Online survey
- Printing and distributing annex to local media outlets
- Annex printed in local newspaper, with an invitation for public comments

Draft Final Annex

After an established period of review and comment has passed, the planning team can meet to determine what, if any, changes should be made to the draft plan. If the team decides that major changes are required based upon the findings of the review and comment period, a subsequent round of review and comment may be necessary. However, if only minor changes are made, or if the planning team feels that the annex is fully suitable, then they should finalize it and distribute copies to all relevant agencies, organizations, and officials.

Validation

No plan is final until it has been tested. To ensure that the planning team has created a usable product, the Children in Emergencies annex should be subjected to tabletop exercises and drills—both individual to the annex itself and as a part of the overall testing of the emergency operations plan. Validation helps to iron out the real-world issues that are difficult to visualize in the abstract planning sessions, as well as to ensure that all participants are familiarized with each other. To maximize the effectiveness of the validation effort, the associated testing interval and schedule should match that of the plan's other components, as stipulated in the basic plan.

Review/Revise the Annex

Like the basic EOP, the Children in Emergencies annex is an ever-changing document, reflective of the community that it serves. Over time, capacities increase or decrease, risks change, populations shift and alter, and new positions arise or disappear. The Children in Emergencies annex is likely dependent upon many aspects outlined in the basic EOP, and it should therefore find inclusion in the cycle by which that document is reviewed and revised.

The Children in Emergencies Annex Template

1. **Introduction**
   a. **Purpose** (A paragraph or two explaining exactly what the annex is, why it was created, and what it does. It provides a brief explanation of each component of the annex.)
   b. **Situation** (Defines the scope of the plan; it allows users to understand exactly for what the annex is needed. Components of the section may include: geographical limit of the jurisdiction affected by the annex; important, relevant information about the area, such as schools, day-care facilities, recreational centers, and shelters; a listing of hazards that could affect children to a disproportionate degree; information on children in the community and their location at certain times [such as when they are in school, and the numbers]; cultural and linguistic factors; maps; and other information as required.)
   c. **Assumptions** (Describes those details the annex template users must assume to be true, or that which they believe would be true during the annex's activation.)

i. Children will remain under the guardianship of their parents or other legal guardians.
ii. The probable location of children during the school year is predictable, as set by the department of education. Outside of regular school hours, the location of children is dictated primarily by families and social networks.
iii. Parents' primary concern during times of emergency or disaster will be to locate and collect their children.
iv. Many providers of children's care, including day care and home care employees, teachers, camp counselors, and others, will be affected by major disasters themselves. Their primary concerns at this time may be the whereabouts and safety of their own families.
v. In events where there are numerous injuries or fatalities sustained by children, local pediatric providers and institutions will be quickly overwhelmed.
vi. Children will suffer the effects of PTSD at rates and severities greater than those of adults.
vii. Institutions normally tasked with the daytime care of children, including schools, daycare centers, and others, are likely to be closed during and following a major disaster.
viii. In certain disasters, children will be required to shelter in place with their families, such as with pandemic flu or bioterrorism.

d. **Special considerations**
e. **Policies**

2. **Concept of operations** (Explains how the actions prescribed in the annex will play out, most notably that of emergency response. Topics covered could include what situations will initiate activation of the annex, when and how the emergency operations center will be staffed by appropriate child-focused officials, what other general actions will be taken [when and by whom], and additional logical, planned sequences actions to take place. Predisaster issues are covered in this section as well, including warning and evacuation, for example.)

a. **Objective** (Describes what the primary and support agencies, organizations, and officials will aim to achieve.)
   i. Physical protection
   ii. Psychosocial protection
   iii. Cognitive protection
   iv. Schools and daycare
   v. Other considerations

3. **Organization and assignment of responsibilities** (Describes and illustrates the actual organizational structure of the disaster management functions. Organizational charts and other illustrative tools may be used. This section includes a detailed list of the actual organizational titles (roles—does not include names) that will be involved in the response to a disaster. To each of those roles, the actual responsibilities assigned to the person filling that role are listed, with information dictating how and when those responsibilities are carried out. In many cases, there are responsibilities that require the involvement of several actors, and in such cases this section stipulates primary and supportive designations to each to clarify leadership.)
   a. **General**
   b. **Organization**
   c. **Responsibilities**
      i. Local level agencies and organizations
         1) Mitigation
         2) Preparedness
         3) Response
         4) Recovery
      ii. State level agencies and organizations
         1) Mitigation
         2) Preparedness
         3) Response
         4) Recovery
      iii. Federal level agencies
         1) Mitigation
         2) Preparedness
         3) Response
         4) Recovery

- **iv.** Other organizations
  - **1)** Mitigation
  - **2)** Preparedness
  - **3)** Response
  - **4)** Recovery

4. **Authorities/references** (Lists statutory authorities upon which the actions listed in the annex are based, and provides references to sources used in the creation of the annex.)
5. **Appendices** (Allow for detailed information that supports actions or other items contained in the annex.)

Appendix F

Emergency Preparedness Planning Resources for Childcare

National Association of Child Care Resource & Referral Agencies (NACCRRA)

www.naccrra.org/disaster (In search box type: Is Child Care Ready?)

- *Is Child Care Ready?: A Disaster-Planning Guide for Child Care Resource & Referral Agencies*
  This guide is a practical toolkit for Child Care Resource & Referral (CCR&R) agencies to help child care programs—both in child care centers and providers' homes—keep children safe and their businesses open during and after natural disasters, terrorist attacks, chemical emergencies, and other catastrophes.

- *Disaster Preparation: A Training for Child Care Centers*
  This guide is designed to assist CCR&Rs and others in training child care centers on disaster preparedness. It includes specific activities for training individuals who direct and work in child care centers.
- *Disaster Preparation: A Training for Family Child Care Providers*
  This guide is intended to assist CCR&Rs and others in training family child care providers on disaster preparedness. It includes activities for training individuals who care for children in their homes.
- *Emergency Planning Forms*
  The user-friendly forms offer templates for child care providers and others to use to fully prepare for disasters.

Emergency Response Planning for Child Care Providers Toolkit
www.naccho.org/pubs/product1.cfm?Product_ID=161 or **www.montgomerycountymd.gov/content/hhs/phs/APC/childcaremanual.pdf**

- This toolkit is designed to prepare childcare providers for emergency events and to assist in he recovery effort by helping children cope with the traumatic event. A train-the-trainer guide is included along with a CD that contains Microsoft PowerPoint presentations. You can download this toolkit for free or order hard copies for a fee on the NACCHO website. The Montgomery County web address will take you directly to the free PDF version.

Emergency/Disaster Preparedness for Child Care Programs
nrc.uchsc.edu/SPINOFF/EMERGENCY/Emergency.htm

- This template was adapted from *Caring for Our Children, National Health and Safety Performance*

Standards: Guidelines for Out-of-Home Child Care. This template was a joint collaborative project of the American Academy of Pediatrics, the American Public Health Association, and National Resource Center for Health & Safety in Child Care.

National Child Care Information Center (NCCIC)
www.nccic.acf.hhs.gov/emergency/

- The NCCIC Child Care Resources for Disasters and Emergencies website brings together information and key resources about emergency preparedness, disaster response, and recovery that relate specifically to child care.

Head Start Disaster Preparedness Workbook
www.cphd.ucla.edu/headstart.html

- This workbook is designed to guide Head Start programs through the development and implementation of comprehensive disaster plans. It is based on information obtained directly from Head Start personnel regarding their disaster preparedness and planning needs.

Ready to Respond Emergency Preparedness Plan
www.brighthorizons.com/talktochildren/docs/emergency_plan.doc

- This plan covers medical emergencies, natural disasters, utility disruptions, fire emergencies, hazardous materials, bomb threats, violent situations, parent/guardian issues, hostage situations, and missing children.

To Hold Safe—Framing a New Era of Disaster Child Care
www.project-kid.org/hold_safe_rev_%202_07.pdf

- This paper draws upon the shared concerns, experiences, and vision of emerging child care leaders to propose a new framework that hinges on recognizing children's distinct needs, fostering resiliency, and providing a continuum of care.

Day Care Planning Tool Kit

www.pema.state.pa.us/pema/cwp/view.asp?A=566&Q=254999

- This kit includes a three-part plan (Basic Plan, Checklists and Supporting Documents), a PowerPoint presentation to use in introducing the planning process and a Daycare Facilities Planning Guide that helps fill in the blanks to complete the plan.

Source: http://www.co.hennepin.mn.us/files/HennepinUS/HSPHD/Public%20Health%20Protection/Epidemiology/Daycare%20Manual/1730_se10bemerprepchildcare.pdf.

Appendix G

The Unique Needs of Children in Emergencies: A Guide for the Inclusion of Children in Emergency Operations Plans—September 2007

Save the Children®

This guide is a project of Save the Children's Domestic Emergencies Unit.

The Domestic Emergencies Unit promotes emergency management practices that address children's needs on the national, state and local levels in the United States, through partnership, advocacy and program implementation.

Save the Children is the leading independent organization creating lasting change for children in need in the United States and around the world. For more information, visit savethechildren.org. Save the Children USA is a member of the International Save the Children Alliance, a global network of 28 independent Save the Children organizations working to ensure the well-being and protection of children in more than 120 countries.

Please contact us if you use any or all of this guide so we may provide you with updates, or to ask questions or offer comments and suggestions.

Mail: U.S. Programs: DEU, Save the Children.
54 Wilton Road, Westport, CT 06880

Phone: (800) 728-3843

E-mail: usemergency@savechildren.org

Download this guide and learn more about our work at:
www.savethechildren.org/usemergency

Disclaimer: This document is intended to be used as a practical and informative guide only, to assist public officials by providing suggestions and ideas for the development of a document to municipal emergency operations plans. It is not intended to replace the actual experience and training that such a task demands, nor should it be used as a legal authority for any purpose.

Contents

Purpose

This guide was created to help local and state emergency managers/coordinators in their efforts to develop and maintain a Children in Emergencies supplemental document to the community's standard

Emergency Operations Plan (EOP) that addresses the special needs of children. This guide is meant to drive the active planning process, not to take its place. There is no single format that can adequately fit every community—developing this capacity is both the legal and the moral responsibility of the community leaders themselves.

This Guide is intended primarily for use by personnel responsible for the development and maintenance of the community's EOP in local emergency management agencies. It is strictly a guide. It establishes no requirements and its recommendations may be used, adapted or disregarded.

Why Develop a Children in Emergencies Document?

Children (0–18 years of age) are a highly vulnerable segment of the population in times of disaster. Under normal conditions, there are components at the governmental, private and non-profit level which together form the networks on which children depend to support their development and protect them from harm. In addition to these systems, children fall under the supervision of their parents, guardians and/or primary caregivers. Once a disaster occurs, however, most or all of these foundations in a child's life may suddenly collapse. The child care centers and schools to which they were enrolled may be damaged, destroyed or used for shelters. Their parents or guardians may be stretched between caring for the needs of their children and addressing the needs of the whole family's recovery. The child victims, who are generally incapable of managing their own needs, can suffer disproportionately and may fall behind their peers in development and education. Additionally, the physical and psychological damage sustained by children can far outweigh the same effects inflicted on fully-grown members of society, often requiring years of physical, psychological and other therapy to address.

The Planning Process in Brief

Form the Planning Team

The planning team for the development of the Children in Emergencies document should be drawn from various groups that have a role or stake in the emergency response needs of children. The list below is by no means to be considered all-inclusive. Nor is it necessary for every community to involve all of these positions in its effort—the key to forming a planning team is for the planning coordinator to ensure that membership represent an accurate cross section of the organizations involved in the jurisdiction's emergency response effort as it relates to children, parents, guardians and pregnant women.

Possible Planning Team Members (Agencies, Organizations and Individuals)

- The Office of the Chief Executive
- Emergency Services (law enforcement, fire/rescue and EMS)
- Emergency dispatchers
- Public health and safety officials
- Social service agencies and volunteer organizations (including a children's services agency)
- Area hospitals (children's and general)
- Urgent care providers
- Suppliers of equipment and materials for the educational, health, hygienic and nutritional needs of children
- Pediatricians
- Educational administrators/Superintendent of schools
- Teachers' organization leaders
- Child care association representatives
- Public Information Officer (PIO)
- Local media
- Jurisdiction's legal counsel
- Emergency managers and agency representatives from neighboring jurisdictions (to establish mutual aid agreements)
- State and/or Federal representatives, as appropriate
- Mass care coordinator and mass care facility managers
- Parent and guardian organization representatives
- Other organizations or agencies involved in the care of children or child/family recreation (e.g., community recreation department, child care licensing agency)
- Organizations managing transient populations that include children (hotel associations, tourism boards)

- Mental health agencies
- Poison control centers
- Social service agencies
- Local Emergency Management Planning Committee (LEPC) members
- Faith-based groups and churches
- School nurses
- Courts (as needed)
- Community zoning officials

Perform Document Research

Once the planning team has been established, the team should begin by assessing all of the information that is available as a result of the Basic EOP development, including (most importantly) the hazard risk assessment, the base map of the community and the inventory of emergency management resources available both within and outside the community.

In addition, the planning team may need to gather information that provides them with insight into the following:

- Statutory authorities (laws, regulations, statutes and other legal information) relating to the emergency care of children in the community
- Base map of the community, upon which all child care facilities are located (e.g. schools, child care centers)
- Population and demographic information for all children in the community
- Number of special needs children in the community and information regarding the kinds of need and the facilities available to attend to those needs
- Community school system information, including:
    - Name, address, and contact information for each school
    - Number and age of students in each school
    - Each school's status as a community shelter (or shelter for neighboring community)
- Child care information, including:
    - List of community child care facilities, including business names, addresses and contact information for each facility

- Capacity of each facility
- Viability of each facility to provide emergency shelter
- Number of children enrolled in each facility

- Hospital and health care information
  - Name, address and contact information for each
  - Number of pediatric beds in each facility
  - Number of pediatric physicians in the hospital system
  - Hospitals in neighboring jurisdictions willing to accept pediatric casualty overflow (including all information above)
  - Name and contact information for all private pediatricians in the community

- Mass care shelter information
  - Shelter administrator name
  - Shelter address and other pertinent information
  - Shelter capacity for children

- Non-Governmental Organizations (NGO) information
  - List of child-focused NGOs operating the community (disaster and non-disaster related)
  - Contact information and area of focus

- Transportation information
  - Inventory of vehicles that would be used to transport children during an evacuation or following a disaster
  - Status of child-safety devices or capacities of the vehicles
  - Address and contact information for transportation providers
  - Probable evacuation routes and plans for facilities serving/housing children

- Resource Database
  - List of suppliers who can provide emergency supplies and equipment related to the care of children (diapers, wipes, formula, feeding implements, etc.), including address and contact information
  - Inventory and pricing information for relevant supplies and equipment

- Emergency management information

    - Equipment, supplies and facilities that meet the emergency needs of children
    - Information regarding emergency services staff training in pediatric emergency response
    - Available courses within and outside the community that focus on pediatric emergency management

- Psychosocial (emotional support) information
    - Name and contact information of community pediatric psychologists
    - Name and contact information of school social workers
    - Name and contact information of local experts on child development

- Hazard Information
    - Community risk as it relates to children, the facilities housing/serving them and neighborhoods where there are notably higher densities of children
- Mitigation options available to minimize the risk to children and facilities housing/serving them

With proper planning and guidance, emergency management agencies can minimize the risk faced by the community's children. Children, families and those tasked with the care of children (teachers, child care centers, etc.), can all take action before disasters occur to prepare for and mitigate their effects. Response and child-stewardship organizations that are most likely to assume the role of protecting children in the immediate aftermath of a disastrous event can be equipped for and provided with proper training to manage the specific needs of this special population. And the community can plan for the specific needs that children will have in the longer-term recovery phase, when these vulnerable lives are gradually brought back to normalcy.

Assumptions

The following list of assumptions is provided only to present examples of the kinds of assumptions that a planning team's efforts may be based on. For any given community these assumptions may or may not be true:

- Children whose parents or guardians are present will remain under parental guardianship or under the care of the legal guardians
- The location of the community's children during the school year and during regular school hours is predictable as determined by the department of education and the individual educational facilities
- Outside of regular school hours, the location of children is dictated primarily by families and social networks
- Parents' and guardians' primary concern during times of emergency or disaster will be to locate and collect their children
- Many providers of children's care, including child care and home care employees, teachers, camp counselors and others, will be affected by major disasters themselves. Their primary concerns at this time may be the whereabouts and safety of their own families
- Institutions normally tasked with the daytime care of children, including schools, child care centers and others, are likely to be closed during and following a major disaster
- In events where there are numerous injuries or fatalities sustained by children, local pediatric providers and institutions will be quickly overwhelmed
- In certain disasters, children will be required to shelter in place with their families, such as pandemic flu or bioterrorism
- In certain disasters, children will be required to shelter in place at daytime care facilities, including schools and child care centers
- Transient children, including the children of tourists, travelers passing through the community, patrons of local businesses and others, may require additional help related to guardianship, especially when parents or guardians are not present
- All schools and many private child care and educational facilities maintain internal emergency operations plans of their own to address the needs of children, although these plans are applicable only while children remain in their care

- Catastrophic disasters may overwhelm the capacity of local facilities to deal with pediatric needs, including medical care, emergency care, special diets, sheltering arrangements and supervision
- Until children are moved from the grounds of a school or child care facility or until assistance is requested from the office of emergency management, children will remain under the care of the school or child care facility administration.

What Emergency Management Measures Can Be Taken to Address the Needs of Children?

There is no definitive list of needs that apply to every community. Rather, this information is generated by the planning team. Each community should already have a person or organization dedicated to these tasks on a daily basis. Ideally, the planning team will include this person or group(s) and identify their role(s) in emergencies.

It is only after a planning team has determined the needs of children in the community that it can begin to determine what actions may be taken (and what actions are feasible) to address the needs and to reduce the vulnerability of children. The following lists provide examples of actions that may be considered by the planning team when developing a document to meet the needs of children in emergencies. This list is by no means complete.

Drafting the Children in Emergencies Document

The following section provides guidelines on how a Children in Emergencies document may be developed by a local community. Each section is described, often with examples of information that may be included. It is in no way prescriptive, recognizing that every jurisdiction is unique in its resources, concerns and needs. Developing a document is a process that relies on the experience and knowledge of the planning team and is driven by their desire to address the needs of children.

Lead and Support Agency Assignment

Lead Agency

A document may have a designated lead agency within the local government. This agency is responsible for managing the development of capabilities relative to the specific function described and for the direction and control of this function when the document is activated. Selection of the lead agency should be based on the applicability of the function to the agency's central mission, the agency's ability to mobilize the necessary support and resources as described in the document, and the agency's willingness to assume the responsibility of such an appointment.

Support Agencies

Each document may also have one or more support agencies drawn from both within and outside the local government structure (including the private sector). These agencies are tasked with providing resource or logistical support to the operation of the document when activated.

Organization and Assignment of Responsibilities

This section describes the responsibilities of tasked individuals and organizations to provide for the special needs of children in emergencies, and it illustrates the actual organizational structure of the disaster management function. It is necessary to include a detailed list of the actual organizational titles (to ensure the continuity of the plan, planners should always use only the titles, not the names, of the officials currently holding positions) that will be involved in the response to a disaster. To each of those roles, the actual responsibilities assigned to the person filling that role are listed, with information dictating how and when those responsibilities are carried out if applicable. In certain cases, there are responsibilities that require the involvement of several actors, and in such cases this section stipulates primary and supportive designations to clarify leadership.

Examples of the officials that might be tasked in a Children in Emergencies document and some of the responsibilities they may be tasked with are presented in the following list. This list is only an example and not a recommendation of what responsibilities should be included or what local agency or official should be held responsible.

Chief Executive Official

- Establish a Government Liaison position for children in disasters issues
- Provide information to the public on the need to take care of children during the disaster

Emergency Manager

- Form and foster community partnerships that help to manage children's issues in disaster response and recovery
- Mitigate known disaster vulnerabilities at schools, child care centers, camps, sporting venues and all other facilities where children congregate
- Educate families on methods to mitigate the disaster risks to children
- Provide families with guidance on home disaster preparedness and encourage families to develop family disaster plans
- Develop a program to educate children about disaster response, including what to do if they are separated from their parents or guardians or if they require rescue
- Establish an Emergency Operations Center (EOC) Children's Issues Coordinator
- Develop systems, protocols and points of contact for sharing information on children between the office of emergency management and facilities that care for children prior to incidents
- Develop systems, protocols, and points of contact for sharing information on children between the office of emergency management and facilities in the care of children with the Children's Issues Coordinator
- Develop systems for identifying responders certified to work with children (such as a "badging" system)

- Develop a system for collating and disseminating all tracking information on children (as provided by facilities that care for children, including hospitals)
- Encourage the use of the NOAA All-Hazards radio system that provides early warning to facilities that care for children (schools, child care centers, recreational programs)
- Assist all facilities that care for children with planning for shelter-in-place scenarios
- Provide guidance or assistance to facilities that care for children about evacuation planning and procedures
- Include pediatric health care facilities (e.g. children's hospitals, pediatric emergency departments and pediatricians' offices) in all aspects of emergency planning and preparation
- Establish agreements with organizations and agencies (government and nongovernmental) who will address the special needs of children following a disaster in the community
- Ensure that all facilities that care for children conduct Continuity of Operations Planning and are prepared for the sudden loss of community services.
- Assist child care facilities and schools in their efforts to develop onsite emergency operations plans
- Integrate schools and child care facilities into local disaster plans, with special attention paid to evacuation, transportation and reunification of children with parents or guardians and incorporate the Incident Command System at these facilities
- Incorporate children into the community donated goods plan (e.g., diapers)
- Conduct drills with federal, state and regional/local emergency managers that include pediatric victims or a majority of pediatric victims in various circumstances (e.g., in schools, child care facilities, school buses, etc.) to adequately test the capacity of the system to handle pediatric patients

- Include child safety and security issues in all drills and exercises
- Conduct disaster exercises and drills at facilities that care for children, in partnership with emergency services
- Include sufficient proportions of pediatric victims and child-related scenarios in all regional disaster drills and actively involve the major pediatric care providers within the community (e.g., children's hospitals, pediatric societies, child care centers, schools)
- Activate the Children in Emergencies document
- Monitor the emergency response needs of children
- Create and distribute situation reports on the status of children affected by the disaster
- Conduct a community-wide, child-focused damage and needs assessment
- Ensure that all emergency vehicles and teams are supplied and resupplied with child-appropriate equipment and materials
- Assess emergency management needs relevant to children's issues at all facilities that care for children

Children's Issues Coordinator (EOC)

- Enact badging, credentialing and background check systems for anyone who will be working primarily with children
- Track all affected children, including those who are evacuated, sheltered at offsite locations, hospitalized or sheltered in place
- Track all children who are sheltered in place and assist the sheltering facilities in providing for the needs of those children
- Develop an accountability system to identify and track the movement and location of children within evacuation effort
- Map all facilities where large numbers of children are likely to congregate, and develops plans to safely evacuate them in the event of a rapid-onset emergency
- Track all evacuated children (in conjunction with the Transportation Coordinator) and provide a central repository of

this information for concerned parents, guardians and family members
- Ensure that the needs of special needs children are met during evacuations

Transportation

- Confirm and log the availability of vehicles suitable for the transport of children and able to withstand many of the consequences of disasters (snow, water, heat, etc.) within the community
- Ensure that vehicles equipped to transport children are available for evacuation and transportation during the disaster response and recovery phases (e.g., vehicles with child restraint devices)
- Provide orientation for all evacuation and disaster transportation personnel on the special safety and security needs of children
- Track all evacuated children (in conjunction with the Children's Care Coordinator) and provide a central repository of this information for concerned parents, guardians and family members
- Ensure that all individuals transporting children have passed background checks

Mass Care

- Develop an accountability system to identify and track the movement and location of children within community shelters and children sheltered in place at congregation points (e.g., child care, school)
- Develop systems that will ensure that security exists for unattended/unsupervised adolescents in shelters and other facilities in that care for children in emergencies
- Ensure that shelters are stocked with or can obtain emergency food, water and nutritional supplements appropriate for children of all ages and feeding implements for children of all ages (including bottle-fed infants and infants on introductory solid food diets)
- Develop a list of sources or providers of child-specific food items in the community and a system to deliver appropriate

and ample stocks of these items to facilities that are likely to need them in an emergency situation
- Establish pre-disaster agreements between facilities that care for children and mass care organizations that determine which shelters children will be brought to in emergencies
- Develop policies on the responsibilities of parents and guardians within shelters
- Establish child-safe storage for cleaning and disinfecting equipment in shelter locations and other locations where children may congregate following disasters
- Establish hand hygiene procedures, adequate sinks, and stockpiles adequate amounts of soap and paper towels
- Develop protocols for diapering in shelters
- Develop protocols for cleaning toys and other shared implements (such as toilets, changing stations, feeding areas, etc.)
- Provide secure transportation within the shelter and the medical care and resources systems (including appropriate official supervision of and accountability for unattended children)
- Track all child-specific information at activated community shelters and report to EOC as required
- Establish routines for children in shelters to foster a safe, calm, nurturing and normalizing environment
- Allow opportunities for children to play and socialize with other children

Superintendent of Schools

- Establish partnerships with all outside groups that will have an impact on your schools during and after an incident
- Become involved with the communities emergency operations planning process
- Utilize internal resources to network externally and assist in the districts emergency planning (e.g., school nurses liaison with public health sector, school psychologist/social worker with local mental health resources)
- Establish pre-disaster agreements between schools and/or facilities to temporarily house children until they can be released to parents/guardians
- Conduct shelter in place planning and drills at schools

- Develop plans for contacting or notifying parents and guardians
- Involve parents and guardians in school-based disaster planning efforts
- Conduct disaster drills in schools
- Plan with local community groups how to place children who have not been picked up after a local disaster
- Develop plans for establishing instant classrooms (including staff, supplies and appropriate curricula) within close proximity to shelter locations, in the event that schools are damaged, destroyed or converted into community shelters
- Develop plans for the replacement damaged or destroyed educational materials
- Ensure that all students' educational records are backed up in a safe, offsite location
- Incorporate materials on the hazards that affect the community in regular curricula
- Plan for the replacement of teachers and child care staff that will leave to deal with their own disaster consequences
- Provide temporary replacements for educators who have been affected by the disaster
- Assist educators in returning to work, and have a system in place to recruit and hire additional staff as needed
- With the district social services office/coordinator, provide training for educators in supporting children facing stress and the signs of potential more serious psychological problems, including anxiety, depression, behavioral problems, and Post Traumatic Stress Disorder (PTSD), and appropriate responses and referrals
- With the district social services office/coordinator, provide support for teachers facing stress

Human Services

- Inventory all child care space available both within the community and in surrounding communities, noting the number of filled and empty slots
- Develop plans for establishing "instant/emergency child care centers" in the event that the child care infrastructure in the community is damaged or destroyed

- Plan for the staffing, operation and equipment of child care centers to be established at community emergency shelters
- Work with local law enforcement to develop protocols for the timely reunification of families
- Establish systems for and conduct pre-disaster identification of children (e.g., name tags, other forms of ID), especially for those who are not verbal or who cannot give their own names, a parent's or guardian's name, or other critical information
- Prepare and provide emergency preparedness and response guidance for families of children with special health care and other needs
- Establish child care facilities at all community shelters
- Perform an assessment of damages to registered child care and other children's infrastructure components
- Establish instant child care centers
- Assist shelters in establishing child care facilities for sheltered residents
- Assist families of children with special health care and other needs
- Coordinate with the EOC Children's Issues Coordinator to report on the status of child care and other children's infrastructure to the EOC
- Assist child care facilities in forming partnerships to assist each other during a crisis

Fire

- Arrange for regular hazard safety inspections of child care facilities and schools and for the provision of structural and nonstructural mitigation advice and assistance as required
- Ensure that emergency vehicles are equipped with rescue equipment suitable for pediatric victims

Emergency Medical Services

- Create plans for transporting injured children to hospital facilities outside the immediately affected area, including routes, destinations, vehicles and safety devices (e.g., car seats)
- Equip emergency response personnel and vehicles with adequate supplies of child-safe and child-dosed antibiotics, antidotes and vaccines

- Purchase pediatric emergency response supplies, equipment and pharmaceuticals sufficient for a mass-casualty incident involving children
- Purchase special decontamination showers that are appropriate for children of all ages (including infants), as well as children without parents or guardians, non-ambulatory children and special needs children
- Make every effort to keep families together within the emergency medical system
- Maintain pediatric pharmaceutical emergency supplies, validating expiration dates regularly
- Provide family-centered emergency care to families with children
- Document all care

Hospitals

- Work with Emergency Medical Services to develop an accountability system to identify and track the movement and location of children from the field to hospital release
- All pediatricians and pediatric hospitals should develop and maintain Continuity of Operations Plans (COOPs)
- All hospitals should be prepared to handle a surge in pediatric patients
- Purchase pediatric emergency response supplies, equipment and pharmaceuticals sufficient for a mass-casualty incident involving children
- Make every effort to keep families together within hospitals
- Prepare for pediatric patients (overflow) in general hospitals not accustomed to child patient issues
- Maintain pediatric pharmaceutical emergency supplies, validating expiration dates regularly in conjunction with public health

Public Health

- Develop an inventory, including contact information and specialty, of all pediatricians in the community (including those who live in the community but work elsewhere or who are retired)

- Include a detailed pediatric component in any Web- or community-based resource networks
- Provide training to ensure that general emergency practitioners are able to recognize and respond to the needs of an ill or injured child at all levels of care—from the prehospital setting, to emergency department care, to definitive inpatient medical and surgical care
- Develop procedures for managing pediatric emergencies at all facilities where care is likely to be provided (in the field, shelters, clinics, hospitals)
- Establish agreements with pediatricians to provide emergency care in the event of a disaster where pediatric emergency care physicians are overwhelmed
- Develop regional mutual assistance agreements to accommodate pediatric victims (with children's hospitals, for example)
- Incorporate poison control centers into emergency medical procedures as a resource and central clearinghouse for toxicological information (including antidotes and contamination procedures that may need to be broadcast to the public in biological or chemical emergencies)
- Provide pediatric disaster-related education to "supplemental response groups" (e.g., school staff, child care personnel, community response organizations, civic organizations, specialty medical services, family practices, hospices, youth organizations)
- Address the pediatric medical needs of special needs children (dialysis, pre-existing physical therapy, disability-related)
- Provide on-site pediatric emergency and primary health care at emergency shelters
- Maintain pediatric pharmaceutical emergency supplies, validating expiration dates regularly in conjunction with hospitals
- Provide informational resources on pediatric emergency care at emergency response facilities (shelters, emergency services offices)
- Establish continuity of nurturing care for children (care by the same person for children between 0–18 months is considered important)
- Document all care

- Encourage parents and guardians to keep backup copies of children's health records in a safe, secure location in case their physicians' records are destroyed
- Make arrangements for children with special health care needs, including arrangements for child patients on long-term medications
- Monitor child health and hygiene in emergency shelters and provide information and assistance to parents and guardians regarding good child hygiene practices
- Assess needs relevant to children's health prior to, during and after an incident
- Enact ongoing child health screening in shelters to ensure that problems are recognized as soon as possible
- Make medical information resources available to parents and guardians (computers, posters, phone referral lines, etc.) to aid in appropriate use of medical resources
- Provide standardized health care data collection for children at shelters and places where children may congregate
- Identify, track and prevent the spread of illnesses more typical in children, in shelters and among the affected population in general
- Ensure that children requiring medication for ongoing health problems (e.g., asthma) are able to replace lost prescriptions and refill them when necessary
- Isolate sick children within shelters to contain the spread of childhood illnesses
- Establish temporary pediatric clinics for the special needs of children (including well-visits)

Mental Health

- Enhance pre-existing children's mental health infrastructure as necessary to handle the surge of need likely to follow a disaster
- Train pediatricians to be able to identify psychological symptoms, perform mental health triage, initiate brief supportive interventions and make appropriate interventions or referrals when necessary
- Provide psychological counseling and care to children during evacuation

- Mobilize the assistance of pediatric psychiatric specialists to assist in the recognition and treatment of pediatric psychiatric trauma and illness
- Perform interventions to minimize pediatric psychological trauma, especially in shelter and school settings
- Incorporate age-appropriate psychosocial interventions into ongoing in-school recovery programs and curricula
- Ensure that children with pre-existing mental health conditions are not excluded from eligibility for mental health care after a disaster or crisis
- Mobilize outreach support teams to go into the community (e.g., schools, child care centers, churches) to provide stress debriefing, triage and long term monitoring
- Conduct community memorial and grieving services geared towards children
- Identify parents and guardians who are having difficulty in coping with the event, and refer them to appropriate support networks (children's recovery depends a great deal upon the status of their parents or guardians)
- Conduct early interventions with all children in the affected area, especially school-based interventions where children are most comfortable
- Inform parents about the immediate and long-term effects of disasters on children to help them identify if their children are suffering from the effects of a disaster
- Ensure that psychological counseling and care are provided to children during evacuation

Social Services

- Develop guardianship protocols to guide the care of children separated from their parents at shelters, schools or child care centers
- Develop plans for placement of children during disaster and terrorist events in case of injured or deceased family members
- Establish pre-disaster agreements between facilities that care for children and mass care organizations that dictate what shelters children will be brought to in emergencies and likely needs of those children

- Develop policies and plans for the ongoing care of children who are separated from their parents and are unable to be quickly reunited, including transportation, supervision, shelter, care and nutrition
- Assist all facilities that care for children with planning for shelter-in-place scenarios
- Identify, track and address the needs of sheltered special needs children
- Provide children with a sense of normalcy as soon as possible after the critical phase of the emergency has ended
- Establish safe play areas in all shelters foster natural childhood development
- Provide communication assistance for children who require it (e.g., children who do not speak English, children with speech or sensory disabilities)
- Assist in the social integration of children, especially those who are separated from their families and friends or who are otherwise displaced
- Minimize parent/child or guardian/child separation
- Maintain strong communication with parents/guardians about the well-being of their children (while the children are in supervised care and while they are with their parents/guardians), to help parents identify and track potential problems.
- Document all activities
- Apply a family-centered approach after a disaster that includes, but is not limited to, assessment, early intervention and treatment with parents, guardians and primary caregivers
- Ensure that transient children (children of tourists, non-residents in facilities including camps and boarding schools) are identified, tracked and cared for

Legal System

- Determine all legal considerations concerning the care and treatment of minor children (including unaccompanied minor children), such as consent, guardianship, decontamination consent, records privacy and photographs of unidentified children

- Appoint lawyers to serve as guardians ad litem for children orphaned or those who have lost a custodial parent
- Include all relevant domestic courts (e.g., family, probate, juvenile) in the planning process to consider children's best interests

Law Enforcement

- Develop a list of all local workers who have already passed criminal background checks and who would be cleared to work with children for both security and other purposes (e.g., teachers, child care center staff, recreational department staff, coaches, etc.)
- Develop plans for quickly and accurately checking the background of and establishing the credentials for all responders, relief providers and volunteers (spontaneous and affiliated) who will be working directly with disaster-affected children in shelters, emergency medical services, psychosocial care and other areas
- Perform security checks on staff and volunteers who wish to work with children in the response and recovery phases
- Provide security to children in shelters
- Work with the National Center for Missing and Exploited Children to reunite families

Public Information

- Develop a system to provide concerned parents or guardians with information regarding the whereabouts and safety of their children
- Warn all facilities that care for children, as required
- Provide parents/guardians post-disaster response and recovery information about the disaster needs of children and the facilities that are currently offering to meet those needs
- Advise parents, guardians, other caregivers, the media and public officials about ways to help children cope during times of stress (anniversaries of the event, holidays, life changes, etc.) after a disaster

- Work with Law Enforcement/EOC Children's Issues Coordinator
- Develop pre-disaster messages on how to help children cope with disaster-related stress and disasters' effects

Community Zoning Officials

- Ensure zoning codes are adequate to protect current child-inhabited facilities
- Author new codes that prevent child-inhabited facilities from building in potentially unsafe areas (e.g. brownfield locations, near hazardous material facilities)

Public Works and Utilities

- Provide emergency support to families of children with special health care needs
- Develop a resource list of all large child care facilities to expedite return of utilities. This includes liaising with private utilities

All Responding Agencies

- Develop systems and policies that protect all children from discrimination based on their age, gender, race, ability, or other factors

Other Agencies, Individuals and Organizations

This is by no means an exhaustive list of the tasks or roles needed for to address children's needs. Other agencies, individuals and organizations that may accept or be assigned responsibilities under the provisions of the Children in Emergencies document include:

- Voluntary organizations
- Local media organizations
- Youth services director
- Recreation departments

Authorities/References

Any statutory authorities, including the Basic EOP, that provide legal basis for the provisions of the document should be listed here. This section should also provide reference to any sources of information from within the municipal government and from independent sources.

Children in Emergencies: Related Appendices

The appendices that follow provide additional information that may be considered when developing a Children in Emergencies document or included as appendices to the document.

Appendix 1: Protocol to Rapidly Identify and Protect Displaced Children

- Survey all children in your hospital, medical clinic or shelter to identify children who are not accompanied by an adult; these children have a high probability of being listed as missing by family members. Find out where they are sleeping/being held and the name and age of person(s) who is/are supervising them, if available.
- Place a hospital-style identification bracelet (or, ideally, a picture identification card) on the child and a matching one on the supervising adult(s), if such an adult is available. Check frequently to make sure that the wristband matches that of the adult(s) seen with the child in the hospital or shelter. If there is no supervising adult, the child should be taken to the hospital's pre-determined pediatric safe play area where he/she can be appropriately cared for until a safe disposition or reunification can be made.
- The names of all children identified through the survey as not being with their legal guardians or who are unaccompanied should be considered at high-risk and immediately reported to the hospital's emergency operations center. Additional

reporting should also be made to the National Center for Missing and Exploited Children (NCMEC) at 1-888-544-5475. The NCMEC can then crosscheck them with the names of children who have been reported missing.

- After the "high risk" children have been reported, a complete list of all children names in the hospital, clinic or shelter should be sent to the office of emergency management or other agency responsible for tracking (if activated and the information is requested).
- Unaccompanied children and those who are not with their legal guardians should undergo a social and health screening taking into consideration an assessment of the relationship between the child and accompanying adult, ideally performed by a physician with pediatric experience.

Adapted from CDC Health Advisory. 2005. *Instructions for Identifying and Protecting Displaced Children*. September 28.

Appendix 2: Child ID Survey

Name:_______________________________Hospital#__________

Age: ___ Months/Years DOB__________________

Gender: Male_____ Female ____________

Is the child currently accompanied by a supervising adult?
Yes No

Name of the currently supervising adult?______________Age___

Is this person a Parent? Yes No

A Grandparent? Yes No

Is this parent the usual guardian? Yes No

Was the child living with this person before the disaster?
Yes No

Does the supervising adult have any proof of legal guardianship or relationship to child? Yes No

If Yes, please describe or attach a copy:

____

If the adult(s) is not a Parent or Grandparent, what is the relationship to this child?

Aunt/Uncle_________________________________Age___

Sibling____________________________________Age___

Friend____________________________________Age___

Other (next-of-kin, teacher)______________________Age___

Was the child treated for illness or have an injury? Yes No

If yes, please describe:_____________________________

Was the child admitted to the hospital? Yes No

If Yes, give room or location:________________________

If No, give location or address where child is currently (lobby, Pediatric Safe Area, sent to shelter, etc.)_________________

Does this child have a history of medical problems? Yes No

If yes, please list:_________________________________

Does this child or family members have special needs? Yes No

If yes, please list:_________________________________

Source: CDC Health Advisory. 2005. *Instructions for Identifying and Protecting Displaced Children*. September 28.

Appendix 3: Psychological Effects of Disasters on Children

Two myths are potential barriers to recognizing children's responses to disaster and must be rejected: (1) that children are innately resilient and will recover rapidly, even from severe trauma; and (2) that children, especially young children, are not affected by disaster unless they are disturbed by their parents' responses. Both of these beliefs are false. A wealth of evidence indicates that children experience the effects of disaster doubly. Even very young children are directly affected by experiences of death, destruction, terror, personal physical assault and by experiencing the absence or powerlessness of their parents. They are also indirectly affected through identification with the effects of the disaster on their parents and other trusted adults (such as teachers) and by their parents' reactions to the disaster.

Another barrier to recognizing children's responses to disaster is the tendency of parents to misinterpret their children's reactions. To parents who are already under stress, a child's withdrawal, regression or misconduct may be understood as willful. Or, parents may not wish to be reminded of their own trauma or, seeking some small evidences that their life is again back in control, may have a need to see everything as "all right." In either case, they may ignore or deny evidence of their children's distress. The child, in turn, may feel ignored, not validated, not nurtured. This may have long-term consequences for the child's development. In the short run, feeling insecure, the child may inhibit expression of his or her own feelings, lest he or she distress and drive away the parents even more.

Most children respond sensibly and appropriately to disaster, especially if they experience the protection, support and stability of their parents and other trusted adults. However, like adults, they may respond to disaster with a wide range of symptoms. Their responses are generally similar to those of adults, although they may appear in more direct, less disguised form.

Among pre-school children (ages 1–5), anxiety symptoms may appear in generalized form as fears about separation, fears of strangers, fears of "monsters" or animals or sleep disturbances. The child may also avoid specific situations or environments, which may or may not have obvious links to the disaster. The child may appear preoccupied with words or symbols that may or may not be associated with the disaster in obvious ways or may engage in compulsively repetitive play which represents part of the disaster experience. The child may show a limited expression of emotion or a constricted pattern of play may appear. He or she may withdraw socially or may lose previously acquired developmental skills (e.g., toilet training).

Older children (ages 6–11 or so) may engage in repetitious play in which the child reenacts parts of the disaster or in repeated retelling of the story of the disaster. The child may express (openly or subtly) concern about safety and preoccupation with danger. Sleep disturbances, irritability or aggressive behavior and angry outbursts may appear. The child may pay close attention to his or her parents' worries or seem to worry excessively about family members and friends. School avoidance (possibly in the form of somatic symptoms) may appear. The child may show separation anxiety with primary caretakers, "magical" explanations to fill in gaps in understanding, and other behaviors usually characteristic of much younger children. Other changes in behavior, mood and personality, obvious anxiety and fearfulness, withdrawal, loss of interest in activities and "spacey" or distractible behavior may appear.

As children approach adolescence, their responses become increasingly like adult responses. Greater levels of aggressive behaviors, defiance of parents, delinquency, substance abuse and risk-taking behaviors may be evident. School performance may decline. Wishes for revenge may be expressed. Adolescents are especially unlikely to seek out counseling.

Children of all ages are strongly affected by the responses of their parents or other caretakers to disaster. Children are especially vulnerable to feeling abandoned when they are separated from or lose their parents. "Protecting" children by sending them away from the scene of the disaster, thus separating them from their loved ones, adds the trauma of separation to the trauma of disaster.

Symptoms Shown by School-Aged Children

- Depression
- Withdrawal
- Generalized fear, including nightmares, highly specific phobias of stimuli associated with the disaster
- Defiance
- Aggressiveness, "acting out"
- Resentfulness, suspiciousness, irritability
- Disorganized, "agitated" behavior
- Somatic complaints: headaches, gastrointestinal disturbances, general aches and pains. These may be revealed by a pattern of repeated school absences.
- Difficulties with concentration
- Intrusive memories and thoughts and sensations, which may be especially likely to appear when the child is bored or at rest or when falling asleep
- Repetitive dreams

- Loss of a sense of control and of responsibility
- Loss of a sense of a future
- Loss of a sense of individuality and identity
- Loss of a sense of reasonable expectations with respect to interpersonal interactions
- Loss of a realistic sense of when he or she is vulnerable or in danger
- Feelings of shame
- Ritual reenactments of aspects of the disaster in play or drawing or story telling. In part, this can be understood as an attempt at mastery. Drawings may have images of trauma and bizarre expressions of unconscious imagery, with many elaborations and repetitions.
- Kinesthetic (bodily) reenactments of aspects of the disaster; repetitive gestures or responses to stress reenacting those of the disaster
- Omen formation: the child comes to believe that certain "signs" preceding the disaster were warnings and that he or she should be alert for future signs of disaster
- Regression: Bed-wetting, soiling, clinging, heightened separation anxiety.
- Post Traumatic Stress Disorder syndromes much like those of adults, although possibly with less amnesia, avoidance and numbing evident.

For an adult, although the effects of disaster may be profound and lasting, they take place in an already formed personality. For children, the effects are magnified by the fact that the child's personality is still developing. The child has to construct his or her identity within a framework of the psychological damage done by the disaster. When the symptoms produced by disaster are not treated or when the disaster is ongoing, either because of the destruction wrought (e.g., by an earthquake) or because the source of trauma is itself chronic (e.g., war or relocation to a refugee camp), the consequences are even more grave. The child grows up with fear and anxiety, with the experience of destruction or cruelty or violence, with separations from home and family. Childhood itself, with its normal play, love and affection, is lost. Longer-term responses of children who have been chronically traumatized may include a defensive desensitization. They seem cold, insensitive, lacking in emotion in daily life. Violence may come to be seen as the norm, legitimate. A sense of a meaningful future is lost.

Source: Ehrenreich, J. H. 2001. *A Guidebook to Psychosocial Intervention*. Mental Health Workers Without Borders. http://www.mhwwb.org/CopingWithDisaster.pdf

Appendix 4: Special Psychological Needs of Children Following Disasters

For the most part, the same principles that apply to adults apply to children, with appropriate adaptations for their age (i.e., use language appropriate to the child's age; be concrete). The various child-specific reactions to disaster discussed earlier suggest several additional principles for work with children:

- Children are affected both directly by the disaster and indirectly, by observing and being affected by their parents' reactions. Unless there are strong reasons to the contrary, such as an abusive parent-child relation or the physical or psychological unavailability of the parents, involving children together with their parents should be a major part of treatment. Encouraging parents to discuss what happened in the disaster with their child, to recognize and accept and understand their child's reactions and to communicate openly about their own reactions, is helpful.
- A barrier to identifying children in need of services may be the parents' ignoring or denying signs of distress in their children or parents or attributing regressive behaviors such as bed wetting or acting out behaviors as "willful." Parents should be educated about these issues and case finding should be pursued through other routes (e.g., schools) as well.
- Parents may benefit from education with regard to appropriate responses to particular behaviors and to the benefits of specific treatments, as well. For instance (a) Regressive behaviors, such as bed-wetting, should be accepted initially. The child should be comforted without demands. He or she should not be shamed or criticized or punished. Later, normal expectations can be gradually resumed. (b) Behavioral interventions (systems of rewarding desired

behaviors, with limit setting on undesirable behaviors) are the most useful responses to inappropriate behaviors. (c) Physical comforting may be useful in reducing anxiety levels among children. One study has shown that regular back and neck massages may be helpful. (d) Children need reassurance and permission to express their own feelings without fear of being judged.

- Children may have special concrete needs—toys, bedding, special foods, availability of age-appropriate activities (play groups, school, chores). Parents also benefit when these are provided, since they help the parents cope with the demands their children place on them. On-going childcare services, to enable parents to return to work or to deal with the practicalities of a return to normal function, are also needed.
- Separation of children from their parents should be avoided, if at all possible. When it is absolutely necessary (for the child's safety or because of the inability of the parents to care for the child), efforts should be made to ensure that the child is accompanied by other familiar and important figures in their life, such as a grandparent, older sibling or teacher.
- Children are especially prone to drawing inaccurate conclusions about the cause of the disaster, their own actions and the normality of their current feelings. For example, they may believe that they are somehow to blame for what happened. Exploration and correction of these ideas is part of treatment.
- Younger children (up to ten or eleven, at least) may not be able to use language effectively to describe their feelings or to work through their reactions. Drawing, play with puppets, role playing or writing which is not specifically focused on the disaster (e.g., poetry, stories) may be a useful way of enabling a fuller exploration of responses. These approaches are discussed in more detail in Chapter VI.
- Children should be given time to experience and express their feelings, but as soon as possible, a return to the structure of household routines should be pursued.
- Schools play a key role. They provide a safe haven for children during the day and serve as locations for case

finding and for intervention and. By providing a structured environment for the child, they help the child regulate his or her reactions. A rapid return of children to school and monitoring of attendance and of unusual symptoms is helpful. (It is not unusual for children to want to be with their parents immediately following a disaster, however. Childcare services may be needed.) When children return to school after a disaster, they should not be immediately rushed back to ordinary school routines. Instead, they should be given time to talk about the event and express their feelings about it (without forcing those who do not wish to talk to do so). In-school sessions with entire classes or groups of students may be helpful. The school can also hold meetings with parents to discuss children's responses and provide education for parents in how to respond to children after a disaster.

- Children, like adults, benefit from feeling a sense of control over frightening situations. Involving children in age-appropriate and situation-appropriate tasks that are relevant to relief efforts (e.g., collecting supplies for disaster victims or taking on responsibilities such as caring for younger children in a shelter) is helpful both to the child and to other victims of the disaster.
- The repetitive graphic images of the disaster shown on television can generate anxiety. Exposure to television accounts of the disaster should be limited. An adult should be present to monitor and protect the child from overwhelming graphic images and to talk about what the child is watching.

Source: Ehrenreich, J. H. 2001. *A Guidebook to Psychosocial Intervention.* Mental Health Workers Without Borders. http://www.mhwwb.org/CopingWithDisaster.pdf.

Appendix 5: Disaster Response Information for School Crisis Teams

Identify children and youth who are high risk and plan interventions. Interventions may include individual counseling, small group counseling or family therapy.

From group crisis interventions and by maintaining close contact with teachers and parents, the school crisis response team can determine which students need supportive crisis intervention and counseling services. A mechanism also needs to be in place for self-referral and parental-referral of students.

Support teachers and other school staff. Provide staff members with information on the symptoms of children's stress reactions and guidance on how to handle class discussions and answer children's question. As indicated, offer to help conduct a group discussion. Reinforce that teachers should pay attention to their own needs and not feel compelled to do anything they are not comfortable doing. Suggest that administrators provide time for staff to share their feelings and reactions on a voluntary basis as well as help staff develop support groups. In addition, teachers who had property damage or personal injury to themselves or family members may need leave time to attend to their needs.

Engage in post-disaster activities that facilitate healing. La Greca and colleagues have developed a manual for professionals working with elementary school children following a natural disaster. Activities in this manual emphasize three key components supported by the empirical literature: (a) exposure to discussion of disaster-related events, (b) promotion of positive coping and problem-solving skills and (c) strengthening of children's friendship and peer support. Specifically:

- **Encourage children to talk about disaster-related events.** Children need an opportunity to discuss their experiences in a safe, accepting environment. Provide activities that enable children to discuss their experiences. These may include a range of methods (both verbal and nonverbal) and incorporate varying projects (e.g., drawing, stories, audio and video recording). Again provide teachers specific suggestions or offer to help with an activity.

- **Promote positive coping and problem-solving skills.** Activities should teach children how to apply problem-solving skills to disaster-related stressors. Children should be encouraged to develop realistic and positive methods of coping that increase their ability to manage their anxiety and to identify which strategies fit with each situation.
- **Strengthen children's friendship and peer support.** Children with strong emotional support from others are better able to cope with adversity. Children's relationships with peers can provide suggestions for how to cope with difficulties and can help decrease isolation. In many disaster situations, friendships may be disrupted because of family relocations. In some cases parents may be less available to provide support to their children because of their own distress and their feelings of being overwhelmed. It is important for children to develop supportive relationships with their teachers and classmates. Activities may include asking children to work cooperatively in small groups in order to enhance peer support.

Emphasize children's resiliency. Focus on their competencies in terms of their daily life and in other difficult times. Help children identify what they have done in the past that helped them cope when they were frightened or upset. Tell students about other communities that have experienced natural disasters and recovered (e.g., Miami, FL and Charleston, SC).

Support all members of the crisis response team. All crisis response team members need an opportunity to process the crisis response. Providing crisis intervention is emotionally draining. This is likely to include teachers and other school staff if they have been serving as crisis caregivers for students.

Secure additional mental health support. Although more than enough caregivers are often willing to provide support during the immediate aftermath of a natural disaster, long-term services may be lacking. School psychologists and other school mental health professionals can help provide and coordinate mental health services, but it is important to connect with community resources in order to provide such long-term assistance. Ideally these relationships would be established in advance.

Important Influences on Coping Following a Natural Disaster

Relocation. The frequent need for disaster survivors to relocate creates unique crisis problems. For example, it may contribute to the social, environmental and psychological stress experienced by disaster survivors. Research suggests that relocation is associated with higher levels of ecological stress, crowding, isolation and social disruption.

Parent's Reactions and Family Support. Parents' adjustment is an important factor in children's adjustment and the adjustment of the child in turn contributes to the overall adjustment of the family. Altered family functions, separation from parents after natural disaster and ongoing maternal preoccupation with the trauma are more predictive of trauma symptomatology in children than is the level of exposure. Thus, parents' reactions and family support following a natural disaster are important considerations in helping children's cope.

Emotional Reactivity. Preliminary findings suggest that children who tend to be anxious are those most likely to develop post-trauma symptomatology following a natural disaster. Research suggests that children who had a preexisting anxiety disorder prior to a natural disaster are at greater risk of developing PTSD symptoms.

Coping Style. It is important to examine children's coping following a natural disaster because coping responses appear to influence the process of adapting to traumatic events. Research suggests that the use of blame and anger as a way of coping may create more distress for children following disasters.

Appendix 6: Hospital Decontamination and the Pediatric Patient

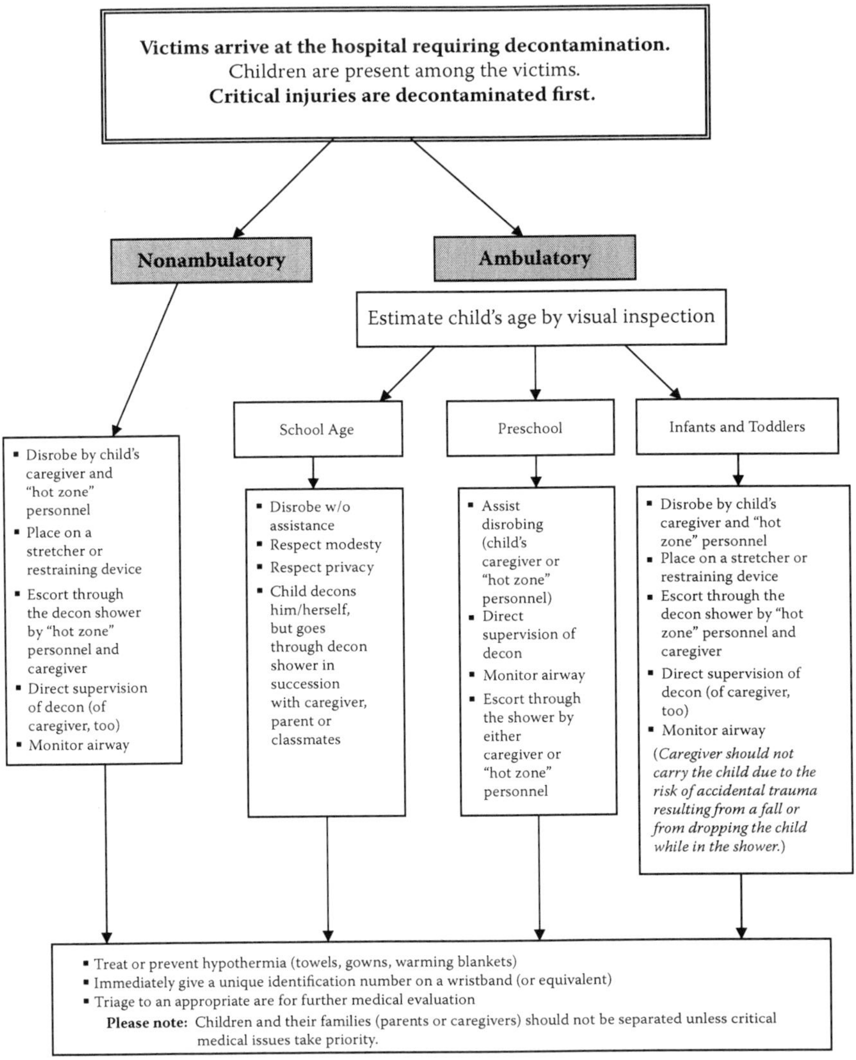

Appendix 7: Legal Considerations for Working With Children in Disasters

The following are legal questions and issues that may arise during a disaster. Having policies and procedures in place prior to an event should be considered.

- For unaccompanied children during a disaster, consent is not needed to treat for a life or limb-threatening situation. Is parental consent needed to treat a child victim with minor injuries? With psychological injuries?
- Is parental consent required to decontaminate an unaccompanied child? What if child is asymptomatic? What if child is refusing?
- What medical or social information can be released and to whom during a disaster?
- Check HIPAA rules and your legal counsel concerning the unidentified patient locator protocols, such as posting Polaroid photographs of unidentified children.
- Who can children be released to and if not the parent or caregiver, what permission or information is needed? What is your protocol for releasing children if no legal guardian or parent can be found or if no permission document is provided?

Source: New York City Department of Health and Mental Hygiene (NYC Health). 2006. *Hospital Guidelines for Pediatrics in Disasters*. Centers for Bioterrorism Preparedness Program Pediatric Task Force.

Appendix 8: Registry Information from Schools, Child Care Centers and Other Facilities that Care for Children

Unlike registries of individuals, which are built through optional self-reporting, a registry for schools and child care facilities is more easily and systematically conducted. Such a registry is composed of a database or spreadsheet that lists each school or child care facility's name, address, telephone number and other vital information. Vital information could include the points of contact (with off-hours contact information for at least 2 senior staff members), licensed capacity or census data, number of staff and any existing transportation capability by the facility using either regular or wheel chair assist vehicles.

The "licensed capacity" census figure is the "worst case" or maximum population at the facility that could require support at any given time. For childcare facilities, this maximum is set by the operating license, generally issued by the State. These facilities may have a smaller number of children on any given day but never more than the license allows. Schools, K–12, are required to report their official headcount to the state on a specified date, (typically in the fall term) to qualify for state funds and this is the number that should be used when planning. The availability of staff members should include food service, custodial workers, volunteers or other people who are generally expected to be on site each day when accounting for the total number of "adults" on site. Summer school programs should be also be identified to the emergency management agency by the school system since the size of the school population and the locations of the school sessions will probably differ from the regular term and the location could change from year-to-year.

If a particular school facility has anything exceptional that other schools do not have, it must be documented in the registry as well. Examples include a higher percentage of children with disabilities or language barriers or possibly a childcare facility within the regular school that supports a large number of infants. It is also important to note if the school is totally dedicated to children with a specific disability, such as a deaf or blind oriented school, since this could require additional or targeted resources.

Children/youth with behavioral or developmental challenges are sometimes adjudicated to residential treatment facilities and removed from parental custody. These individuals usually stay in the facilities at night and attend school or training activities during the day. Like schools, residential treatment facilities should register with emergency management and provide the same information as schools.

References

Agency for Healthcare Research and Quality (AHRQ). 2006. Pediatric Terrorism and Disaster Preparedness: A Resource for Pediatricians. US Department of Health and Human Services. http://www.ahrq.gov/research/pedprep/pedresource.pdf

American Academy of Pediatrics. 2002. The Youngest Victims: Disaster Preparedness to Meet Children's Needs. Physicians Fact Sheet. February. http://www.aap.org/terrorism/topics/PhysiciansSheet.pdf

American Academy of Pediatrics. 2002. The Youngest Victims: Disaster Preparedness to Meet Young Children's Needs. Children, Terrorism and Disasters Toolkit.

Early Childhood Institute. 2006. Systematic Emergency Preparedness for the Child Care Sector. Mississippi State University.

Ehrenreich, John H., Ph.D. 2001. A Guidebook to Psychosocial Intervention. Mental Health Workers Without Borders. http://www.mhwwb.org/CopingWithDisaster.pdf

Federal Emergency Management Agency. 1996. Guide for All Hazards Emergency Operations Planning. State and Local Guide 101.

Johnston, Carden, MD, FAAP, FRCP and I. Redlener, MD, FAAP. 2006. Critical Concepts for Children in Disasters Identified by Hands-on Professionals: Summary of Issues Demanding Solutions Before the Next One. Pediatrics. V.117. Pp. S458–S460.

Krug, Stephen, MD, FAAP. 2006. Testimony of Steven Krug, MD, FAAP on Behalf of the American Academy of Pediatrics. Homeland Security Subcommittee on Emergency Preparedness, Science and Technology. "Emergency Care Crisis: A Nation Unprepared for Public Health Disasters". July 26.

Gurwitch RH, Kees M, Becker SM, Schreiber M, Pfefferbaum B, Diamond D. 2004. When disaster strikes: Responding to the needs of children. Prehospital Disaster Medicine. V.19(1). Pp. 21–28.

Lazarus, Philip J., S. Jimerson and S. Brock. 2003. Responding to Natural Disasters: Helping Children and Families. National Association of School Psychologists.

Mailman School of Public Health. 2003. Pediatric Preparedness for Disasters and Terrorism: A National Consensus Conference. National Center for Disaster Preparedness. Columbia University. http://www.ncdp.mailman.columbia.edu/files/pediatric_preparedness.pdf

National Advisory Committee on Children and Terrorism (NACCT). 2003. Recommendations to the Secretary, June 12, 2003. US Department of Health and Human Services.

New York City Department of Health and Mental Hygiene (NYC Health). 2006. Hospital Guidelines for Pediatrics in Disasters. Centers for Bioterrorism Preparedness Program Pediatric Task Force.

Nicolai, S., Triplehorn, C. 2003. The Role of Education in Protecting Children in Conflict. Humanitarian Network. Paper 42.

Save the Children. N/d. Introduction to Safe Spaces. Save the Children, Protection Unit. Internal Reference Document.

Vermont Child Development Division. 2002. Emergency Response Planning Guide for Child Care. North Waterbury.

Source: Save the Children. 2007. *The unique needs of children in emergencies: A guide for the inclusion of children in emergency operations plans*. September. http://www.savethechildren.org/publications/ emergencies/Children-in-Emergencies-Planning-Guide.pdf.

INDEX

A

B

C

D

I

N

R

S

T

U

V

W

Z